THE ISRAELI–PALESTINIAN PEACE PROCESS

OSLO AND THE LESSONS OF FAILURE
Perspectives, Predicaments and Prospects

Studies in Peace Politics in the Middle East

1 *The Palestinian Refugees: Old Problems – New Solutions*
Edited by Joseph Ginat and Edward J. Perkins

2 *The Middle East Peace Process: Vision versus Reality*
Edited by Joseph Ginat, Edward J. Perkins and Edwin G. Corr

3 *The Israeli-Palestinian Peace Process: Oslo and the Lessons of Failure – Perspectives, Predicaments and Prospects*
Edited by Robert L. Rothstein, Moshe Ma'oz and Khalil Shikaki

Volumes 1 and 2 are published in association with the University of Oklahoma Press

The Israeli–Palestinian Peace Process

Oslo and the Lessons of Failure

PERSPECTIVES, PREDICAMENTS AND PROSPECTS

ROBERT L. ROTHSTEIN, MOSHE MA'OZ AND
KHALIL SHIKAKI

sussex
ACADEMIC
PRESS

BRIGHTON • PORTLAND

Preface, Introduction and Conclusion, and Editorial Arrangement,
Copyright © Robert L. Rothstein 2002

The right of Robert L. Rothstein, Moshe Ma'oz and Khalil Shikaki to be identified as
editors of this work has been asserted in accordance with the Copyright,
Designs and Patents Act 1988.

2 4 6 8 10 9 7 5 3 1

First published 2002 in Great Britain by
SUSSEX ACADEMIC PRESS
PO Box 2950
Brighton BN2 5SP

and in the United States of America by
SUSSEX ACADEMIC PRESS
5824 N.E. Hassalo St.
Portland, Oregon 97213-3644

British Library Cataloguing in Publication Data
A CIP catalogue record for this book is available from the British Library.

Library of Congress Cataloging-in-Publication Data has been applied for.

Hardcover ISBN 1 903900 093

Typeset and designed by G&G Editorial, Brighton
Printed by TJ International, Padstow, Cornwall
This book is printed on acid-free paper.

Contents

Preface   vii
Acknowledgments   xvii

1   A Fragile Peace: Could a "Race to the Bottom" Have Been
    Avoided?   1
    Robert L. Rothstein

2   The Pursuit of Israeli–Palestinian Peace: A Retrospective   31
    Aaron D. Miller

3   Ending the Conflict: Can the Parties Afford It?   37
    Khalil Shikaki

4   Domestic Israeli Politics and the Conflict   47
    Abraham Diskin

5   Foundering Illusions: The Demise of the Oslo Process   59
    Yossi Ben-Aharon

6   Islamic Perspectives on the Oslo Process   78
    Mustafa Abu Sway

7   From Oslo to Taba: What Went Wrong?   88
    Ron Pundak

8   Why Did Oslo Fail?: Lessons for the Future   114
    Manuel Hassassian

9   The Oslo Peace Process: From Breakthrough to Breakdown   133
    Moshe Ma'oz

Contents

10 The Middle East Peace Process – Where to Next?   149
    Ziad Abu Zayyad

11 A Fragile Peace: Are There Only Lessons of Failure?   161
    Robert L. Rothstein

The Contributors   170
Index   172

Preface

The chapters in this book were prepared for a conference held at Colgate University in late March 2001. More than nine months have elapsed since the conference, nine months in which momentous events have occurred. Any book about an evolving international issue, such as the Oslo peace process, runs the severe risk of becoming irrelevant or "overtaken by events" before it appears in print. This seems especially true when the intervening developments have been as shattering as the brutal terrorists assaults of September 11, 2001, and the continued and accelerated "race to the bottom" in the Israel–Palestinian relationship. Nevertheless, however grim the prospects may now seem, since there is no alternative (or no better alternative) to the resumption of peace talks at some point in the months ahead, I would submit that the developments of the past nine months have made the effort to understand the Oslo process even more crucial and the lessons that we have attempted to extract even more (potentially) useful to future negotiations. Providing evidence for this argument necessarily means that this Preface is also a Postscript.

I want to comment here, if very tentatively, about three post-conference developments that have affected or may affect the future of the Oslo peace process: first, a venture into "second-track" diplomacy that emanated directly from the conference; second, the effects of September 11th on the political dynamics of the Israeli–Palestinian relationship; and third, the effects of the escalation of Palestinian terrorism, especially the suicide bombings in Jerusalem and Haifa on December 1st and 2nd, on the peace process. One hardly needs to add that, as I write on December 6th, the after-effects of these terrorist actions remain unclear. Optimists might argue (or hope) that the worldwide condemnation of these attacks might finally induce Arafat to act against terrorism and Sharon to retaliate judiciously, but optimists are an endangered species in the Middle East.

As frequently happens at conferences, what goes on out of the public eye (in the corridors or on social occasions) may be as important as what goes on when papers are formally presented. That was true in the Colgate conference circumstance. In private conversations some of us came to two conclusions. The first was that, despite many disagreements, there were surprising elements of agreement or near agreement on some of the most controversial issues left unresolved at Oslo or Camp David II or Taba (at the end of the Clinton administration). Private positions seemed more flexible and more amenable to compromise than anything either side was prepared to say publicly, at least before the resumption of formal negotiations. This suggested that a venture into "second-track" diplomacy – a private, semi-official negotiation between a small group of well-connected individuals – might be useful. Such diplomacy became possible because of the generosity and vision of Colgate's Dean and Provost who quickly offered to support our venture.

Our second conclusion was that since this was not going to be an academic conference and since we needed participants who had access to top decision-makers and who were also committed to a negotiated settlement, we needed to revise the list of participants. In the end, five of the nine participants (including this writer as a "facilitator") were from the original conference and our four new participants are very well-known political and military figures. The willingness of these individuals to participate is testimony to the fact that thoughtful people are very aware that continued deterioration of the peace process could be disastrous for both sides and that efforts have to be made to achieve a cease-fire and to reach mutually bearable compromises on the very tough final status issues that remain unresolved.

Our meeting was held in July. I cannot reveal the names of the participants or the terms of the documents that we produced, in part because our efforts have not entirely ceased and in part because some of the participants strongly prefer anonymity. But I do want to say something about our efforts in general because I believe they reveal something about both the limits and the possibilities of second-track diplomacy.

We had, in discussing our agenda for the July talks, felt that both sides would have agreed to or been compelled to accept a cease-fire at some point in the ensuing three months. Thus it was our original intent to concentrate on two of the key final status issues that had generated so much conflict at Camp David II and Taba: Jerusalem and the right of return for Palestinian refugees. In the event our optimism about a cease-fire proved sadly naive, the violence continued and even escalated, and we were forced to refocus our efforts on the terms of a deal that might generate a real commitment on both sides to ending the violence and resuming the negotiating process.

Our talks were initially tense and confrontational but gradually the outline of a potentially important joint statement began to emerge. We took as our baseline the recently published Mitchell Report, since both sides had made ostensible commitments to implement it, but we felt that we could strengthen it by removing some of the ambiguities and by being more precise about who should do what and when. Perhaps even more importantly, we felt that a joint statement involving *major* substantive concessions by both sides that was signed by figures of such eminence – individuals who were well known in both camps and who were not identified and discounted as the usual "peaceniks" – might galvanize the moribund peace process. Apart from the debate that would have been generated by the statement, we also felt that the reputation of the irreproachable signees of both sides would provide cover for Mr Arafat and Mr Sharon to make the concessions they were unable or unwilling to make on their own.

Unfortunately, our effort floundered at the very last minute because one of the key Palestinian participants decided, after a night's sleep, that he could not sign the statement because of the commitment to take very strong action against terrorism. There is some irony in the fact that after September 11th Arafat was compelled to accept even stronger anti-terrorist actions, but too late to be very convincing. There were indeed risks in signing not only for this participant but also for Mr Arafat because the use of violence had become so popular in the Palestinian community (and well beyond the extremist movements), and because no other strategy seemed likely to achieve the maximalist gains that Mr Arafat apparently felt he had to achieve. This episode may also have revealed one of the hidden costs of inviting participants to a second-track negotiation that are *too* well-connected: they may find it more difficult to take positions that are unpopular at home or that stray too far from a previously articulated stance. Still, an opportunity to move back toward the negotiating table may have been lost, as all the participants subsequently recognized. It may also be worth noting that subsequent official efforts to restore the peace process were actually more modest in aim than what we almost achieved in the summer of 2001, if unofficially.

Second-track diplomacy can be both intensely frustrating and intensely exciting. The private and informal nature of the talks permits possibilities to be explored that would be impossible in an official setting where the fear of appearing weak inhibits a willingness to move away from fixed positions. In any case, what this participant found most valuable – and also most maddening – about our discussions was that they revealed that reasonable men on both sides were far closer to an agreement on the issues than the public debate might suggest. But when leaders are too weak or too fearful to make compromises that meet the minimal substantive needs of the other side, second-track diplomacy cannot move the game forward. This does not mean that it is useless: it does create a small network of influential people on both sides who are aware of new possibilities, who can communicate these publicly or privately at home, and who have a better sense that the "other" is more diverse than first appears. This may help to diminish the ever-present fear that the other side is not really prepared to negotiate seriously and will renege on all commitments.

The peace process continued to deteriorate during the summer months and there was no obvious way out, especially with a new administration in Washington that was not willing to risk much political capital on restarting it. In effect, the Bush administration's foreign policy team seemed more interested in proving how different from Bill Clinton they were than in working to resolve one of the world's most critical conflicts. To give them their due, however, the risks of engagement were high (as were the risks of non-engagement as became quickly apparent), and peacemaking with reluctant peacemakers was, and is, notoriously difficult, indeed perhaps impossible without very strong external pressure. Leaders who use the peace process as a different way to carry on the conflict or to score political points at home or abroad (seeming tough for home consumption, seeming moderate and flexible for external audiences) cannot sustain the momentum behind a fragile peace process. Both leaders had also backed themselves into a bargaining corner by establishing prerequisites for the resumption of negotiations that would involve great risks for the other. Testing the credibility of the other by posing questions that the other – as one knew – could not answer was not sensible unless the whole effort was an elaborate charade to ensure that the other was blamed for the failure of the peace process. Or perhaps this is merely another way of saying that peace processes are popular because they bring status, resources and time, but that peace agreements, which require both sides to make difficult concessions, are an entirely different matter.

The horrendous assault on the World Trade Towers and the Pentagon on September 11th by Osama bin Laden's Islamic terrorists created a genuine "day of infamy," the full implications of which are still unclear. The United States (and its friends and allies) certainly learned how vulnerable they are to terrorists who are willing to sacrifice their lives in order to instill fear and destabilize Western societies in the name of some paranoid – if not psychotic – fantasies disguised as "Islamic." And the fears have escalated as we contemplate even small groups of terrorists armed with chemical, biological and nuclear weapons. The United States – and Israel with it – have also been shocked at the hatred that has been vented against them by hysterical mobs of Islamic extremists in a variety of countries, ostensibly because of US military assaults against the Taliban and bin Laden's Al-Qaeda terrorists and US support for Israel. On one level, these events have made many commentators aware of the need to fight terrorism by a variety of means in a variety of places – because the victims are no longer just "elsewhere" – but, on another level, they have made many begin to question (as yet quietly) the wisdom of supporting authoritarian regimes in the Middle East that style themselves as friends and as supporters of Israeli–Palestinian peace but meanwhile quietly support terrorist groups, ruthlessly repress freedom in their own countries, and fill their controlled media with the most vile anti-Semitism and anti-Americanism. With friends like these . . .

The events of September 11th and their aftermath also had, and will continue to have, a profound effect on the disintegrating Israeli–Palestinian peace process, although the effects (at least at the time of writing, December 2001) are partially contradictory and may end once the Taliban and Al-Qaeda have been defeated. After all, short of compelling the Israelis and the Palestinians to accept an imposed settlement, which some on both sides have begun to advocate out of a sense of desperation, the constraints and conditions that have made peacemaking so difficult have escalated sharply in the last few years; gaps between the two sides have widened and frustrations, resentments, and grievances are growing deeper and more entrenched. Needless to say, neither leader has made any effort to educate his people for peace – Arafat has in fact done quite the opposite – and it seems unlikely in any case that many could hear or be willing to listen as the bombs explode. Moreover, an imposed peace could become a recipe for disaster since neither side might be fully committed to a peace they had not created (and thus did not "own"). Furthermore, the willingness of the United States to stay the course with sustained political, military and financial support is always contingent on the next change in administration or the shape of the new systemic crisis. New leaders in the two communities might also help to sustain the peace, especially as Arafat's credibility and support continue to erode, but there is hardly a guarantee that they will be an improvement on the incumbents. Put differently, Arafat is the worst of all leaders, except for the alternatives, and Netanyahu – if he returns to power – could make Sharon look like a moderate.

In short, pessimism about the short-term prospects for Israeli–Palestinian peace is surely warranted. Still, there were a few *small* signs that burying the peace process might be premature, although the terrorist attacks on December 1st and 2nd, the Israeli reaction, and the potential for civil war within the Palestinian communities if Arafat finally does act seriously against the terrorists he no longer seems able to control, may extinguish even these signs that the door to peace has not been slammed shut. In any event, we ought at least to make note of these signs.

In the first place, the United States has been forced back into the peace process because of the need to keep the coalition against the Taliban and Osama bin Laden together: Muslim allies have demanded movement on the Palestinian–Israeli front in order to diminish protests in the "street" against support for the United States and its allies. It is, of course, far from clear that even a successful peace process between the Israelis and the

Palestinians will diminish the wave of protests because brutal, corrupt and incompetent regimes will not suddenly become democratic, responsive and prosperous because of a peace agreement that is bound to leave many on both sides unhappy and willing to go on fighting. Ironically, the autocratic regimes may in fact be most at risk if they lose the ability to use Israel as a rationalization of repression and ineptitude.

Whatever the long-term consequences, the short-term effects of a more active role by the United States, signaled by Secretary of State Powell's address of November 19th, are as yet unclear. But the potentially beneficial effects are great because progress without a strong US role is unlikely. In any case, the coalition against the Taliban and Al-Qaeda seems to be holding together reasonably well, although this may be due more to the apparent rout of the enemy forces than to the US diplomatic initiative. If the war drags on and the Taliban and Al-Qaeda succeed in launching a guerrilla war, and Osama bin Laden evades capture or death, strains on the coalition are inevitable. Nevertheless, for the moment, the return of the US to the peace process in the Middle East may be the catalyst necessary to restart the peace process. But it takes three to tango, so to speak, and success is likely only if one can also foresee changes in policies and perspectives by Arafat and Sharon.

Are there any signs that the failure of the peace process and the events of September 11th have generated a degree of learning in both communities and their leaderships? No clear and simple answer is possible because the peace process has become a prisoner of events – the next terrorist incident, potential leadership changes, a new international shock, whatever. The initial reaction of Arafat and some part of his community to the events of September was radically different: while large numbers of the Palestinian citizenry was reported to be dancing in the streets, joyful at the death and pain inflicted upon thousands of innocent Americans and others, Arafat – presumably having learned from his incredible blunder in rushing to support Saddam Hussein's brutal invasion of another Arab country – ordered his security forces to crush any further demonstrations of support for the terrorist assault and tried to align the Palestinian movement as rapidly as possible behind the anti-terrorist campaign. This kept the Palestinians in the game as possible beneficiaries of US pressure to restart the peace process.

These benefits presupposed, however, that Arafat could or would make a genuine effort to stop Palestinian terrorism and arrest and punish any individual or group that refused to desist. Arafat had made many promises to do so in the past but had always broken those promises, presumably because the use of violence was popular and efforts to stop it could be risky. Doubts had also grown that Arafat, a product of his past, was neither capable of nor willing to accept a compromise settlement – except perhaps as a stage to launch demands against Israel itself. Thus the credibility of his promises either with the Israelis or the Americans was nil. What was potentially different now was that worldwide condemnation of terrorism was much stronger. These two factors gave Arafat a degree of leverage to crack down on terrorism and to make the case to his own people that suicide bombers could not bring peace. The terrorist strategy had surely inflicted pain on Israelis and greatly increased psychic insecurity about daily living, but is joy at inflicting pain worth the cost of very high numbers of Palestinian deaths, increasingly impoverished standards of living, children on the street rather than in the schools, the virtual destruction of the Israeli peace movement, and the disintegration of a peace process that nearly brought the Palestinians a relatively good settlement at the end of the Clinton administration – a settlement that may no longer be available? Arafat's response to that question has never been satisfactory but the intense pressure that has been put on him after the terrorist attacks of December 1st and 2nd may finally compel him to act – or perhaps, conversely, as is his usual style, to promise anything and to deliver only more promises.

Unfortunately, Arafat is caught on the horns of an agonizing dilemma. As terrorist assaults lead to increasingly severe Israeli reactions, death and destruction mounts and so do the demands for increased compensation to make it seem as if the deaths were meaningful and heroic. Caught between his own people's support for the continued use of violence and their opposition to action against the extremist groups and the demands of Israel and the United States to take strong action immediately to stop additional terrorist assaults, he has no safe options. Why risk a civil war to get to a bargaining table that might not have much on it? The likely response, if the past is a guide, is that he will hedge and waffle and dodge and divert in the hope that something will turn up to eliminate the need to do anything drastic. The notion that this time – finally – faced with threats to his survival from both Hamas and Israel, Arafat will have no choice but to act decisively is superficially appealing but may yet again run aground against familiar obstacles: the lack of alternative leaderhip, the fear of civil war, Arafat's skill as a survivor. The US initiative is thus not likely to get very far unless the pressure on Arafat is intensified (say, by a cutoff of US and European financial support) and unless Israel is willing to offer him some concession (say, on settlements) to justify taking a big risk for peace – something that Israel does not yet appear willing to do.

(The latest twist in the plot, after the above was written, was the sudden announcement by Hamas and Islamic Jihad that they were suspending – not ceasing – terrorist activities, presumably to avoid civil war, and in response to Arafat's pleas. This is a rather typical Arafat tactic to deflect pressure and to avoid the necessity of actually destroying the terrorist networks, but it is hardly likely to satisfy the Israelis who know that terrorism will return when the pressure is lowered.)

Israel, conversely, initially reacted to September 11th on the basis that it now had free rein to go after the Palestinian terrorist network as if it were an outpost of Bin Laden's Al-Qaeda. The Israeli response to continuous terrorist actions had been relatively restrained – at least in Israeli eyes – because the military had not attacked in force and because the targeted but extra-judicial killing of known terrorists was not very different from President Bush's call to get Osama "dead or alive" or Bush's willingness to suspend or threaten various civil liberties in order to make it easier to pursue and prosecute terrorists.

Israel soon discovered, however, that what the United States could or would do was not what Israel could or would do. The imperatives of keeping the coalition together against the Taliban and Al-Qaeda, and thus restarting the peace process, prevailed over the feeling of Sharon and many Israelis that their terrorist threat was structurally similar and justified similarly severe responses to Palestinian terrorism. Sharon was publicly rebuked and the President and the Secretary of State broke new ground in talking openly about the West Bank and Gaza as occupied territories and the creation of a Palestinian state. In short, the retaliation against Al-Qaeda's terrorism did not give Israel carte blanche against the Palestinian terrorist networks, but the outrage of December 1st and 2nd may have created a new dynamic. The latter atrocities occurred just after an American mission arrived to try and move the peace process back on track – an all too direct and insulting response by the terrorists. But the mission surely must continue for there is no sensible alternative to a cease-fire and the resumption of negotiations which might restore some hope to the Palestinians that a renewed peace process just might produce widespread gains (and not merely for Arafat's coterie), and to the Israelis that living a normal life will become possible once again. Terrorism for terrorism's sake, merely to enjoy inflicting pain on the other, is unlikely to bring the Palestinians nearer to any of their (reasonable) goals; and more force and more targeted assassinations by the Israelis succeed only in keeping a losing game going.

Finally, another dynamic in Israeli public opinion may also justify a degree of hope. The outpouring of hatred against Israel from the Arab (and Muslim) "street" and the demand by the fundamentalists for the destruction of Israel increases doubts in Israel that a genuine peace would ever be possible or that the Arab world would ever accept a Jewish, democratic and prosperous Israel as a legitimate Middle Eastern state. From this perspective, any concessions to the Palestinians would simply be used as a platform to make new demands until Israel itself was at risk. Arafat's maximalist demands at Camp David and his popularity for rejecting a very generous offer by Clinton and Barak seemed to confirm this ominous view of Palestinian intentions. Still, Israeli intentions have evolved. A recent poll (reported by J. J. Goldberg in *The International Herald Tribune*, November 30, 2001, p. 6) found 55 percent of Israelis still saying Israel's best option was an accelerated effort to make peace and only 20 percent favoring an intensified war against the Palestinians. A substantial minority of Israelis (44 percent) even favored the idea of a peace imposed on both sides by the United States. This suggests there is more room for a serious effort at peacemaking than might at first seem evident, but the opportunity may be lost – again – despite or perhaps because of Arafat's weakness, his demanding too much too soon, or his loss of control, a leader without followers. If any or all of these possibilities prove true, the peace process may be doomed until new leadership emerges, perhaps in both countries.

*   *   *

It would take a very brave or a very foolish person to make a strong prediction about the near term course of events, let alone anything long-term. We have become prisoners of events and prisoners of our anxieties, an extraordinary accomplishment for an evil fanatic in control of a relatively small group of men willing to die as a complex expression of their hatred for the West, the United States, Israel and the Jews, and Muslims who do not share their vision of Islam or the evils of the modern world. Whatever happens to Osama bin Laden and his key collaborators in the present conflict, enough of these people seem likely to survive, to pursue the acquisition of the most destructive weapons, and to remain intent on killing as many "enemies of Islam" as they can. This presumably implies that the terrorist threat will be the defining security threat for at least the next few years or longer. It also seems likely to mean that the conflict within the Islamic world is likely to escalate, a conflict not only between two different versions of Islam but also between the brutal reactionary regimes still in power in the Middle East and the forces of democracy and modernization that are desperately seeking to emerge and triumph.

The peace process between the Israelis and the Palestinians has been buffeted by the turmoil generated by the events of September 11th and their aftermath. But that peace process also runs on its own track, and local and regional developments are likely to remain more powerful and consequential than events elsewhere, which is not to deny the importance of the latter. And it is a peace process too important on its own terms to become a residual of policy needs elsewhere in place or time. It is also too important to be left as a residual of the play of domestic politics, as has been true in both camps for more than a year. The struggle of old war horses to stay in power, helped by the ability to blame the other for everything, has come to dominate the need to break out of the inherited constraints of the past.

Pessimists and realists always seem to win the battles in the Middle East but the war still goes on. I have suggested that a small and perhaps fleeting window of opportunity may have opened for progress in the peace process because of the interaction of a number of factors: the return of the US as an active player, perhaps some rethinking of the utility and wisdom of a terrorist strategy, perhaps some willingness on the part of thoughtful elites on both sides to rethink what peace will require and what it might bring, and perhaps simple battle fatigue in (parts of) both camps. But the window of opportunity can quickly shut because the men of violence can drag everybody down with them and because no one has learned to trust the possibility of peace – to "give peace a chance", as that old cliché goes.

If the conflict continues to escalate, the race to the bottom may culminate in an all-out war that kills many and settles nothing. But the imminence of catastrophe may finally shock even weak leaders, fearful followers, and uncertain external supporters to look for a different route. It is my hope that if and when the peace process is resurrected, the chapters that follow will provide the peacemakers with some important lessons about what to do and not to do to deepen a peace that will be fragile and at risk for years to come.

Acknowledgments

The Conference at which these papers were presented was held at Colgate University in late March 2001. There would have been no conference without the strong intellectual and financial support of Jane Pinchin, then Colgate's Dean and Provost and now Acting President. Jane also offered extraordinary financial and moral support for an ensuing venture into "second-track" diplomacy, which I shall briefly discuss in the Preface. All of us who participated in the conference are very grateful for Jane's support. I also want to thank my colleague Professor Steve Kepnes for the many intellectual and practical contributions he made to the Conference.

RLR
London, December 2001

A Fragile Peace: Could a "Race to the Bottom" Have Been Avoided?

Robert L. Rothstein

The Oslo peace process is near death and even its most fervent supporters have almost lost all hope. The "race to the bottom" began almost immediately after the famous handshake on the White House lawn (September 1993) but the pace of deterioration reached near warp speed after Ariel Sharon's infamous visit to the *al-Haram al-Sharif* / Temple Mount. It was a match thrown on a smoldering fire. The opposition to the Oslo Accords, which has been widespread from the beginning, has been more than happy to insist that failure was inevitable: the Israeli right (both secular and religious) because it felt too much had been given away, and the Palestinian left and the Islamic fundamentalists because not enough had been gained (or guaranteed in the future) to justify entering an uncertain peace process. The opposition hardened and deepened as the peace process lost momentum and staggered from crisis to crisis for a variety of reasons: the continuation of pervasive mistrust, the continual failure to meet deadlines, the failure to improve standards of living for the Palestinian people, the dismal and disappointing performance of Mr. Arafat's Palestinian Authority, the petty harassments and humiliations imposed by heavy-handed Israeli soldiers and police – the list could go on.[1] A dismal process produced a dismal outcome, perhaps a paradigm of how not to run a peace process.

This seems to imply that Oslo was a "bad" peace, a peace that was bound to disappoint expectations, or that could not be effectively implemented, or that demanded a degree of compliance that asked too much too soon from one or both parties, or that one or both parties signed only to get breathing space to rearm or to increase external support, or that was forced upon the parties by an external patron with its own agenda. Since a peace with any or all of these characteristics may increase the probability of a return to violence and may make it even more difficult for the next attempt to jump start a peace process to work, and since any or all of these accusations have been made against Oslo, a bad peace might seem an apt description.

This argument, however, seems misleading and insufficiently contextual. There are surely differences in quality between different peace agreements and some may be more equitable than others or more closely approximate the minimally acceptable terms of agreement for both sides. Nevertheless, all peace agreements that attempt to start the process of resolving protracted and sometimes existential conflicts are inevitably flawed, fragile, and incomplete. Such agreements should not be criticized for failing to do the impossible or failing to more fully approximate either side's ideal notion of what should or can be done. No preliminary peace agreement – or exploratory truce, perhaps more accurately – in this context is going to meet all the demands or needs of both parties or clarify and resolve the central symbolic and substantive issues that have driven and continue to drive the conflict. And no peace agreement should be called "bad" for only beginning and not completing the process of making peace or for only creating new opportunities not new guarantees. Note here that the point is not merely that such peace processes are bound to be fraught and difficult but rather that the peace processes themselves are going to be affected in fundamental ways by the characteristics of the conflict and the way in which it has evolved (a point to which we will return in detail below).

In short, such agreements are largely blank canvases or canvases with only a few faint lines drawn in. What happens next awaits the skill and imagination of the painters/peacemakers. Only a victor's peace could promise more and, apart from the fact that neither side has conceded defeat, such a peace may only create more long-run problems than it resolves. Moreover, the alternatives offered by the naysayers are hardly superior: we are now witnessing a return to violence, to the desire to inflict pain on the other even if the inevitable retaliation is even more painful, a "politics of the last atrocity."[2]

The argument thus far necessarily implies that the standards we should use in evaluating Oslo and other such agreements must be as tentative, provisional, and open-ended as the agreements themselves. We can really know whether Oslo is good or bad only after some time has passed and we can assess how well our painters/peacemakers have implemented the agreement, taken advantage of opportunities to deepen it, and understood the need for new patterns of thought and action in the post-peace period. This period, rather like the period after a new democratic government has been established, has both dangerous continuities with the past and new opportunities that can be grasped or ignored. Ignoring either the continuities or the opportunities can turn a protracted conflict into an insoluble one.

The limiting case argument here is something of a paraphrase of

Churchill's famous comment on democracy: Oslo is no one's idea of a good peace, except for the alternatives. Oslo was a product of its times, a period when both sides for different reasons were willing to explore the possibility of a new relationship but were also still distrustful and suspicious, not in full control of their domestic constituencies, not fully convinced that painful compromises were necessary or wise, ever ready to interpret the failings of the other as a justification for using the peace as a new means of carrying on the old conflict, and unwilling to risk much or to gamble on a high risk/high gain strategy. Indeed, in light of prevalent beliefs and attitudes and in light of how much was left unresolved by Oslo – nearly everything of substance – ambivalence and caution were rational and prudent.

The disastrous deterioration of the Oslo process has generated a search for scapegoats: the "usual suspects" include Arafat for the Israelis (and many US officials), Netanyahu, Barak and Sharon for the Palestinians, and Bill Clinton for some on both sides.[3] The burden of my argument is that we need to get beyond scapegoating to ask why leaders felt the need to act as they have. When we get to this level, we will find that a large part of the answer lies in the nature of the peace process in protracted conflicts. Still, while the task of transforming an exploratory truce into a genuine peace process was and is bound to be tense and difficult, the descent did not have to be as profound and bitter as it has become. Individual leadership does make a difference: context is important but not solely determinative. Thus a profound failure of leadership on both sides has made a bad situation worse and turned a peace process into a tragedy. And the hope that such leaders will at least learn from their mistakes seems entirely illusory – as yet.

I want in the rest of this chapter to discuss a number of inferences that can be drawn about the kind of peace process that we can expect to emerge during a protracted conflict. Before doing so, however, it is necessary a few brief comments about the general characteristics of protracted conflict.

Protracted Conflict: Existential Fears, Distrust, and the Absence of Empathy

The costs of protracted conflict are devastating, from brutal and unending violence to the perversion of civic values, psychological traumas, profound economic losses, and the shame of pariah status or the sorrows of a life on the run in exile. Why, then, with elites and publics – if not the "hard men" with the guns and bombs – increasingly desperate to find a way out and increasingly affected by battle fatigue and a sense of the futility of more of the same, has it been so difficult to negotiate compromise settlements more bearable than an ugly status quo.[4] And even an ugly status quo may seem preferable to relinquishing deeply held and sometimes theologically ordained maximalist goals of victory, even victory in the far-off future – however bad the present, it is impossible to disprove the belief that victory by a "long war" strategy of attrition is possible.[5] Moreover, the limited offers that weak leaders can make to each other and the uncertainty that such offers will be implemented or produce enough benefits quickly mean that what can be offered and what can be gotten seem insufficient. Thus it seems more prudent to complain bitterly about the status quo but to risk little to change it. Each side, ever distrustful, fears that compromise offers will lead only to new demands or to an appearance of weakness. There is something akin to what economists used to call a low level equilibrium trap or a bad status quo without any obvious exit option.

Protracted conflicts develop other, deeper characteristics that help to explain why it is so difficult to embark on a peace process. I will only briefly list some of these characteristics because my primary focus is on how – taken as a whole – they affect the negotiating process, not on the characteristics themselves. Thus a conflict syndrome, or a set of long-lasting structural conditions, emerges that sustains and intensifies the conflict: economic inequalities, the isolation of the warring communities from each other, an indifference to learning about an "other" who is to be destroyed, the misuse of history for entirely partisan purposes, the feeling on both sides that they are embattled minorities, and the development of a "conflictive ethos" that fuels animosities, demonizes the other, and strengthens each group's sense of identity and separateness.[6] At some point, after an exchange of atrocities and a hardening of views, such conflicts may become existential: each feels that its very existence is at stake and that any or all means are justified to destroy the other before being destroyed.[7] It hardly surprises that empathy is absent in these circumstances, a factor of some consequence because empathy is the basis of most moral judgments and its absence may also impede the process of learning about the other.[8]

One result of the creation of a deep-seated conflict syndrome is that something akin to a prisoner's dilemma game develops: distrust is so pervasive and the lack of information about the other is so profound that sub-optimal outcomes are inevitable – they are expected and not an aberration. The trick may be to avoid turning a prisoner's dilemma game into a totally irrational game of chicken, of bluffing with lives at stake, which may describe the latest stage of the Oslo process. Another consequence is that "normal" conflicts of interest become more difficult to resolve because they can be transformed into conflicts of symbol and icon that cannot be compromised. In any case, since most peace negotiations focus on compromising the issues on the negotiating agenda, and not on dealing with the subjective or long-run issues that are part of the underlying conflict syndrome, there may be a bad fit between what gets discussed and perhaps resolved during the peace negotiations and the conflictual factors that persist and may – if not dealt with as rapidly as possible – undermine the peace process itself or its aftermath. It is a staple of conflict analysis to argue that both levels of conflict must be dealt with but it is not sufficiently stressed that the long-run issues must be confronted and dealt with from the start to strengthen the constituency for peace, to provide evidence of good intentions to the masses, and to provide immediate, tangible benefits that people do not want to lose.

The very fact that the conflict is protracted and that neither side can achieve some of its central aims or defeat the other side also usually means that both leaders have been weakened (threatened by extremists who promise more and denounce the possibility of a compromise agreement) and that a kind of Gresham's Law of conflict operates with extremists driving out or eliminating moderates. Leaders begin to focus narrowly on staying in power and containing extremists at the expense of exploring a substantive compromise with the enemy. At a minimum, this implies that any peace process that emerges will be tentative, that posturing for domestic constituencies to prove that the leader is not giving away too much and that he is bargaining hard to achieve maximal gains will dominate, and that the process will be slow, crisis-driven, and always in danger of destruction.[9]

At the height of the conflict, in its most existential phases, pessimism abounds and the conviction grows that "no solution is immediately practical."[10] This view is too stark because some movement or some improvement in current conditions is always possible – even between bitter enemies; not everyone is always a "true believer" in apocalyptic visions of the conflict, and taking the "no solution" view too literally may miss important changes that are occurring in both communities.[11] Still, when the conflict is at its most intense stage, suggestions of compromise are likely to seem treasonable, opposition to compromise may be the only position that can maintain domestic unity, the stakes of the conflict seem so high that it becomes an article of faith that the other is completely untrustworthy and always seeking to do the worst, and thus constant demands for quick and strong evidence that any tentative explorations of compromise by the other side are meant seriously are prevalent.

At some point, when both sides realize that they have reached a military stalemate, when the costs of going on seem to weigh more than the ever-receding potential benefits of victory in the "long war," and when the simple desire to begin living a "normal" life becomes increasingly attractive, a "window of opportunity" may open to begin exploring the possibility of peace.[12] This changes the terms of the conflict, opens new opportunities for movement, and may even begin to reorient some cognitive maps but it is obviously a long way from a genuine peace settlement that resolves substantive issues.[13] The road ahead is perilous in large part because the initial agreement and subsequent agreements are largely procedural, because they are not self-executing and terms are constantly exposed to divergent interpretations, the persistence of old attitudes means that the post-peace period will have many continuities with the pre-peace period, and the extremists will be energized to destroy an already fragile peace. In short, the period after a weak peace agreement has been negotiated is potentially transformational or potentially regressive: the conflict can return (as in the Middle East now) or the peace can be slowly strengthened. The key factors in determining which outcome will ensue are likely to be joint efforts to reduce the negative effects of the structures of conflict that still persist and joint efforts to establish new patterns of thought, new styles of interaction, and new cooperative institutions more appropriate for peaceful coexistence.[14] None of these efforts were seriously attempted in the Oslo years and instead each side signaled the other that the conflict was still on – and thus generated a negative self-fulfilling prophecy that quickly came to pass.

I want now to discuss what the foregoing arguments imply about what we should expect or anticipate from any peace process that does begin.

Fragile Peace and the Management of Expectations

There follows **six** conceptual points about what we can reasonably expect from very fragile peace processes.

1 As I have already suggested, we cannot expect that either side will make a full commitment to the peace process because initial offers are likely to be minimal, doubts about the other's willingness or ability to offer more or to implement promises will be great, there will be widespread (and not unreasonable) fear about either's ability to get a substantive agreement through domestic political processes, and both will be unhappy about the terms of any agreement and constantly seeking to push its limits or renegotiate its terms. Since these fears and doubts are rational, given the context discussed earlier, reluctant and tentative commitment to a low risk/low gain strategy is intrinsic to the end game of a protracted conflict. Generosity will be limited, demands to dot every "i" and cross every "t" will be pervasive, and haggling over every inch of territory or every symbolic concession will be nasty. Risk aversion will be high because fear of failure will be high and leaders will seek to protect themselves against these risks (to themselves and to the peace process, in that order) rather than to increase the chances of success by altering attitudes and patterns of behavior. In short, there is a strong likelihood that the temporary truce will revert quickly to renewed conflict because each seeks to manipulate the peace process to gain more or to be stronger at the next stage – faith in the possibility of real peace is too weak to expect much more than a defensive posture.

Perhaps one lesson of this is to avoid the (premature) euphoria that is generated by ceremonies on the White House lawn or grand statements about the establishment of "peace in our time." Expectations are obviously easier to manage if they are not blown out of proportion. This point is worth special emphasis if only because the peace process is shadowed by the ineradicable risk that any apparent shift toward peace is merely tactical, a platform to raise new demands or to achieve ancient goals by slower and at least momentarily less violent means. The fear of being duped is especially strong in the early stages because distrust is still pervasive and the consequences of being wrong about the intentions of the other could be catastrophic for both leaders and followers. These suspicions explain why demands for strong, tangible, and early indications of a serious commitment to peace are inevitable – but also dangerous when the other leader is weak, confronts dangerous rivals, and has an insecure domestic base.[15] In any case, the potential conflict between what each leader needs to do to bolster domestic support and to increase his own willingness to run risks and what he needs to do to convince the other side that the peace process is genuine and that momentum needs to be maintained is severe. The results can be disastrous if either or both leaders are unaware of or indifferent to these concerns-which in the case of Arafat and Netanyahu led to the joint conviction that the other was not serious about peace.[17]

2 The second point follows from the first but is frequently ignored, especially by commentators intent on blaming a convenient scapegoat for the latest disaster in the peace process. The point is that the stop/go, off/on, crisis-driven negotiating process that developed after Oslo (and after the Good Friday agreement in Northern Ireland) is not simply the result of flawed leaders and unpredictable political events. This kind of process is not an aberration but rather intrinsic in this context: we can bemoan but we should not be surprised that leaders won't risk more – there is no clear reason whey they should – or that they act with mental reservations, implicit doubts, and a readiness to pull back quickly. We should anticipate a peace process that loses momentum and can easily become a prisoner of events, that is dominated by last-minute decisions on the edge of an abyss, and that moves – forward and backwards – in an erratic and inconsistent fashion.[18] There is a willingness to explore but with an escape hatch to the comforts of the familiar – and leaps of faith into a brave new world are likely to seem bearable risks only to strong leaders very sure of their domestic base.[19]

If weak leaders can only hedge their bets, move slowly, and be excessively optimistic about what benefits can be expected (and how soon) from any tentative agreement, one needs to understand that such behavior is intrinsic to this kind of peace process. In effect, it is neither an aberration, nor irrational, nor the result simply of weak and ambivalent leaders. I do *not* mean to exculpate such leaders: as with Arafat and Netanyahu, they can make a bad situation much worse, they can fail to adopt new patterns of behavior, and they can accelerate the race to the bottom. Nevertheless, understood contextually, we can better understand why they act as they do, why asking them to risk more or to take actions that threaten their basic power positions is unlikely to work and why other leaders should be careful not "to set them an exam that they can't pass."[20]

* * *

On one level, the first two points might seem another way of making a simple point: the peace process that seeks to end a protracted conflict will be fraught. The points are still worth making, however, because they are so frequently forgotten by leaders overcome by premature euphoria (or by weak leaders who must promise too much to doubtful followers) and by external supporters intent on disengaging as rapidly as possible. On another level, the points have even greater significance. It is at least arguable that the most important task that leaders confront in the aftermath of the initial agreement is the management of expectations. If the latter are too euphoric, if hopes have risen unrealistically, a rapid descent into despair and disillusionment is inevitable. This can easily destroy the peace process because it will become impossible to build a wider constituency for peace, the top/down elite-driven peace process will not begin to generate grassroots support, and momentum will rapidly dissipate. Negative outcomes are especially likely when the lack of empathy means that one or both sides is unaware of, or indifferent to, what the other needs.[21] Each side can well end by sending the signal that the conflict continues, peace is a sideshow. Thus the presentation of the peace process – the way we "frame" it and set out what can be the expected from it – is not an exercise in public relations but is rather a major factor in determining whether it will succeed or fail.

3 The third point is to some extent implicit in the first two but it also begins to lead us into a crucial issue: the domestic politics of peacemaking. In conventional, interest-based conflicts the most important level of interaction is usually between the parties themselves as they engage in a process of concession/convergence. However, in the conflicts that concern us here it is usually two other levels that dominate. Because there is so much doubt about the commitment of the other side and so much fear of being duped,

leaders (especially leaders weakened by past failures or unstable domestic coalitions) are likely to focus primarily on not getting too far ahead of a domestic constituency that may still believe in promises of ultimate victory or in a demonic view of the other.[22]

Weak leaders may also view the third level of interaction with actual or potential external patrons as more critical than face-to-face negotiations with the old enemy. Thus Arafat might have signed the Oslo agreement not because of any substantive gains – which were minimal – but because it meant that he and the PLO were recognized as the legitimate representatives of the Palestinian people and he might gain status and resources from a new access to the White House. And he might have been reluctant to compromise at Camp David II for fear of negative reactions from the Arab world. On the Israeli side, there has not only been an obvious reluctance to alienate the United States but also a reluctance to use its military power fully for fear of losing moral legitimacy among other democratic states.

The key point here, details apart, is that the most essential bargaining level – face-to-face with the enemy – may become a residual of the other levels and almost epiphenomenal to other bargaining games that are important, but not as important as the face-to-face game. Perhaps another way of making the point is to note that the game is not just about ratifying an agreement between two parties but is also a rolling, multidimensional effort to keep the game going – managing crises, building support, monitoring compliance – that requires all three levels to work together or at least not at cross purposes.

The argument here suggests that the peace process is really a three-level bargaining game. If the interactive effects of two-level games are complex and indeterminate, how much more so are three-level games?[23] Whatever the answer, one thing should be clear. Awareness that the other leader may be posturing for the domestic audience or for the support of external patrons means that there is added uncertainty and distrust at the face-to-face level: how committed can the other be if he seems more focused on different bargaining arenas?

4 The domestic politics of peace is so important that it requires separate treatment. But, given the increasing tendency to argue that domestic politics is always dominant (especially in international political economy), one needs to emphasize that the argument here is more differentiated.[24] Domestic constraints and opportunities can obviously be critical but it seems to me that most leaders involved in peace processes make their choices based on a complex assessment of potential support or opposition on all three levels – not to mention their cognitive biases, the history of the conflict, and their sense of whether or not time is on their side. Out of this conceptual maze – which might make any choice seem extremely risky, including procrastinating – I would guess that the dominant form of decision-making is likely to be a form of "negative satisficing." In short, the leader will make a last-minute decision, fudged as much as possible, that offends the least number of actors who have the power to do him harm.[25]

One needs also to note that the phrase "domestic politics" can mean many different things in many different contexts. One obvious point to keep in mind is that the domestic politics of a democratic state like Israel and the internal politics of a rebel group are very different things, apart from the generic notion that each leader needs to secure his domestic base. Thus the leadership of the rebel group may get its legitimacy from its image of militancy for the cause, not from a free vote, and the notion of a "loyal opposition" is unacceptable because the rebel group values (and needs) unity above all else. In any case, in what follows I do not seek to discuss all the analytical complexities of the notion of domestic politics but rather only to highlight certain aspects that are relevant to the peace process in protracted conflicts.

Oslo was a top/down peace, driven by elite calculations and perceptions.[26] An elite consensus on the need to try the peace track, even if the two elite groups do so for different reasons, may be a necessary first step to break through a stalemate. But at some point the peace process must be broadened and deepened so that grassroots support grows. This complex process has only recently begun to be analyzed in depth but it is clear that it is multidimensional: for example, quick improvements in standards of living, the creation of new institutions to foster cooperation, and longer term efforts to change attitudes, perceptions, and behavior.[27] This process failed dismally after Oslo as neither Arafat nor Netanyahu made much effort to educate their constituencies about the sacrifices necessary for peace or the need to think and act differently in the post-peace period. As a result, as conditions deteriorated the masses began to see the peace as increasing dangers and decreasing standards of living. The pressure from below that did emerge was largely negative: to be tougher, to offer less, to retaliate harshly.[28] The "peace process" became a dangerous farce and its supporters began to abandon ship.[29] Perhaps even worse, because the capacity to make credible promises is an important component of any bargaining relationship, the fact that Arafat had lost total credibility with the Israelis – he had lied too often – and various Israeli leaders had lost credibility with the Palestinians (even Barak who went far toward meeting their demands) meant that the peace process might not be resurrected until new leaders emerged.[30]

Why did the Oslo process deteriorate so rapidly and so profoundly? Peace was never going to be easy but it was not inevitable that the difficult would become the disastrous. One *part* of the answer is that two weak leaders cannot make a strong peace. A leader in a very fragile peace process must accomplish two tasks: first, he must create, sustain and enlarge his domestic constituency for peace; and second, he needs to understand and act on the knowledge that his fate and the fate of the other leader are linked together – to borrow a phrase, they will hang together or hang separately. The leader who can only hide behind his extremists (and even urge them on as Arafat has done in supporting the use of violence after Sharon's visit to the Temple Mount/*al-Haram al-Sharif*) fails in the first task. A leader with no empathy for, or understanding of, the other side or the requirements of a peace process fails in the second task.[31]

A crucial problem that weak leaders face is that internal unity is likely to crumble as a peace process develops and the possibility of controversial and painful compromises suddenly becomes real. The masses, still committed to ancient rhetoric about ultimate victory and perhaps unaware of all the factors pushing toward peace, may well slow the process down and threaten the leadership with severe sanctions. Other elites may also threaten the leader by denouncing compromise and maneuvering to be in a good position if a succession crisis arises. A weak leader, caught between rising domestic opposition and an offer that seems inadequate may see his only choice as negotiating by exchanging atrocities, which may generate internal unity but at the cost of destroying the peace party on the other side – not to mention the rising death toll on both sides.[32]

One tactic that weak leaders can try is to give any group powerful enough to undermine a compromise agreement a seat at the bargaining table (both internally to develop a consensus and externally when negotiating with the other side). It is not clear that this is wise since it gives the outriders a potential veto over the negotiating process or at least the ability to delay it dangerously. In South Africa, where the ANC and the National Party were the dominant players, analysts and practitioners developed the idea of "sufficient consensus" to isolate and control extremists but to allow them also to join the consensus should they decide to accept its premises.[33] But where each side is more divided and the extremists are relatively more powerful, it may not be possible to construct such a consensus – except behind the continuation of the conflict and the rejection of compromise. In such circumstances, the best option may be to create a "coalition of the willing," isolate the extremists, and seek support from the other side to help contain violence and limit the cycle of retaliation. In effect, the "sufficient consensus" may have to cross boundaries.

Perhaps we can get a better sense of the consequences of weak leadership if we briefly comment on the domestic constraints on Prime Minister Barak and Chairman Arafat. Both were weakened by the growing disillusionment with the peace process, although they reacted to this situation in a completely different fashion. The dismal performance of Arafat's Palestinian Authority obviously meant that his popular support declined, that he was fearful of making any of the concessions necessary for peace, that he felt threatened by and thus impelled to undermine an emerging trend toward democratization in the Palestinian community, and that he encouraged the use of violence to bring him what diplomacy could not.[34] It is undoubted this record that led Dennis Ross, the US negotiator in the Middle East, to say of Arafat that "I have come to the conclusion that he is not capable of negotiating an end to the conflict because what is required of him is something he is not able to do. It's simply not in him to go the extra yard."[35] This criticism may be well-founded but it needs to be leavened by an awareness of Arafat's domestic weakness and by an awareness that *all* the choices he faced were risky and unclear.

Barak, in contrast, reacted to domestic weakness in almost exactly opposite terms. While initially strongly supported, his support began to evaporate as the extent of the concessions he was prepared to offer Arafat became clear, as Arafat seemed to increase his demands with each concession, and as Arafat ultimately turned to violence to elicit further concessions. The Israeli public seemed to offer majority support for the peace process but that support was thin because most of that majority did not believe that Oslo would in fact bring real peace.[36] Thus support was neither widespread nor stable. And as violence intensified so did pressures from below, but not for more concessions but rather for fewer concessions and increased toughness. In effect, the domestic risks of peacemaking obviously grew as Oslo produced increased violence, increased insecurity, and increased demands.[37] Perversely, Arafat's tactics seemed designed to destroy a potential partner for peace and to guarantee the return to power of a much harder opponent. Barak responded to declining support for the peace process and for himself by staking everything on a gamble for a "final" settlement at Camp David. When this was rejected by Arafat (and might have been rejected by the Israeli public in a referendum), Barak himself paid a high political price for getting too far ahead of his own constituency or not producing results to justify his risk-taking.[38]

5 The argument that I have made necessarily implies that it is a dangerous illusion to argue that the kind of peace or peace process described will produce "peace in our time" or a quick and easy "normalization" of a relationship that has been dominated by total distrust and deep and unresolved grievances. Thus the kind of rhetoric that President Clinton and Prime Minister Barak used to describe the failed efforts at Camp David II was not only naive but also guaranteed to raise expectations that were bound to disappoint. Dreams of the perfect may harm the possibility of the "merely" good.

Perhaps we can get a better sense of the dangers of raising expectations if we think about the peace process in terms of three levels that are not easily synchronized. The initial level – say, Oslo in 1993 and 1994 – frequently involves a crucial trade-off: an end to violence (at least temporarily and by most combatants) in exchange for recognition of each other as legitimate and necessary bargaining partners. This is crucial, particularly in terms of potential, because it changes the terms of the conflict (what each now might consider) and opens new opportunities for movement. But it is obviously a long way from a genuine peace settlement because few substantive issues have been resolved, the process of implementation of even minimalist terms is likely to be erratic and uncertain, and the number on each side genuinely committed to the process is likely to be small and mostly among the elite.[39] It is at this level that the management of expectations may be most crucial not only because they have probably escalated with the signing of an agreement but also because disappointed expectations can destroy an already fragile peace.

The second level usually involves an important and potentially forcing agreement on how to begin bargaining on substantive issues and some sort of explicit timetable to avoid deliberate delays and compel movement away from extreme demands. One hopes during this period for both substantive progress on key issues and an effort to isolate extremists and to show the masses that there are real benefits from peace that they do not want to lose. Perhaps also some joint institutions can be created that widen the constituency for peace and begin to show some of the beneficial possibilities implicit in mutual cooperation. Presumably expectations and achievements should begin to converge at this stage – at least if some improvements have occurred. It suffices to say that Oslo was an unmitigated disaster at this level.

The third level is more long-term in intent and focus. Given the failures at the second level, this level never became operational but this hardly means it is inconsequential. Since many of the structural problems that have driven and deepened the conflict over the years still persist – even if the peace process has reached substantive agreement – the process of reconciliation can hardly have begun.[40] The problems that remain are thus deep-seated, they will not disappear because a "scrap of paper" has been signed, and it may take decades before success at this level can be achieved. Nevertheless, even if reconciliation can only be built brick by brick through an accumulation of small actions that show mutual respect, a commitment to equity, and a willingness to atone for and apologize for the atrocities of the past, it remains true that efforts need to commence at once. The leaders on both sides obviously never gave this level the slightest thought and began running backwards as rapidly as possible. Expectations that the relationship would begin to change and that each would value the benefits of peace were completely thwarted.

One result was that leaders lost any credibility they might have had (or built up) with the other side. Since the ability to make credible promises is essential for an effective bargaining relationship, and since this no longer seems possible with the present leadership, we confront the grim reality that peace may have to be put on hold. However, the necessity of constructing and maintaining a stable coalition against terrorism after September 11 may finally have forced the Bush administration in November 2002 to make its first serious venture in Middle East peacemaking, with results that are as yet unclear. Finally, one should note that the ultimate aim at this level is not the elimination of conflicts of interest, an obvious impossibility, but rather a commitment to resolve all disputes peacefully and by political means. That this is now utopian should not be an excuse for wallowing in cynicism or insisting "nothing can be done." Some small steps of progress are always possible, indeed necessary, even at the darkest moments.[41]

6 The violence and hatred that have virtually destroyed the peace process in the last six months (since Ariel Sharon's infamous visit to the Temple Mount in September 2000) have had one potentially salutary effect. Both sides have learned, at an unnecessarily high cost, that current strategies are not working.[42] They have not, however, learned how to improve their performances and thus far we have seen only tactical maneuvering and not new strategies. In effect, we have evidence of a negative learning curve: the worse things get, the worse each side behaves. According to one analyst, for learning to occur a sense of urgency, of feasibility, and of desirability must converge. Only the first has spread widely among the elite communities on both sides, which implies that the deeper assumptions about the relationship are unlikely to be changed but that tactical shifts are possible – and at least potentially useful for averting some crises or managing those that do occur.[43] There are many reasons why learning is difficult (complexity, different interpretations of past, present and future, the rapidity of change, etc.) but it may be especially so in an intense, virtually existential conflict. As noted earlier, it is a crucial issue, if complex and elusive, because many key values that can sustain a peace process – trust, cooperation, empathy – must be learned: they do not always come naturally in the present context.

In the current situation (April 2001) it has become nearly impossible to end the violence and restart the negotiating process because both Arafat and Sharon have locked themselves into a bargaining straitjacket. Sharon says no talks until the violence stops but Arafat seems to think only violence can get him *all* of his goals – i.e., more than Barak offered at Camp David – and thus insists the violence will continue until he gets what he wants (a negotiating process that *begins* where Barak's last offer left off).[44] Either doing what the other wants would thus seem a loss of face and an enormous risk domestically.[45] The only winners are the extremists opposed to any peace agreement: "meaningless" atrocities, as one observer has called them, in fact are very meaningful if they can derail a fragile peace process. What do these comments suggest about appropriate bargaining strategies? There is a grand debate between two schools of thought – leaving aside the third option of staggering on with a deteriorating status quo until both sides (presumably) come to their senses, an option that is both dangerous and unattractive to all. The first school insists that incremental, brick-by-brick bargaining will not work because of the intensity of the conflict, the total absence of trust, and the pervasive fear that concessions will be interpreted as weakness. Thus only a "big bang" strategy will work. The model here is familiar from Camp David I and II and Dayton: lock the leaders away in some isolated venue, heavy involvement and pressure from a powerful mediator (the United States), the rising political costs of failure for leaders on both sides as expectations rise and their reputations are at stake, and the alluring vision of a reputation as a peacemaker or a candidate for a Nobel Peace Prize. But sometimes the big bang fizzles (as at Camp David II) or continued disagreement on critical issues is obscured or inability or unwillingness to fully implement vague terms is ignored. The high risk/high gain strategy is attractive because it apparently leaps over the usual obstacles by getting the big chiefs into a setting where the costs of failure may seem, at least momentarily, to be greater than the risks of compromise agreement.[46] But if there is no "contract zone" on key substantive issues, if emotions are running too high, and if the enemies of the compromise are strong, not many leaders are going to take the big risks or believe in the big gains.

The alternative seems to be incrementalism, leaving the big issues aside until conditions are more promising and pursuing limited goals that, brick by brick, build bridges to coexistence. Perhaps some limited political agreements will become possible (if initially on peripheral issues) and perhaps even a code of conduct will gradually develop that creates new rules on how to carry on the relationship.[47] But by its very nature an incremental process can be derailed by its slowness in the face of high levels of distrust or by limited gains that do not seem to accumulate or spread to the masses or by the anger generated by terrorist actions or by the lack of clarity about where the process is meant to go. Low risk/low gain may come to seem high risk, no gain.

If these alternatives seem inadequate, what is left? One possibility is to suggest a compromise that might be called "incrementalism plus": an agreement on the minimal long-term goals of both sides (a Palestinian state in nearly all of the West Bank/Gaza and East Jerusalem, and an Israeli commitment to stop all settlement activity in exchange for a strong commitment to stop the violence, stop the illegal purchase of arms, and cease all future demands on Israeli land), with this goal to be pursued in a phased fashion and with strong sanctions for non-compliance. Issues for which no agreement was possible (like the right of return or control of the Temple Mount/*al-Haram al-Sharif*) would require continuous negotiation for a period of time, after which they could be submitted to a mutually-agreed arbitration panel. This kind of agreement would diminish Israeli fears that Arafat would continually raise new demands – the infamous "salami" tactic – and it would provide a period in which (perhaps) enough progress could be made to cool down the "hot" issues and make them amenable to compromise. It would also make clearer what compliance and good behavior would produce and it might generate incentives to comply and not disincentives to cheat. Unfortunately, this argument begs a key question: How do you stop the currently escalating levels of violence so that enough stability can be restored to begin even thinking about bargaining strategies, not win-the-war strategies? (Or the desperate "strategy" of hanging on until the other cracks or something turns up). Given the hard trade-off between guaranteed short-run costs and short-run political risks and the uncertain long-run benefits, this outcome is unsurprising. Still, front-loading benefits, meeting early deadlines, being careful about rhetoric, may at least send some useful signals.

There is another point about bargaining strategies that may be worth mentioning. When the conflict is at its most intense and apparently insoluble state, the only kind of bargaining game that is likely to work is distributional: the narrow exchange of like for like on largely procedural issues. When there is a move toward peace, one hopes to see some form of integrative bargaining emerge in which trade-offs between issues and perhaps resource commitments from external parties permit the size of the pie to be increased. This did not happen either during the initial Oslo negotiations or in the aftermath, perhaps because so little of substance was actually decided by Oslo or perhaps because the United States and other potential donors were not directly involved in the process. In any case, the delays in implementation and the continual accusations of bad faith and non-compliance hardly created an environment conducive to moving beyond distributional bargaining or indeed counterfeit bargaining designed largely to make the other side seem duplicitous.

There is another perspective on the negotiating process in protracted conflicts that may be worth noting, even if its relevance remains to be proved. If the period after a weak peace agreement has some unique characteristics, mixing together persisting conditions of the old conflict and the new conditions or possibilities generated by an initial step toward peace, perhaps we could argue that this period also requires a new approach to bargaining and negotiations, one that builds on but is different from integrative bargaining.[48] This new approach might be described as "transformational bargaining" because the central aim is neither winning the game nor increasing the size of the pie but rather generating new rules and codes of conduct to facilitate long-term peaceful coexistence. This is bound to be an evolutionary process but one that needs to begin affecting behavior in the peace process very quickly – lest we recapitulate the cumulative disasters of the post-Oslo years.[49]

What one needs to try to do in the post-peace agreement period is to deal with the changes that are occurring and the changes that have not yet occurred. Morley argues that negotiations are not about resolving issues or managing a conflict but rather about creating a formula to link what is happening now to what happened in the past and what will happen in the future.[50] Creating an "agreed story" may indeed be helpful over the long term but in the present context it might be considered too abstract or insufficiently aware of the elements of the "conflict ethos" that still persist. It may be more realistic or prudent to suggest that what needs to be done is to shift the bargaining focus from a sole concern with gains for each to a joint concern with individual gains *and* gains for the relationship itself so that each side sees the survival of a viable relationship as a value in itself.[51] This also implies understanding that an important part of the bargaining is subjective and is largely about recognition of identities, status, and legitimacy; once this understanding is achieved, implementation of rules of conduct becomes much easier. This does not imply an effort to deemphasize the importance of gains for each side but rather an attempt to broaden the definition of interests and to weight future gains more heavily.[52]

There have been a number of efforts to suggest rules or codes of conduct for former enemies but most seem to focus on cases where power needs to be shared in a single state between relatively equal partners.[53] Here I am concerned with a related but distinct case: the partitioning of territory between relatively unequal partners. I will merely suggest, tentatively, some possible rules for transformational bargaining. I should emphasize that all these points merely summarize lessons from prior analysis. First and most obviously, there must be an agreement, preferably explicit, to settle all future conflicts of interest peacefully and through a mutually agreed political process. There is usually a willingness to make this pledge when an initial agreement is being negotiated (as with Arafat's commitments at Oslo) but an equal willingness to abandon it when gains seem insufficient or domestic pressures mount. This is a make-or-break issue and perhaps one ought to consider sanctions for non-compliance, especially by mediators, aid agencies, and guarantors. Such sanctions ought to be limited to publicity for early violations but ought to rise in severity with later or more serious violations. Second, borrowing from the theory of consociational democracy, there must be a mutual veto over actions that affect both communities or that have significant cross-border effects. Israel's continual expansion of settlements illustrates the dangers here. Third, despite the mutual recognition implicit in the initial peace agreement, the de facto inequality between the two partners suggests the need for asymmetrical reciprocity: the stronger must be willing to sacrifice some short-run gains for the long-term benefit of the relationship. Fourth, as noted above, while the leader's first task is to ensure that he can increase his own constituency for peace, it is also critical that he understands the needs (and thoughts) of the other leader and is willing to offer support – perhaps hanging together may avert hanging separately. Fifth, leaders must try to avoid forcing confrontations or crises or pushing every dispute to the edge of the abyss – the fabric of the relationship may be too weak to withstand such pressures. Sixth, building peace brick by brick obviously takes time but actions that seem small and insignificant by themselves can accumulate and have significant substantive effects – akin to what happens with the idea in economics of a "cascade of information."[54] Doing things like rewriting biased histories and school texts and changing the rhetoric of confrontation in various arenas can show benign intentions and affect the atmosphere of the relationship. Finally, it helps to build joint institutions that can facilitate cooperation, learning, and mutual awareness. And they may increase the number of people with a felt stake in the peace process.

None of these rules, of course, guarantee a stable peace but implementing them does seem likely to increase the probability that the peace can be strengthened. This is especially true if implementation is accompanied by substantial external financial and political support, providing that support is not wasted in corruption and misconceived expenditures.[55]

Conclusions

Oslo was an exceptionally fragile peace but perhaps the best that could be gotten (or expected) at the time. It gave Arafat and the PLO substantial benefits but it did not provide many benefits to the Palestinian people, it promised negotiations on all the critical issues but it could not and did not guarantee any of the outcomes each side desired, and neither side was able or willing to take the risks implicit in betting on the success of the peace process. As noted, the result was a peace process that became the continuation of conflict by other means. The context of peacemaking was so difficult that failure could easily have been anticipated. Only a different, wiser, and more powerful leadership might have averted the worst.

Given the fact that agreements like Oslo or the Good Friday agreement or the Dayton agreement will always have high risks of failure, why sign them? All of these agreements were top/down agreements and there was very little pressure from below or from the demonstration effect to take the plunge. Still, the elites on both sides, if for very different reasons, could have concluded that even a weak agreement that is badly implemented was a better risk than a status quo that seemed likely to deteriorate. Even if they fail, such agreements may create a floor on which to anchor later negotiations; they break through the immobility, and they may compel some on both sides to begin thinking about what peace is worth and what must be sacrificed to get it. Moreover, some of the risks may be bearable – not all failures to implement are crucial. Agreements are exchanges of conditional promises and there are many reasons to comply with them (including testing the intentions of the other or preserving a reputation for trustworthiness). There are also a variety of means available to decrease vulnerability or to increase the costs of non-compliance.[56] Increasing the incentives to comply may be necessary, especially in the early post-peace period, but if expectations are effectively managed, if some beneficial learning does occur, and if external support is generous, incentives may come to outweigh disincentives.

Nevertheless, gaining sufficient support for the peace process is always going to be a hard sell. Apart from the fact that old attitudes and beliefs will not disappear quickly and that the immediate gains from peace are not likely to be great, there is the intrinsic dilemma of such peaces: there is no way to guarantee that the old enemy is able or willing to implement the peace (let alone deepen it) or that he will not swallow today's concessions and then ask for more. In such circumstances both sides may find it easier to make a case for fighting on because the risks are known and the costs seem bearable and victory – someday – may be possible. And a risky peace process does not have the cognitive legitimacy, especially with the masses, of more, but familiar, conflict.

Thus signing with the full intention of implementing commitments may require a leap of faith.[57] That leap may be justified if the risks of not seeking peace are seen as worse, if some means of reducing the risks (phased implementation, demilitarization, third party guarantees, etc.) are built into the process, and if key leaders recognize (and act on) the belief that the future is not determined – that bad things are possible but not certain. And, presumably some on the other side are likely to see it as in their interest to accept the terms and implement them effectively. In the end, there are no risk-free choices and gambling on a prudent, phased peace process may be as (or more) reasonable than gambling on a crumbling and dangerous status quo.

The gloom and doom surrounding current circumstances is surely justified. At a minimum, an opportunity has been lost; at a maximum, both sides might slide even deeper into violence and hatred and perhaps even generate a regional war. Nevertheless, it is very important to emphasize another aspect of the Oslo process. A few years ago a US official was asked to assess the progress in Bosnia since the signing of the Dayton agreement. He replied:

> If you judge by Dayton [that is, the terms of the agreement] there is noncompliance everywhere you look . . . But if you judge by the standard of a peace process [over twenty or thirty years], this thing is going at warp speed.[58]

There is a useful lesson implicit in this comment. The terms of Oslo have obviously not been met but Oslo also has a deeper layer of meaning. If one looks beyond the violence, one could argue that Oslo broke the mold and forced each side for the first time to confront questions obscured by the conflict itself: how much is peace really worth and how much can we or must we give up for an opportunity to live in peace? Confronted with these questions both sides – leaders and followers alike – have retreated into the comfortable pieties of the past and into mutual accusations of deceit and bad faith. When and if the peace process is revived, it may well be that both sides will have learned useful lessons about how to run and not run a peace process. In effect, even if Oslo is in ruins, it will have left traces in the sand that future peacemakers will not be able to ignore or forget.

There are a few simple and obvious precepts that might make future negotiations more likely to succeed. Simple and obvious they may be but they are too often forgotten or ignored in the context of intense conflict. Most of these precepts refer to attitudes that both sides need to bring to the negotiations or priorities that they need to set. In a sense, they seek to broaden the cognitive legitimacy of the peace process to both sides, elites and public alike.

(1) Borrowing from a literary expression – synecdoche – do not mistake the actions of a part for the actions of the whole. We all "know" on some intellectual level that not all Palestinians are terrorists and not all Israelis are Baruch Goldsteins. But we also speak loosely when we say "the Palestinians" or "the Israelis" do not "really" want peace, when in fact some do, others don't, and yet others shift attitudes quickly in response to what the *other* does do. We forget all these distinctions too easily in the context of the latest atrocity, especially when media and texts depict the other as evil and corrupt. It pays to remember that peace will always be opposed by some and that the peace does not require unanimity in either camp but rather enough on both sides to form a viable (and, one hopes, growing) coalition for peace. In any case, neither will be able to see potential partners for peace if neither can differentiate between potential allies and real enemies.[59]

(2) A second precept borrows from the first rule of medicine: do no harm. Joining a peace process merely to gain leverage in the conflict or with no intention of full implementation or with the intention of using violence as a means to force concessions can only succeed in destroying the peace.

It is a useless counsel of perfection to insist that none of these should be done, given the inevitable doubts that a fragile peace can survive. Still, if the leaders at least are genuinely committed to the peace process, destabilizing and destructive actions may be limited, contained, and unnecessary. As noted above, failure here means that the leader will lose credibility with the other side and lose also the ability to make the necessary conditional promises that are the basis of any agreement. Failure also means later agreements will be progressively harder to negotiate.

(3) Everyone agrees that the peace process requires strong leaders that are willing to talk truthfully to their followers, that have the courage to do more than hide behind their extremists, that understand that the post-peace period will require new patterns of thought and action, and that have the courage to make clear that there is no such thing as a cheap peace, a peace without painful compromises. The conflict between Israel and the Palestinians has had only caricatures of this ideal, although Rabin might well have risen to the occasion had he lived. The problem is that the evolution of the conflict tends to generate weak leaders limited by ambivalent domestic support and rising opposition to compromise. Perhaps only a mediator who provides strong cover for necessary compromises and strong promises of aid can help this situation. The other apparent option, increasingly discussed in recent months, is to await the arrival of a new generation of leaders, which could be a costly wait – and there is no guarantee that they would be much better. One needs also to be aware that talk of the need for a new leader may only further weaken support for the existing leader, thus making the negotiating process even more unstable. Perhaps trying to strengthen the old leader may be a more prudent course than waiting for salvation by the arrival of a new savior.

(4) There is widespread agreement among analysts of the negotiating process that any agreement will be unstable unless it is perceived as fair and equitable by both sides. The problem with this, of course, is that there is usually complete disagreement between the parties about what equity or fairness means. The problem is compounded by the lack of empathy, which implies that each dismisses the other's claims as spurious or irrelevant.[60] Here asymmetrical reciprocity by the stronger side could be helpful in smoothing over subjective conflicts, as could an emphasis on apologies for past sins.[61] Perhaps also this could be joined to a sense of asymmetrical equity: the grievances and resentments of the rebel side may be deeper and thus unilateral gestures by the stronger may have a disproportionately beneficial impact. In the short run, given the complexity of this issue, perhaps it would be better to try to avoid focusing on fairness and equity, and instead concentrate on practical compromises that can produce quick benefits for the public at large.

(5) One problem has been intrinsic to the kind of peace process described

above. This is that all the short-run calculations of interests and actions work out the wrong way. It is rational to make only tentative commitments, to delay implementation, and to cheat where the likelihood of being caught and the penalties for being caught are small, if you distrust the other side and if you doubt his willingness or ability to offer a compromise more attractive than the status quo. In these circumstances any agreement is likely to unravel before it can produce enough benefits to begin to seem valuable. In effect, to borrow a term that is currently fashionable at the World Bank with regard to structural adjustment programs, no one seems to "own" the peace agreement in the sense of feeling it is a valuable possession that should be protected and nurtured.

This brings us to the final precept, one that is endlessly relevant for problems of cooperation in an anarchic world: take the long-run seriously or as the economists say, lower the discount rate on the future. If both sides remain entirely focused on short-run, zero-sum games or games of chicken or blind man's bluff, the prognosis is for more of the same (if we are lucky) or a steadily deteriorating blood bath with potentially disastrous regional consequences. Decisions that seem too painful or even dangerous to make now might be calculated differently if each side thought more about what the relationship might look like in ten years if such decisions are not taken now and such risks run now before they become much worse in the years ahead. This little exercise in mental gymnastics is unlikely to affect the calculations of the extremists who believe that both God and time are on their side but whether it can somehow intrude on the calculations of weak leaders intent, above all, on retaining power is unclear. Unless it does, however, whether from the emergence of new leaders, or severe pressures from key patrons, or from a terrible "shock" that finally generates enough pressure so that most come to believe "enough is enough," the race to the bottom may not be over.

Notes

1 Complaints about the corruption, brutality and incompetency of Mr. Arafat's regime have been widespread even within the Palestinian community. For example, see the severe criticisms in a joint statement by twenty Palestinian notables reported in *The New York Times*, November 29, 1999, p. A7. Mr. Arafat provided abundant evidence of the accuracy of the indictment by promptly jailing seven of the signers, shooting another, and threatening the rest.

2 Edward Said has long advocated the creation of a binational state in which Israelis and Palestinians share power and live together peacefully. See Edward W. Said, *The End of the Peace Process – Oslo and After* (New York: Pantheon Books, 2000). Since this would involve the destruction of the idea of a Jewish state and since it would give the Palestinians only shared sovereignty, this is a

peace proposal with a unique characteristic: it is completely rejected by both sides. Apart from the obvious fact that the escalation of violence and radical rhetoric has made living together peacefully seem ever more utopian, the pursuit of this "solution" and the dismissal of the Oslo process and whatever succeeds it loses the opportunity to make moderate gains that can be built on and generates more support for extremist options that could destroy any hope of progress toward peace.

3   For criticism of Arafat by the former US Negotiator Dennis Ross, see Clyde Haberman, "Dennis Ross's Exit Interview," *The New York Times Magazine*, March 27, 2001, pp. 38–9. For a bizarre assault on former President Clinton, who pushed the Israeli government to make the Palestinians the most generous offer they have ever received, see the excerpts from a memorandum issued by the Palestinian Media Center under the auspices of the Palestinian Authority in *The New York Times*, January 23, 2001, p. A10.

4   The violence is embittering and polarizing but it does not always impinge heavily on daily life and adaptations have been made to the other costs. As one analyst said of Northern Ireland, "the current situation is unsatisfactory to all the contending parties, but it is not the worst conceivable. [The parties] hold on to what advantages they have, lest in the course of bargaining they lose even more than they already have." John Whyte, "Dynamics of Social and Political Change in Northern Ireland," in Dermot Keogh and Michael H. Haltzel, eds., *Northern Ireland and the Politics of Reconciliation* (Cambridge: Cambridge University Press, 1993), p. 116. One ought not leave the impression here that the domestication of protracted conflict – learning to live with its traumas – is cost free: *inter alia*, there is a coarsening of civic virtue, a devaluation of democratic norms, and a destruction of empathy.

5   A number of rebel groups, after discovering victory is not imminent, have adopted a "long war" strategy to minimize short-run losses and keep the "dream" alive. See for example Brendan O'Brien, *The Long War: The IRA and Sin Fein, 1985 to Today* (Syracuse: Syracuse University Press, 1995).

6   For a more detailed treatment of these conditions see my essay "In Fear of Peace: Getting Past Maybe," in Robert L. Rothstein, ed., *After the Peace: Resistance and Reconciliation* (Boulder, CO: Lynne Rienner Publishers, 1999), pp. 1–25. On the "conflictive ethos" and the way in which it enables a society to adapt to conflict, see the interesting piece by Daniel Bar-Tal, "From Intractable Conflict Through Conflict Resolution to Reconciliation: Psychological Analysis," *Political Psychology*, Vol. 21, No. 2 (2000), pp. 351–65.

7   See Meron Benvenisti, *Intimate Enemies – Jews and Arabs in a Shared Land* (Berkeley, CA: University of California Press, 1995), pp. 77–88 and 199–200, for an argument about the existential nature of the Israeli–Palestinian Conflict.

8   The absence of empathy is also part of the reason why the response of one side to an atrocity committed against the other is rarely an expression of genuine sympathy but rather a restatement of what has been done to us by them in the past – if not an actual expression of joy at the suffering of the other, as if it allayed my own pain.

9   The dilemma is that a gradual, incremental peace process is likely to fail because of the use of violence by the extremists, the slowness in achieving significant material benefits from peace, and the inability of weakened leaders to manage rising expectations effectively. Conversely, the conditions necessary for successful "big bang" negotiations are rarely present. Thus neither a low risk/low gain nor a high risk/high gain strategy seems likely to work, a point to which we shall return.

10 Richard Rose quoted in John McGarry and Brendan O'Leary, *Explaining Northern Ireland – Broken Images* (Oxford: Blackwell Publishers, 1995), p. 354. Note that Rose seemed largely correct for about two decades but that gradual changes were occurring – politically, psychologically, economically – that finally led, as with Oslo, to a tentative breakthrough in the mid-1990s.

11 While the existential elements of the conflict seemed to abate immediately after the Oslo Accord was signed, the resumption of terrorism, armed attacks, and riots has regenerated feelings about an existential threat – particularly in Israel where the feeling that "we are back to 1948" has grown even among some of the people who were once among Oslo's strongest supporters.

12 Much of the literature on internal conflicts, borrowing a term made popular by I. W. Zartman, uses the term "ripe moment" where I have used the term "window of opportunity." I prefer the latter for a number of reasons that I will discuss in a forthcoming piece but note here only that Zartman's term is something of a tautology, that the notion of a specific "moment" is misleading and not well specified, and that it misses the complexity of the different strands that must come together to get a tentative break-through toward peace. Zartman also argues that the ripe moment will come when there is a "mutually hurting stalemate" but this too is not well specified: the mutually hurting stalemate can go on for a long time before a ripe moment suddenly appears. See I. William Zartman, "Dynamics and Constraints in Negotiations in Internal Conflicts," in Zartman, ed., *Elusive Peace: Negotiating an End to Civil Wars* (Washington, DC: The Brookings Institution, 1995), pp. 3–29.

13 Trade-offs in the initial stage will be discussed below.

14 I shall discuss later how such efforts might be generated and strengthened.

15 Demands for full and complete implementation of all Palestinian commitments at Oslo (especially on terrorism) might seem reasonable in this context but asking for too much too quickly, as Prime Minister Netanyahu did with Chairman Arafat, may thus be a disguised way to undermine the agreement or to weaken the enemy leader. For an interesting discussion of this argument, see Ian S. Lustick, "Ending Protracted Conflicts: The Oslo Peace Process Between Political Partnership and Legality," *Cornell International Law Journal*, Vol. 30, No 3 (1997), pp. 741–57.

16 In this regard Arafat failed miserably as his rhetoric in private ("the struggle continues," etc.) differed from his rhetoric in public (constant assertions about the need for a "peace of the brave," which rapidly became a joke on both sides), which greatly increased suspicion and doubt about Oslo. His creation of a corrupt, brutal, and incompetent PA did not help matters. On this, see Glen E. Robinson, "The Growing Authoritarianism of the Arafat Regime," *Survival*, Vol. 39, No. 2 (Summer 1997), pp. 42–56. Robinson says that the fact

that Arafat has become a despot is surprising but I do not find it surprising given his background, his experiences as a frequently challenged rebel leader, the weakening of his position (especially after support for Saddam Hussein's invasion and brutalization of Kuwait), and the lack of strong popular support for Oslo.

17 Conviction about the other's lack of seriousness and the fear of being duped are, as noted earlier, intrinsic to these kinds of peace processes. The lack of trust thus generates negative self-fulfilling processes, which implies that both sides (and external supporters) must be aware of this and understand the need to take actions that generate increases in trust. Since building trust is obviously time-consuming and since cooperative policies must be implemented from the beginning of the peace process many analysts argue that overlapping interests must be and can be a sufficient basis for cooperation. I am doubtful, however, that in the fraught context of protracted conflict a sense of shared interests will suffice (or perhaps even be perceived). This suggests that, since trust and cooperation are largely learned patterns of behavior, a successful peace process will require leaders who seek to generate a learning process that sends the proper signals or lessons to the other side – which did not happen after Oslo. On learning trust, see Kenneth Clark and Martin Sefton, "The Sequential Prisoner's Dilemma: Evidence on Reciprocation," *The Economic Journal*, Vol. 111 (January 2001), pp. 51–68.

18 If leaders on both sides understood this context more clearly, they might also understand a crucial piece of tactical advice: don't push to the edge of the abyss because there may not be any exit strategy. This seems to be the situation that Arafat and Sharon have now blundered into: extreme statements about what the other must do or commit to before talks can begin again. On how stronger and wiser leaders in South Africa avoided going over the abyss – although they got close to it at times – see Pierre du Toit, "South Africa In Search of Post-Settlement Peace," in John Darby and Roger MacGinty, eds., *The Management of Peace Processes* (London: Macmillan, 2000), pp. 30–1.

19 Lustick has argued for a high-risk, high-gain strategy in the Oslo process but my argument attempts to explain why it is very likely that a low-risk, low-gain strategy will be chosen and, indeed, why the high-risk strategy, were it to be chosen by both sides, might end very badly – as happened with Arafat, Barak, and Clinton at Camp David II. For the counter argument, see Ian S. Lustick "Necessary Risks: Lessons for the Israeli-Palestinian Peace Process from Ireland and Algeria," *Middle East Policy*, Vol. 3, No. 3 (1994), p. 42ff.

20 The quote is from Eamonn Mallie and David McKitrick, *The Fight for Peace – The Secret Story Behind the Irish Peace Process* (London: Heinemann, 1996), p. 349. I shall speak further below about the contrast between what strong and weak leaders can risk.

21 Yossi Beilin notes that Abu Mazen, a very high-ranking Palestinian official, told him (Beilin) at Oslo that the Palestinian leadership before Oslo took pride in knowing nothing about Israel and the Israelis: why bother if Israel was to be destroyed? So Israel was demonized and no distinction was made between different views or perspectives. See Yossi Beilin, *Touching Peace – From the Oslo Accord to a Final Agreement* (London: Weidenfeld and Nicolson, 1999),

p. 168. Perhaps this commitment to ignorance about the enemy helps to explain why Arafat took so many actions that undermined the Israeli peace movement. In any case, ignorance and demonization do not encourage empathy.

22 There will be more discussion of this level with the fourth point below.

23 For two-level bargaining games, see Peter B. Evans, Harold K. Jacobsen, and Robert D. Putnam, eds., *Double-edged Diplomacy: International Bargaining and Domestic Politics* (Berkeley: University of California Press, 1993). Note that even the notion of a three-level game may sometimes oversimplify, as in Northern Ireland where one could specify a direct Loyalists–Nationalist level, a Belfast–London level, a Belfast–Dublin level, and a London–Dublin level – not to mention the domestic levels for all the parties to the conflict.

24 For one interesting example of the current focus on the importance, if not the dominance, of domestic politics, see Helen V. Milner, *Interests, Institutions and Information: Domestic Politics and International Relations* (Princeton: Princeton University Press, 1997).

25 For testimony in this regard about Arafat, see Haberman, "Dennis Ross's Exit Interview" and Mohamed Rabiel, *US–PLO Dialogue – Secret Diplomacy and Conflict Resolution* (Gainesville, FL: University of Florida Press, 1995, pp. 46–56. It is unclear whether rebel leaders, always insecure and threatened, exhibit these tendencies in a more flagrant form than government leaders – as the economists say, it all depends.

26 Most peace processes in protracted conflicts are top/down in form, which also generates the common problem of how to develop grassroots support. One apparent exception is the Basque conflict, where pressures for peace were driven by both popular demands and the "demonstration effect" of the Good Friday agreement in Northern Ireland. See Ludger Mees, "The Basque Peace Process, Nationalism and Political Violence," in Darby and MacGinty, *The Management of Peace Processes*, pp. 172–4 and 175–6.

27 We shall return to these issues below.

28 See Tamar Hermann and David Newman, "A Path Strewn with Thorns: Along the Difficult Road of Israeli–Palestinian Peacemaking," in Darby and MacGinty, *The Management of Peace Processes*, pp. 43–5.

29 Even prominent peaceniks like the novelist Amos Oz began to express serious doubts about whether Arafat was ever serious about peace or – worse yet – whether peace with the Palestinians would ever be possible. More and more people began to refer to the years of struggle after 1948 as if the past had been resurrected in an even more malignant form.

30 The political philosopher Hannah Arendt was one of the first to point out the importance of being able to make credible promises in politics. It is especially important in the present context where doubts about the other's true intentions are inevitable. For a brief discussion of Arendt's views, see Ronald A. Wells, *People Behind the Peace: Community and Reconciliation in Northern Ireland* (Grand Rapids, MI: Wm. B. Erdmans, 1999), pp. 40–1.

31 The leader's primary initial task is obviously to rally domestic support for peace, without which he will quickly fall – or quickly have to abandon the peace process. But it takes two leaders and two constituencies for peace to

stabilize and deepen. Thus, each leader is also a key figure in helping (or hurting) the other's efforts to build support. The leader's task is dual because he has so much at stake in how well the other performs, something which neither Arafat nor Netanyahu seemed to understand or care about. In addition, neither Arafat nor Netanyahu made even minimal efforts to educate their own people about the compromises necessary for peace, whether from weakness or lack of conviction about peace is unclear. Or perhaps it was simply too dangerous in terms of each's domestic constituency, which offered support based on an image of militancy.

32 The dilemmas faced by weak leadership also raises questions about the commonsensical notion that the longer a peace process goes on, the more the leader has invested in it and the more he needs some face-saving compromise. But the situation is more complex than this because it depends on the alternatives available, the nature of the gains in the compromise, the extent of internal and external pressures to reach agreement, and subjective judgments about whether time is or is not on one's side.

33 See du Toit, "South Africa: In Search of Post-Settlement Peace," p. 29.

34 For an excellent review of the weaknesses of Palestinian institutions, see *Strengthening Palestinian Public Institutions* (Report of an Independent Task Force sponsored by the Council on Foreign Relations, with Yezid Sayegh and Khalil Shikaki as Principal Authors, New York, 1999) and Glen E. Robinson, *Building a Palestinian State: The Incomplete Revolution* (Bloomington, IN: Indiana University Press, 1997).

35 Haberman, "Dennis Ross's Exit Interview," p. 38.

36 Hermann and Newman, "A Path Strewn with Thorns," pp. 119–20.

37 When Arafat publicly raised demands for a "right of return" for several million Palestinian refugees to Israel itself and for complete sovereignty over the Temple Mount/*Haram al-Sharif*, which was obviously also a revered religious site for Jews, he was not only falling in behind his own extremists but also signaling the Israelis that he had lost interest in peace and wanted only victory. One is reminded here of a statement by Heinlein, the leader of the Czech Germans, in 1938: "We must always demand so much that we cannot be satisfied." Quoted in Arthur Aughey, "A New Beginning? The Prospects for a Politics of Civility in Northern Ireland," in Joseph Ruane and Jennifer Todd, eds., *After the Good Friday Agreement* (Dublin: University College Dublin Press, 1999), p. 140.

38 Note that the divergent responses to weakness – one seeking to use more violence to get more gains, the other offering more concessions in hopes of overcoming domestic dissent by reaching a comprehensive settlement – suggests the difficulties of deriving simple propositions about the varied effects of domestic politics on peace processes.

39 To return to an earlier metaphor, the painters/peacemakers in Northern Ireland drew a few more lines (about power sharing, peaceful resolution of disputes, a principle of majority consent), but left the big issue of Northern Ireland's political fate unsettled. Oslo was a more problematic agreement because its initial benefits were largely procedural, it settled nothing of substance, and it provided no picture of a final agreement or of a principle to

guide the decision-making process. In part, this reflects the difference between a case where power-sharing in one entity is an obvious choice and the more difficult and complex issues involved in dividing a territory both consider their own.

40 For discussions of the requirements of this stage, see my "Fragile Peace and Its Aftermath," in Rothstein, *After the Peace*, pp. 223–47 and Bar-Tal, "From Intractable Conflict Through Conflict Resolution to Reconciliation."

41 This is one of the benefits of the many "second track" negotiations that may occasionally benefit the peace process itself but are probably more important in keeping lines of communication open even in the worst of times and in exploring options that are difficult to deal with in formal talks because of fears of losing face or appearing weak.

42 Some Palestinians are even beginning to question the use of violence as a bargaining tactic, "gingerly asking if their leaders have a strategy that justifies the devastating loss of life, property, mobility and income." Deborah Sontag, "Palestinians Delicately Begin Debate on Circle of Violence," *The New York Times*, March 9, 2001, p. A1 and p. A8. There are obviously risks in doing so because even the appearance of disloyalty has been punished severely – including assassination.

43 See George W. Breslauer, "What Have We Learned About Learning?" in George W. Breslauer and Philip E. Tetlock, eds., *Learning in US and Soviet Foreign Policy* (Boulder, CO: Westview Press, 1991), pp. 830–51. Since it seems clear that deeper assumptions about the enemy and about appropriate behavior are unlikely to change until the peace process is widely perceived as stable and beneficial – which may take more than a decade – the crucial immediate question is whether and how the peace process can survive when old ideas still prevail and new ideas are largely about tactical adjustments. Perhaps adapted behavior-choosing new means but not new ends-will suffice until the peace process begins to show its worth.

44 The latter demand, of course, violates standard bargaining rules (nothing is decided until everything is decided, which implies partial concessions in a failed negotiation do not bind later negotiators), rules that the Palestinians themselves insisted on (according to an Israeli negotiator). Arafat's use of violence brings to mind an old Arab proverb: When the only tool you have is a hammer, every problem looks like a nail.

45 The fact that both sides have backed themselves into a rhetorical corner is rather like the current crisis over decommissioning of arms in Northern Ireland. Either the relinquishing of arms by the IRA or acceptance of the fact that they will not relinquish them by the Protestant community will be seen as a defeat: thus stalemate and a growing threat to the peace itself. Making one demand too far can turn a practical issue, about which some compromises are possible, into a symbolic issue that cannot be compromised.

46 I pointed out earlier that it is not always true that leaders will finally compromise because their reputations will suffer if a prolonged and highly publicized negotiation fails. Much depends on the available alternatives, propensity for risk, and other factors.

47 For suggestions in this regard by Dennis Ross, see Jane Perlez, "U.S. Mideast

Envoy Recalls the Day Pandora's Box Wouldn't Shut," *The New York Times*, January 29, 2001, p. A4.

48   The period after a weak peace agreement has been signed thus has some unique characteristics-which also bear some resemblance to the period after a new democracy has been established on rather shaky grounds. For more detailed comment, see my "Fragile Peace and Its Aftermath."

49   I should hasten to add that the comments that follow are very tentative and incomplete. They are provided here only indicatively.

50   One example of Morley's argument is in Ian E. Morley, "Intra-organizational Bargaining," in Jean F. Hartley and Geoffrey M. Stevenson, eds., *Employment Relations: The Psychology of Influence and Control at Work* (Oxford: Blackwell, 1992), pp. 203–24.

51   This is akin to the notion that the states in the nineteenth-century balance of power system sought individual gains but not to the point that such gains would threaten the system itself. A sense of restraint, of playing by mutually agreed rules, of trying not to push potential allies to the edge kept conflicts – most conflicts – from getting out of hand. It helped, of course, to have a common enemy in mind: revolutionary threats to political stability.

52   Where power is asymmetrically divided it might also imply the need for asymmetrical equity (a willingness by the stronger to accept lesser gains in the short run).

53   There is an interesting discussion of the need for a "politics of civility" in Northern Ireland in Arthur Aughey, "A New Beginning? The Prospects for a Politics of Civility in Northern Ireland," in Ruane and Todd, *After the Good Friday Agreement*, pp. 122–44.

54   This fits with the notion that small actions can, over time, produce larger than anticipated effects.

55   Arafat insisted that a substantial portion of the aid he received be invested in the creation and arming of eight security forces (over 40,000 individuals). According to Israeli sources, he spent even more on secret and illegal imports of other weapons. This has increased the ability of the Palestinians to engage in armed conduct or to undertake terrorist actions. But the opportunity costs have been great: money diverted from more productive efforts to accelerate development, an escalation of the level of violent exchanges with the Israelis, and the conviction in Israel that Israeli citizens would not get security from peace-and that Arafat had proved that he could not be trusted.

56   For a useful discussion of this issue, see Richard B. Bilder, *Managing the Risks of International Agreement* (Madison, WI: University of Wisconsin Press, 1981).

57   Suspicion that the rebel side is only accepting today's offer as a stage before asking for more later is widespread: a compromise agreement reflects momentary inability to achieve all goals but not a relinquishing of those goals. As fears grew in Israel that the use of violence and the hatred pouring out of the "street" (and Arafat's media) meant that the Palestinians would never accept Israel's right to exist in peace, questions also began to grow about giving up anything new if it was to be used only as a platform for more demands. Similar fears arose in Northern Ireland about the IRA's view that the Good Friday agree-

ment was only a stage on the way to Irish unification. See Jennifer Todd, "Nationalism, Republicanism and the Good Friday Agreement" in Ruane and Todd, *After the Good Friday Agreement*, p. 57 ff.

58 Quoted in R. Jeffrey Smith, "U.S. Sees Long Foreign Role in Bosnia," *The International Herald Tribune*, December 29, 1997, p. 5.

59 I already have noted that I am doubtful about the workability of the common-sense notion that all who have the power to overturn the peace process ought to be brought into it. The cost may be too high if they demand too much or if they intend to act as "spoilers." In such cases, they need to be isolated and fought.

60 The problem is especially severe with apparently indivisible and symbolic issues like the Temple Mount/*Haram al-Sharif*. The sensible advice to turn such issues into pragmatic, divisible issues is not easy to follow. The complex issue of what constitutes a just or fair settlement deserves more detailed comment than I can give it here. For a useful analysis, see David A. Welch, *Justice and the Genesis of War* (Cambridge: Cambridge University Press, 1993).

61 There is an interesting discussion of this issue in Donald W. Shriver, Jr., "The Long Road to Reconciliation: Some Moral Stepping-Stones," in Rothstein, *After the Peace*, pp. 207–22.

2

The Pursuit of Israeli–Palestinian Peace: A Retrospective

Aaron Miller

The purpose of this chapter is to look honestly, openly, and critically at the Oslo Process – what it achieved, what it didn't achieve, what about it is worth preserving and what must go by the wayside. It is essential that before we know where we are going, we try to understand where we have been.

First and foremost, I believe it is inappropriate and irrelevant to talk about whether or not Oslo as a process is alive or dead. It is too late for that. The legacy of Oslo, for good or for ill, has shaped the pursuit of Israeli–Palestinian peace in a way that will be very hard to reverse. The legacy of Oslo will likely provide the foundation and to some degree a measure of direction for the future. There are *six aspects* of this legacy that deserve to be discussed. The *first* is the issue of mutual recognition, when in September 1993, Israel and the embodiment of Palestinian nationalism, the organizational embodiment of Palestinian nationalism, the PLO, recognized one another's mutual right to exist. They converted an existential conflict over physical and political identity into a political conflict over borders, over refugees, over security, over Jerusalem, that could be resolved. The issue of mutual recognition is almost irreversible. When you recognize an adversary it is very hard to unrecognize, to take back what you have given, and in recognizing the fact that they were partners Israel and the Palestinians in their own way transcended and undermined a generation of mythologies and ideology. The partnership is definitely uneasy at this point, and indeed it could be described as adversarial, but it is impossible to deny the issue of mutual recognition.

Second, permanent status negotiations, deferred according to an Oslo timetable but ultimately joined, were one of Oslo's most fundamental and radical departures. An Israel and Palestinian commitment for the first time in their history to put issues that were heretofore unthinkable on the negotiating table was very hard to do for each side. For Israelis to put an issue like Jerusalem on the table, for Palestinians who believe in implementation more than in the negotiation process, to discuss territory was very hard. Once an issue is on the table, neither side is going to get everything they want. My perception is that as a result of Oslo, it is impossible to reverse this process now.

Third, Oslo reflected a fundamentally imperfect relationship between two people who were trying desperately to find a way out of a historic struggle. But it changed the situation on the ground, if very imperfectly. Current realities reflect broken commitments and promises, mutual anger and mutual resentment. But two basic facts and processes were created. (1) Israel, to use the words of Oslo, redeployed from the West Bank and withdrew from Gaza, and (2) the Palestinians began to create institutions, however imperfect they may be, of their national life. The realities on the ground are now fundamentally difficult if not impossible to alter.

And *fourth*, what was Oslo a response to in the end? It was a response to one basic reality: that the Israeli–Palestinian problem has no status quo. It will not stay the way it is because Israelis and Palestinians – unlike Israelis and Syrians, unlike Israelis and Jordanians, unlike Israelis and Egytians, and unlike Israelis and Lebanese – are both products of proximity. Proximity is what mandates no status quo. And if there is no status quo in a problem, there has to be change. Change can be bad and violent, tragic and sad. But change can also produce opportunities for accommodation. Oslo was more about starting than it was about continuing or ending. And this in essence was its logic. Oslo was built on the logic of transition. How else do you overcome the complicated situation that Israelis and Palestinians found themselves in? It is all very well to talk about incrementalism or transition. But first you have to talk about how to start a peace process. Later transition brought with it uncertainty and ambiguity; with the result of no clear objective or goal. As a consequence, inevitably, Oslo was flawed because it offered Palestinians and Israelis a departure point but it could not promise or guarantee, either in the negotiations, the agreements themselves, or the implementation of those agreements, where they would ultimately go.

Oslo also had to contend with one fundamental fact that neither Israelis nor Palestinians could change, namely an asymmetry of power. In most negotiations, an asymmetry of power has to somehow be converted into a balance of interests. But this was impossible under the Oslo circumstances. Even prior to Oslo, this issue was particularly difficult for Palestinians. I recall that in the eight or nine negotiating sessions that were held in Washington after the Madrid Conference in October 1991, how difficult it was to watch Israelis and Palestinians deal with each other, but how uplifting it was also to watch Israelis and Palestinians come to Washington and negotiate around a table as equals, with respect and a measure of dignity that was hitherto lacking. It was distressing to observe that once the negotiations adjourned, Israelis and Palestinians returned to an active lower level but ongoing conflict. I do not wish to moralize or to assign blame, but the *reality of an asymmetry of power, which could not be converted into a balance of interests*, made it extremely difficult for both sides.

Settlement activity was a major problem from the Palestinian perspective. In 1992 there were 100,000 Israelis living beyond the Green Line, in 2000 there were 200,000; that is a doubling of the population during the period of the negotiations from 1993 to 2000. Settlements, territory, and borders were issues that were to be addressed in permanent status negotiations. They were not to be prejudiced and predetermined before those permanent status negotiations began. This was one feature of an asymmetrical situation which bred frustration and mistrust, and I believe severely handicapped the Oslo process.

If asymmetry of power was a problem from the Palestinian point of view, then Palestinian behavior during the course of the Oslo process was a huge problem for the Israelis, particularly on the security side. And here there was another asymmetry. If, in fact, renunciation of violence and terrorism was the entry card – the entry point, reflected in the exchange of letters between Rabin and Arafat in September 1993 – then from the Israeli perspective there was little sense of delivery. Albeit that there was security cooperation, and at times there was a unilateral effort on the part of the Palestinian Authority to deal with the activities of Hamas and Islamic Jihad. But from the Israeli perspective, while 100 percent results were not expected, 100 percent effort was expected. And that is not what the Israelis believed was happening. It was episodic at best. And as a consequence of that fact, even though between 1998 and 2000 Israeli experienced the fewest number of terrorist attacks and fatalities in Israel's history, Israeli fatalities doubled during the period 1988 to 1993, and doubled again from 1993 to 1997. This was a major problem because it cut at the core of what the Israelis believed they expected form the Oslo process.

Another issue was the socialization of hostility and grievance, as reflected in Palestinian media treatment. If the Palestinians couldn't abide by Israeli settlement activity, because it prejudged and predetermined issues reserved for negotiations, Israelis increasingly asked themselves the question, Why are our partners continuing to socialize hostility and grievance? And even though most Israelis were prepared to accept the fact that there was resentment and anger as a consequence of Palestinian dependency, this could not excuse the Palestinian Authority's seeming acquiescence or support for this kind of media education. Hence the asymmetry of power and the asymmetry of behavior when it came to security and issues like socialization of grievance made it extremely difficult to create trust and confidence. The logic of Oslo was to defer for now issues that could not be resolved on the assumption that over time confidence and trust would be deposited in the bank. This pool of currency would grow so that even while Jerusalem could not be resolved in 1993, a solution could be worked out later. This was a huge problem because from the perspective of the respective Israeli publics and Palestinian publics a huge gap existed between the world of negotiatiors and the populations on whose behalf they were acting on.

Fifth, the Oslo process created for the first time in the history of the Israeli–Palestinian conflict a process between the Israelis and Palestinians in which they were both heavily invested. There is no question about it. However imperfect the process, four Israeli prime ministers accepted grudgingly, perhaps unwillingly, certain aspects of the Oslo Accords. And the PLO and the Palestinian Authority invested in this process even when their critics and opposition told them that they shouldn't. The process created sufficient basis for cooperation for both parties to enter into permanent status negotiations. But it wasn't enough. There wasn't enough trust and confidence to allow Palestinians and Israelis, when it came time as it did in the spring and summer of 2000, to begin addressing and dealing with the core issues. The Oslo process did not provide the trust and confidence that was required. There was the gap between the world of the negotiatiors and the world on the ground. Then there were two fundamental different points of departure, which psychologically made permanent status negotiations very difficult. The points of departure are not intractable, but they are extremely difficult. The Palestinian departure point, at least among those that accept the notion that a Palestinian state should be created alongside of, instead of in place of Israel, was that a Palestinian state would be the outcome of the peace process. This Palestinian viewpoint is that 78 percent of historic Palestine is gone, 22 percent is left. "It is ours by right, it is ours through a sense of entitlement, it's our." Therefore any fundamental compromise from the 22 percent is a major problem for Palestinians. The Israelis start from a different point of departure. "Yes, we are willing to engage in a political process, yes we are willing to negotiate a permanent status agreement with you, and yes we understand your logic, but you have to accept the fact that our security and demographic needs and requirements will have to come out of your peace." Those two departure points ensured, with or without a successful Oslo process, that the logic of permanent status talks would be very difficult. The issues that Israelis and Palestinians were negotiating were fundamentally different than the issues that Arabs and Israelis had negotiated, either in the first Camp David, the Israelis–Jordanian Peace Treaty of 1984, or the episodic but very serious efforts between the Israelis and the Syrians to negotiate which concluded in March 2000. That is because, of the four core issues that constitute the Israeli–Palestinian permanent status issues, security and territory are negotiable and tractable, but the issues of refugees and Jerusalem are virtually intractable because they involve issues of identity. They are in essence identity issues that don't lend themselves to maps and security arrangements. They cut to the core of the conflict and the sense of history and religion and historical consciousness of both peoples. And as a consequence the burden on the permanent status negotiations of these two issues is tremendous.

Sixth, if you had a process that achieved much but didn't achieve all, was there an alternative? It may be a historical question but it is still a fundamentally important question because it gets to the issue of whether the perfect is in fact the enemy of the good in a conflict where there is no perfect justice. This concept seems to me quite compelling, for there will not be perfect justice from both sides, only imperfect solutions in an imperfect world. Policy is often a choice between imperfect alternatives: pick one, it's better than the other; or don't pick any and sit there and just wait. In my judgment the issue was not whether or not there was another alternative to Oslo, there was no other alternative than to start.

Nevertheless, it is pertinent to ask whether Olso could have been improved. Could confidence and trust been increased, the process of implementation improved, a better relationship between Israelis and Palestinians established, a variety of people to people programs created to address the issues of images and stereotypes? The chapters that follow will address some of these issues.

So where does Oslo fit in the grand scheme of things? I would argue, and have argued, that over the last fifteen years there have been three departure points in the Arab–Israeli conflict, subsequent to the first Camp David, which have created a critical mass of formal and informal agreements. This makes it very difficult for Israelis and Palestinians, or Arabs and Israeli, to go back. An Arab–Israeli peace is not inevitable, but what has been achieved is not easily reversed. The first departure point was Madrid in October 1991, which transformed the whole process of Arab–Israeli negotiations because, whatever excuses or justifications the Israelis and Arabs wanted to use after Madrid as to why there couldn't be a dialogue, why there couldn't be a negotiation, the one justification they could never use again, and they still can't use it to this day, is that there is nobody at the other end of the table. Madrid shattered that excuse forever.

Both sides might not like what they hear but they are partners. In my judgment, Oslo was the second departure point, particularly in view of what it did for Israelis and Palestinians. Finally, what happened in 2000, even though it did not succeed, that is an effort by the Israeli government of Ehud Barak to negotiate permanent status agreements with both Syria and the Palestinians within a six-month period of one another, boggles the mind in how ambitious and bold an undertaking it really was. Barak's purpose has, in my judgment, reshaped the negotiating landscape in the Arab–Israeli conflict in a way that it is not going to be easily reversed.

It may be the cruelest of paradoxes that the Oslo Process, currently criticized and opposed by both the Israelis and Palestinians, for all of its imperfections, may well provide a point of departure for the foreseeable future for some engagement between Israelis and Palestinians. It is a cruel paradox that eight years after Oslo, when permanent status negotiations and agreement was supposed to be a reality, after events of 2000 on the ground, we may in fact be faced with a return to what is incremental and what is partial. But that won't be enough because in the end Israelis and Palestinians need a strategy ultimately to address the core issues that have fueled their conflict. That strategy, I would argue, needs to have three components. *First*, there will have to be a compelling change in the realities on the ground in terms of Israeli and Palestinian behavior. *Second*, there will have to be a negotiating process that fundamentally cuts to the core of the issues that have fueled their conflict, and it will have to be one that is supported by the Arab states. And, *third*, as naive and foolish as it may appear, there is going to have to be a process of education, and it may be generational, which fundamentally changes the attitudes and images that the Israelis and Palestinians currently have toward one another. And maybe perhaps, one day, if Israelis and Palestinians can find a way to address all of these components, they may succeed in negotiating with one another a lasting and a durable peace.

3

Ending the Conflict: Can the Parties Afford it?

Khalil Shikaki

The failure of the Camp David summit in July 2000 to produce a Framework Agreement on Permanent Status left Palestinians and Israelis in a difficult impasse, dashing Palestinian hopes for an end to the Israeli occupation of Palestinian areas in the West Bank and the Gaza Strip. The eruption of popular and armed confrontations later in September ended a seven-year Oslo process and ushered in a process of violence and radicalization. Both sides have different perceptions of the nature of these two events that came to characterize an end of an era.

The Israelis portrayed these events as involving a generous Israeli offer, a stretched hand, and an unparalleled compromise that was met by Palestinian violent rejection. This violence has been portrayed by Israel as being deliberate and orchestrated and sustained by the Palestinian leadership and the Palestinian security services. This violence, Israel claims, has revealed the true face of Palestinians: they are unwilling to accept Israel and are not capable of making peace with it. Israel has particularly focused on the Palestinian insistence on the "right of return" and sought to portray it as reflecting a Palestinian hidden agenda and real intention, which is to dismantle the State of Israel.

The Palestinian perception is different. In the beginning, when Oslo's Declaration of Principles was signed in 1993, Palestinians expected the peace process to lead to the end of occupation. In the end, Palestinian disillusionment and frustration with the peace process led the public to see Oslo as a cover used by consecutive Israeli governments to colonize the land and transfer Israeli civilians into it, confiscate land to build homes for Jewish settlers, build bypass roads that criss-cross Palestinian territory in a way that make contiguity impossible and prevent the implementation of any national developmental project, thus turning Palestine into more than a hundred small enclaves in a sea of Israeli-controlled territory. In other words, the Palestinians saw the peace process as providing Israel with the means to consolidate, rather than end, occupation.

This chapter examines the causes for the failure of the Palestinian–Israeli peace process, which led to a second Palestinian Intifada, violent confrontations, and a breakdown in a relationship that built up over a seven-year period.

The Failure at Camp David

The Oslo process was not without successes. It transformed the *strategic* environment for Israel and the PLO, leading to the signing of the Israeli–Jordanian peace treaty and the creation of the Palestinian Authority, thus opening the way for improved Palestinian political relations with the US and Europe. Public opinion surveys among Palestinians and Israelis during the period between 1993 and 2000 indicate a transformed *psychological* environment. The two societies supported the process and accepted each other. Willingness to compromise and accept an eventual reconciliation was evident in many areas. Israelis came to recognize the need for the establishment of a Palestinian state and the Palestinians came to recognize the need for the establishment of two states in historic Palestine. Both sides supported many forms of reconciliation, including living in peace and cooperation with open borders, joint economic ventures, and a certain level of political and social normalization. The Oslo process led also to the creation and the institutionalization of an extensive network of legal and political norms that came to govern and organize their relationships. The process affirmed, even if implicitly, the commitment of the two sides to the eventual creation of two political entities. These successes were not sufficient, however, to lead to an agreement on permanent status or prevent the eruption of the second Palestinian Intifada.

Internal Palestinian and Israeli debate about the failure of Camp David and the eruption of the Intifada and violence reveals *three* strands of thought on its causes.

(1) The collapse revealed an existing fundamental clash of interests that diplomacy alone cannot bridge. The Israeli insistence on annexation of vital parts of the West Bank and Arab East Jerusalem, and sovereignty over *al-Haram al-Sharif* (the Temple Mount), and the Palestinian insistence on the return of four million Palestinian refugees to Israel are seen as the two most prominent examples of this unbridgeable clash of interests. In other words, continued conflict, in this view, is seen as inevitable and the best one can hope for is a long term truce or interim agreement. The Camp David summit failed because it went too far; it was too ambitious. This view is

particularly adhered to by right-wing groups in Israel and by Islamists and national opposition within the Palestinian camp.

(2) A second view argues that the failure at Camp David was merely temporary and in fact "technical." Lack of sufficient time, complexity of the issues, misperception, and personality factors have all been mentioned by Palestinian and Israeli negotiators as factors contributing to the failure. In this view, Camp David ushered in significant progress on all issues of permanent status; further negotiations and perhaps another summit would have produced a Framework Agreement. Although this view is not widely shared, senior officials from both sides, with intimate knowledge and involvement in the negotiations, have repeatedly publicized it.

(3) A third view, argued in this chapter, takes a middle road between the two. In this view, the failure of the peace process has been the product of four interacting dynamics: underlying structural difficulties, the open-ended nature of the Oslo agreement, domestic political constraints, and problematic negotiating techniques. In this view, progress has been possible; but it has not been sufficient to sustain a successful process. Indeed, during 2000, and contrary to the expectations of many, Palestinians and Israelis made significant progress on all issues of the permanent settlement including Jerusalem and refugees. Nevertheless, by the time this historic achievement was coming to light, neither side was able to endorse it: Barak was on his way out of office and Arafat and the Palestinian leadership were too weak to endorse it. Public opinion on both sides, enraged by months of violence and mass confrontations, shifted in a very short period to hawkish positions thus greatly reducing their leaders' room for maneuver. The cost of ending the conflict has proven to be too prohibitive for either side to contemplate. Both sides contributed to this outcome.

Structural difficulties

When the Palestinian national movement altered its political national ideology in the mid-1970s, abandoning the slogan of "liberation and return" and adopting the "two-state solution," it failed to fully grasp the implications and the critical requirements of such a fundamental transfor-mation. The transformation itself was motivated by pragmatic considerations. Searching for survival, the PLO, in a preemptive step, sought to capitalize on socioeconomic developments on the inside, and to present itself as a serious potential negotiator in a competition against actors on the outside.

The Palestinian national movement never seriously debated the implica-tions of that change on three issues: the "right of return" as understood up until that point by the refugees; the Palestinian relationship with the "other" state, Israel; and the nature of the Palestinian state itself. The failure to do so was motivated by political calculations: the PLO did not want to lose the support of its largest constituency, the refugees; and it did not want to weaken its negotiating position *vis-à-vis* Israel. Israel, on the other hand, preferred for too long to ignore the Palestinian national movement. When it did finally recognize the PLO and the legitimate political rights of the Palestinians, Israel nonetheless sought to mitigate the consequences of such recognition on all issues vital to the Palestinians: the state, the land, and the people. Israel continued to view the Palestinian entity-state as an Israeli protectorate that must be kept under security control. Disagreement over Palestine's sovereignty, its control over its own borders, its military capability, and its external security and foreign policy poisoned relations between the two sides. On the issue of land, Israel never ceased settlement activities believing that occupied Palestinian territory were war spoils that could be colonized. As the size of the "cake" began to quickly shrink while the two sides negotiated its fate, the overwhelming majority of the Palestinians lost all confidence in the peaceful intentions of Israel. But perhaps it was Israel's failure to treat the Palestinian people with dignity that made reconciliation impossible. It rarely treated them as equal; instead daily suffering and humiliation for the man and women on the street continues unabated.

For the Palestinians, the inability to live up to the requirements of a two-state solution created a barrier threatening to block the fulfillment of their national aspirations. For the Israelis, the inability to treat the Palestinians as people with equal rights led to more hate and violence. The unintended outcome of the deliberate policies of the two sides led to a prolonged political stalemate.

The open-ended nature of Oslo

The open-ended nature of the Oslo agreement postponed for up to six years the resolution of the vital issues of the conflict. As a means to resolve a protracted conflict, Oslo's open-endedness only exacerbated an already existing uncertainty. It meant that neither side would make a full commitment to the peace process. As a result, three dynamics were encouraged. First, both sides wanted to keep their options open, thus leading to an Israeli determination to transfer to the Palestinians as little land as possible, and to a Palestinian unwillingness to completely revise the educational system. Secondly, since the major vital objectives of one or both sides were not achieved during the transitional phase, neither side was willing to completely give up its negotiating assets, including the ability to inflict violence, pain, and suffering. Thirdly, since "real" negotiations have not even started, both sides sought to improve their negotiating positions. Since

Israel was stronger and controlled the land in question, its settlement policy proved most effective in prejudicing final status negotiations.

Creating "facts on the ground" poisoned Palestinian–Israeli relations, an outcome that was the exact opposite to the logic of transitionalism. That logic was simple: the transitional process was expected to transform the political and psychological environment, making possible the resolution of very difficult problems. However, by the time the two sides met at Camp David, the size of the settlements' population had doubled in comparison to what it was when the Oslo process began. Israelis were now more determined than ever to safeguard and develop their settlement enterprise, while Palestinians were more determined to oppose it.

The triumph of domestic political constraints

Three domestic factors proved instrumental in constraining the abilities of the two sides to make the necessary compromises for peace. First, the peace process continued to suffer from a lack of legitimacy in the eyes of a significant sector of the population on both sides. Israeli settlers and extreme right-wing elements opposed it and resorted to violence to stop it, culminating in the assassination of the Israeli Prime Minister, Yitzhak Rabin. This lack of consensus influenced the Israeli leadership's willingness to confront the settlers; in fact, it forced that leadership to seek to appease the settlers in order to gain their approval. On the Palestinian side, the Islamists and the national opposition refused to recognize the legitimacy of the peace process or the Palestinian Authority it created. The Palestinian opposition resorted to violence against Israelis in search for means to bring an end to the peace process. The PA, perceiving a lack of legitimacy, was constrained in its ability to confront the opposition for fear of internal strife.

Second, neither side was able to put together a stable peace coalition capable of governing and at the same time of making difficult compromises. The Israeli labor government lost the critical 1996 elections just as the components of the Interim Agreement were being put in place. Right-wing governments were not willing to implement Israel's commitments and in fact sought to reverse the process by accelerating the pace of settlement expansion. Ehud Barak invited the Shas religious party and a centrist Russian immigrants party to join his left-wing government in the second half of 1999, believing that he could count on them to support his peace policy. But he lost both parties even before reaching Camp David in mid-2000. Internal political and personal rivalries among Arafat's senior colleagues, particularly Mahmud Abbas (Abu Mazin) and Ahmad Qurie (Abu Ala) left him almost alone at Camp David.

Third, public opinion on both sides remained reluctant to accept the painful compromises required for a lasting and comprehensive peace.

Despite the tremendous progress in public attitudes among Israelis and Palestinians regarding many peace related issues, some positions remained almost unchanged. As the two leaderships were meeting at Camp David, neither public was willing to entertain compromise on the issues of Jerusalem or refugees. Indeed, these two particular issues of final status negotiations remained outside public discourse throughout the seven years of the interim period between 1993 and 2000. It is not surprising then that little progress in Camp David negotiations was registered on these two issues.

Flawed negotiating techniques

The Oslo negotiating framework suffered from a serious flaw. It demanded that the Palestinians pay a price for peace twice: once for admission to the negotiating table, and once again for reaching a peace agreement. The Palestinians conceded only to the first price, believing that they were simply being asked to make their peace-making concessions in advance. To them, the price for making peace has been the recognition of the state of Israel in 78 percent of their homeland and the establishment of a Palestinian state in the remaining 22 percent, a price they have paid long before sitting at the final status negotiations. The Israelis, however, saw this Palestinian conces-sion as a precondition for talking to the Palestinians. When the Palestinians at Camp David rejected an Israeli offer that failed to meet Palestinian expectations, Israelis began to doubt Palestinian peace intentions.

At Camp David, once serious final status negotiations started, Israel demanded the annexation of several settlement blocs, the imposition of security arrangements that would have allowed Israeli military forces to "enter" the state of Palestine during times of Israeli-declared "emergen-cies," and the imposition of severe political restrictions on Palestinian sovereignty, including the Israeli right to freely use Palestinian airspace. Moreover, Israel refused to recognize Palestinian sovereignty over the Muslim holy place of *al-Haram al-Sharif* in Jerusalem and rejected the recognition of the refugees' right of return. While the Palestinians were willing to accept some of those Israeli demands, if proper *quid pro quos* were offered, they could not renounce sovereignty over *al-Haram* or the right of return.

Specifically, Israel offered to end its occupation on 75 percent of the Palestinian territory leaving 12 percent of the West Bank under Israeli sovereignty and 13 percent under Israeli military control for an indefinite period of time. Israel refused to accept the notion of an equal exchange of territory. The Palestinian state could not have territorial contiguity under the Israeli proposal, as Israel would annex or have access to settlements (such as Ariel) deep inside the West Bank heartland. With regard to

Jerusalem, the Israeli initial offer included demands for Israeli sovereignty over Islam's second holiest place on earth, *al-Haram al-Sharif* (Noble Sanctuary) with its two mosques that were built some 1,300 years ago, an Israeli right to build a Jewish synagogue in *al-Haram*, and the right of Jews to pray inside *al-Haram*. Israel may have later dropped or toned down the second and third demands. Occupied East Jerusalem was to remain under Israeli sovereignty, except for unspecified areas in the northern part of the city which were supposed to come under Palestinian sovereignty or self-rule; other Palestinian areas in the occupied Eastern part were to be given self-rule under Israeli sovereignty. With regard to refugees, Israel refused to acknowledge its role and responsibility in creating the refugee problem; refused to acknowledge the right of return; and refused to take full responsibility for refugee compensation. Israel also refused to turn over to the Palestinian side the documents and the value of the assets controlled by the Israeli Absentee Property Authority. On security arrangements, Israel demanded full demilitarization of the Palestinian state, the continued deployment of its military in the Jordan Valley for an unlimited period of time, and the right to send its full army into the territory of the Palestinian state whenever the government of Israel declared an emergency.

The Palestinians insisted on an Israeli withdrawal to the 1967 borders but were willing, nonetheless, to accept of the notion of an equal territorial "exchange" or "swap" within parameters that would not threaten the contiguity of the state or disenfranchise its citizens. On Jerusalem, the Palestinians agreed to allow the Jewish settlements in Arab East Jerusalem, the "Wailing Wall," and the Jewish Quarter of the Old City to come under Israeli sovereignty as part of the territorial exchange. On refugees, the Palestinian position accepted the principle that the Palestinian state would become home to all refugees choosing to exercise the right of return in Palestine and that the implementation of the "right of return" in Israel proper would take into account the realities and sovereignty of the Jewish state. On security, the Palestinians accepted the principle that the State of Palestine would not possess major weapon systems and that Israeli armed forces would withdraw gradually from the Jordan Valley, and that an international force would be deployed in the Valley.

A second flaw in the negotiating technique was Israel's insistence on the phased implementation of its obligations under the Interim Agreement. Gradually, Israel lost any incentive to implement those obligations, such as the "further redeployments," the release of prisoners, the return of displaced persons, and other obligations. Israeli leaders began to view these as "assets" Israel needed as part of expected trade-offs in the final status negotiations. The implementation of these Israeli interim commitments always provided the two sides with a much-needed time to reach a permanent agreement and a cushion to fall back on in case of failure in the final status talks. Throughout 2000, Israeli Prime Minister Ehud Barak refused to implement the so called "third redeployment" or to release Palestinian prisoners, hoping to use these two issues as a leverage in the ongoing permanent status negotiations.

A Second Palestinian Intifada

The Palestinian public negatively perceived the Israeli proposals presented at Camp David. Israel's public presentation of its position as "take it or leave it" deepened Palestinian despair and disbelief in the ability of the peace process to yield results culminating in the end of occupation and establishment of a sovereign independent state.

The Israeli demands for sovereignty over *al-Haram*, the right to build a synagogue, and praying rights heightened Palestinian public fear of Israel intentions and designs for *al-Haram*. Continued debate between mainstream and extreme religious and political groups in Israel about a possible location for the synagogue in the plateau of *al-Haram* only fueled the Palestinian's perception regarding the future of their sacred religious place. Ariel Sharon's visit to *al-Haram* was seen by the public as further evidence of Israel's real intentions to unilaterally implement its designs over *al-Haram*. It provoked an angry and frightened response.

The use of excessive force by the Israeli police against demonstrations of unarmed civilians in *al-Haram* and elsewhere in the West Bank and the Gaza Strip led to deaths and the injury of thousands. The Israeli policy of massive and excessive use of force coupled with an extensive system of collective punishment, closures and siege, destruction of homes, agricultural land, factories, and other property helped to sustain the Intifada.

While expressing Palestinian frustration with the failure of the peace process and affirming Palestinian demands for an end to occupation and settlement construction and expansion, the Intifada led also to several unintended consequences that impact on the ability of the two sides to revive the peace process. Many PA institutions failed to function under the pressure generated by the Israeli restrictions. The failure of the peace process, coupled with the failure of PA institutions to deliver services to the civilian population, led to serious questioning of PA legitimacy.

Other sources of legitimacy began to surface. Fatah, claiming "revolutionary legitimacy," Hamas, claiming "Islamic legitimacy," and the PLO, claiming "national legitimacy," began to assert themselves at the expense of the PA. The challenge to PA's legitimacy could lead to its collapse if and when Israel begins to seriously threaten its infrastructure and when the PA runs out of financial resources. The ability of the PA to generate revenues has been severely restricted as a result of rising unemployment and the halt to economic activity due to closures and siege. One of the other outcomes of the Intifada has been the negative impact it had on Palestinian and Israeli public opinion. Each society perceived the action of the other as highly threatening. This mutual threat perception elicited highly hostile responses, leading, among Palestinians, to a rise in support for armed attacks against Israelis, including civilians. In June 2001, support for attacks against Israeli civilians, including suicide attacks, soared to more than 70 percent. When compared to the level of support to such attacks in 1996, which stood then at 20 percent, one can see the difference generated by the Intifada and the failure of the peace process. Similarly, more than 80 percent of the Israeli public supported the use of massive military force against the Palestinians and in fact wanted the imposition of even more severe collective punishment measures. The two publics show less willingness than ever to compromise on the difficult issues of refugees and Jerusalem.

What Way Out?

The success of the Israelis and Palestinians in moving the peace process forward in significant ways at the Taba talks in January 2001 indicates that progress was attainable despite the breakdown in the relationship between the two sides. The results of these talks show that the ultimate Palestinian objective is not to deny or threaten the existence, peace, or security of the Jewish state. Palestinians want an independent state in the West Bank and Gaza, and to live in peace and cooperation with Israel. This has been the paramount Palestinian national objective since the mid-1970s and has not changed since. It has been enshrined in the Algiers' PNC 1988 resolution and cemented by the PNC annulment of the PLO charter since Oslo. The Palestinian state, as agreed by the two sides at the Taba talks, would pose no threat to any of its neighbors and would rely on international guarantees and good neighborly relations for its security and the safety of its citizens. Palestinian–Israeli success at the Taba talks indicate that the two sides believe that achieving a permanent peace, putting an end to the conflict, and starting the process of reconciliation is an achievable goal that can be obtained now, not later.

Palestinians intend to build a state that would, just like Israel, welcome all its Diaspora, all those Palestinians who aspire to self-determination, peace, and security in a state of their own. This state would particularly welcome all those Palestinians who suffered most from the historic conflict and lived in poverty and dispossession in refugee camps. Palestinian demands for an Israeli recognition of the principle of the refugees' right of return to their homes is not meant to threaten or undermine the national identity or security of the state of Israel. To the contrary, it seeks to close the file on the historic conflict and thus assure all Israelis of their future and the future of their state.

Israeli refusal to implement the main clauses of Oslo (by refusing to withdraw from Palestinian areas and by expanding the settlement process) has confronted the Palestinians with grave threats to their security, existence and aspiration for freedom and independence, leading to desperation and disillusionment among the majority of Palestinians. Continual confrontation and bloodshed have demonstrated that neither violence nor military campaigns can bring about peace. Palestinians do want to put an end to the violence, as they are the ones who suffer the most from it.

The path to peace starts by a return to cooperation between the two sides, full implementation of previous agreements under international monitoring and supervision, cessation of all settlement activities in occupied Palestinian land, and a return to the negotiating table with the aim of putting an end to the conflict by signing and fully implementing a permanent peace agreement.

Specifically, the two sides need to embrace a package of stabilization that would contain three elements: reduction of threat perception, restoration of confidence in the peace process, and a mechanism for monitoring and verification. Once in place, the two sides can then return to final status negotiations.

Reducing threat perception

The rise in support for violence and military strikes among Israeli and Palestinian publics can only be stabilized by ending violence and freezing settlement expansion. If achieved, stabilization makes people willing to take risks and accept compromises for the sake of peace.

Restoring confidence in the peace process

As in the past, the implementation of the remaining items in the Interim Agreement can restore confidence in the peace process and make people more willing to support negotiations and oppose violence.

Verify intentions through an international role

The deployment of monitors to verify implementation of the agreement can give each side confidence that the other is serious about respecting its obligations and the commitments enshrined in signed agreements.

4

Domestic Israeli Politics and the Conflict

Abraham Diskin

A Personal Note

Whenever I think about the Arab–Israeli conflict, a family story about the 1929 riots in Jerusalem comes to mind. At that time, my father, who was very young, worked in my grandfather's office in the old commercial area of Jerusalem. This is the area, at a top of a hill, located between the walls of the Old City and the Jaffa Road. Almost every day when I drive to the Hebrew University on Mount Scopus, I go through that area, on the imaginary borderline between the Arab and Jewish parts of Jerusalem.

When my father heard Arab cries "Atbakh-al-Yahud" (slaughter the Jews), he went out, weaponed with the curiosity of a young and naive person, to find out what was going on. After a few hours the riots came to an end. Everybody went home, but my father disappeared. "The worst has happened," everybody thought. Then came the telephone call. There were not too many telephones in Jerusalem at that time, but the story tells that "our" telephone number was 23. On the other side of the line was no other than the most extreme religious and political leader of the Arab community in Palestine, the initiator of the riots, Haj Amin al Husseini. He came from an affluent family that had several business ties with the Jewish community. The Husseinis also had business ties with my grandfather. Haj Amin spoke Arabic: "your son is in my hands," he said. "Don't worry, I guarantee that he won't lose a single hair on his head." "Tomorrow morning, he will return home, accompanied by my bodyguards." He kept his promise, and thus I can claim that, in a way, I owe my life to Haj Amin, the man who directly and indirectly was responsible for the violent deaths of so many Jews and Arabs in Palestine.

I remember this story because of many personal emotional reasons, but I also believe that it reflects the fact that the Palestinian–Israeli conflict is characterized by contradictions, many of which continue to dictate the political agenda of the Middle East and the whole world. In the following pages some of these contradictions will be discussed.

The Micro-political Level

There are four basic concepts that characterize the nature of the Israeli political system.

One characteristic – *the quest for security* – is quite unique to Israel and can hardly be found in other Western democracies. It has to do with the fact that Israel has faced existential threats ever since its establishment. At times, all of its neighbors called for its elimination. Today, such threats are less frequent, but unfortunately they may express even greater dangers because of a number of developments such as the proliferation of mass-destruction weapons. I regret that even one of the participants at the Colgate conference consistently calls for the elimination of the State of Israel. At the same time, I respect him for his sincerity. The intention, he is ready to admit, is shared by others, who are not as sincere, and who prefer to hide their true beliefs behind a peaceful mask. The existential security issue is not only national. It is also personal, given, among other reasons, the continuing terrorist attacks against Israeli citizens and Jews outside Israel. The present war of attrition, which was launched against Israel in late September 2000, is apparently based on the assumption that the personal threats to the security of Israelis will have national consequences.

Another important feature of the Israeli polity is the *quest for peace*. For most Western democracies peaceful relations with neighboring countries and other nations is a fact, not a problem. In the Israeli case, while most politicians and their followers support the desire for "peace and security," some may question whether peace is possible at all or whether the desire for peace (and the "costs" of peace) contradicts security needs.

In a number of most important constitutional norms, including several basic laws and the Declaration of Independence, Israel is depicted as a "democratic-Jewish" state. The democratic nature and the Jewish nature of the State of Israel are two other basic features of Israel. Many Arabs claim that the Jewish nature of Israel contradicts its democratic nature. A number of model stable democracies do mention in their laws the national nature of the system. It is interesting to explore what Israeli citizens reflect on this issue. Today, many Israelis argue that Israel is a Jewish-Democratic state, but that it is also a "state of all of its citizens." Are we dealing here with slogans, a real problem, or a contradiction?

In a public opinion poll conducted prior to the 1999 general elections, respondents were asked several questions about such issues: 995 citizens, who represent the whole population (including non-Jews), were interviewed face-to-face between April 29 and May 5. Four statements to which the respondents were asked to react were:

1. It is important that the government will make any effort possible in order to achieve peace (hereafter "Peace");
2. It is important that the government will make any effort possible in order to guarantee security (hereafter "Security");
3. It is important that the government will make any effort possible in order to preserve the Jewish nature of the state of Israel (hereafter "Jewish nature");
4. It is important that the government will make any effort possible in order to preserve the democratic nature of the state of Israel (hereafter "Democratic nature").

Table 4.1 depicts the distribution of answers of the respondents, who could "absolutely agree" (1), "agree" (2), "maybe agree" (3), "disagree" (4), or "absolutely disagree" (5).

Table 4.1 Public positions concerning statements on peace, security, the Jewish nature and the democratic nature of the State of Israel

	N	1	2	3	4	5	Mean
Peace	988	63.7%	27.0%	5.4%	2.6%	1.3%	1.51
Security	979	80.4%	15.2%	2.8%	0.7%	0.9%	1.27
Jewish Nature	989	39.2%	29.7%	14.2%	8.5%	8.4%	2.17
Democratic nature	985	91.2%	15.6%	2.1%	0.4%	0.7%	1.24

It is evident that Israeli citizens support very strongly all four positions. In fact, 61 percent of the respondents either "agreed" or "absolutely agreed" with all the statements. This is quite surprising given the fact the only 69 percent supported the "Jewish nature" statement and given the possible contradictions between some of the statements.

In order to compare different groups of respondents the absolute value of the difference between the mean responds of the groups was divided by 4 (the maximal difference possible). The result is a set of "polarization" coefficients. The maximal polarization, 1, is achieved when all the members of one group "absolutely agree" with a given statement, while all the members of the other group "absolutely disagree" with the same statement. The minimal polarization, 0, is achieved when the mean respond of the two examined group is identical. Table 4.2 represents the level of polarization between Jewish respondents and Arab respondents, and the level of polarization between Netanyahu supporters and Barak supporters in the 1999 elections.

Table 4.2 The Jewish–Arab polarization and the Netanyahu followers–Barak followers' polarization concerning statements on peace, security, the Jewish nature, and the democratic nature of the State of Israel

	Jewish–Arab polarization	Netanyahu followers–Barak followers polarization
Peace	0.12	0.15
Security	0.31	0.02
Jewish Nature	0.65	0.27
Democratic nature	0.11	0.08

It seems clear that the polarization between "right-wingers" (Netanyahu supporters) and "left-wingers" (Barak supporters) tend to be marginal. The only issue where one finds a more considerable polarization between these two groups of voters is the question of the "Jewish nature" of Israel. It seems that many interpreted this statement in religious terms. Hence, secular Jews tended in some cases not to agree. The share of religious Jews among Netanyahu supporters is higher than among Barak supporters. Polarization between Jews and Arab voters tends to be more significant. It is most prominent as far as the "Jewish nature" of the state is concerned. It is also evident concerning the security issue. This results from the fact that Israeli Arabs do not perceive "other" Arabs as threatening as they are perceived by most of the Jewish citizens.

In fact, this question of "enemy image" seems crucial in Israeli politics, in spite of the relatively minimal polarization between "hawks" and "doves." Jewish–Arab polarization on the statement "the Palestinians would have wanted to destroy Israel had they had the chance to do so" was at a level of 0.61 prior to the 1996 elections and 0.42 prior to the 1999 elections. Now it is at its peak, but even before the 1999 elections only 20 percent of all the respondents (including Arabs) "disagreed," 20 percent hesitated and approximately 60 percent either "agreed" or "absolutely agreed."

It should also be noted that when people are asked to rank themselves on a Left–Right dimension, more people identify with either the Right or the Left on questions related to the Arab–Israel conflict then those identifying with one of the camps on questions related to social and economic policies. Obviously, this puts Israel in a unique position compared with other Western democracies. It is also important to note that when concrete questions, such as specific policies or specific territories are concerned, the polarization between left-wingers and right-wingers tends to grow.

In the public opinion poll mentioned above, the respondents were asked to specify whether they "agreed" to the following statements:

1. Within the framework of a peace agreement with the Palestinians, Israel should evacuate settlements (hereafter "Settlements").
2. Within the framework of a peace agreement with Syria, Israel should agree to full withdrawal from the Golan Heights (hereafter "Golan").
3. Within the framework of a peace agreement with the Palestinians, Israel should give up the Jordan Valley (hereafter "Jordan Valley").
4. Within the framework of a peace agreement with the Palestinians, Israel should agree to the partition of Jerusalem (hereafter "Jerusalem").

Public stands on concrete issues tend to be far less stable than the stands on more general questions. The general rule is that the public tends to follow the government (and to change positions) whenever the government (be it a dovish or a hawkish government) makes a dramatic move on questions of war and peace. Thus, only a slight minority supported full evacuation of the Sinai Peninsula prior to the Begin–Sadat Camp David agreement. After the 1978 agreement, a clear majority, which included many right-wingers, supported it. It should be remembered that the territories returned to Egypt consist of 90 percent of all the territories occupied by Israel in the 1967 Six Day War. Likewise, only a few supported the penetration to Lebanon prior to the "Peace for Galilee" operation of 1982. A clear majority, which included many left-wingers, supported the government once the war in Lebanon started. Prior to the first Oslo agreement (September 1993), a vast majority of Israelis objected to the idea of any form of negotiations with the PLO, which was commonly perceived as an extreme terrorist organization affiliated with the most extreme Arab regimes such as Saddam Hussein's Iraq. Only a minority supported such stands in the following years.

The distribution of stands depicted in table 4.3 below reflects the situation prior to the 1999 elections. Positions during the Arafat–Barak Camp David talks tended to be far more dovish. After the failure of the talks, and following the outbreak of Palestinian violence in late September 2000, many returned to views more hawkish than those depicted in table 4.3.

In general, one may claim that a majority of Israelis supports withdrawal from most of the territories – and even the evacuation of at least some of the settlements – but only a minority supports full withdrawal from the Golan Heights and the Jordan Valley. There is also a very clear objection to the idea of partition of Jerusalem.

Table 4.3   Public positions concerning statements on Settlements, the Golan Heights, the Jordan Valley, and the Partition of Jerusalem

	1	2	3	4	5	Mean
Settlements	31.6%	21.2%	17.0%	16.0%	14.2%	2.60
Golan	9.2%	7.8%	17.5%	28.7%	36.8%	3.76
Jordan Valley	7.4%	8.2%	16.3%	36.5%	31.6%	3.77
Jerusalem	9.6%	8.4%	11.0%	19.4%	51.6%	3.95

Table 4.4   The Jewish–Arab polarization and the Netanyaku followers–Barak followers polarization concerning statements on Settlements, the Golan Heights, the Jordan Valley, and the Partition of Jerusalem

	Jewish–Arab polarization	Netanyahu followers–Barak followers polarization
Settlements	0.67	0.55
Golan	0.63	0.33
Jordan Valley	0.63	0.21
Jerusalem	0.72	0.31

Israeli Arab citizens, unlike most of the Jewish citizens, tend to support very strongly a full withdrawal from all the territories including the Golan Heights, the Jordan Valley and Jerusalem, and the evacuation of the Jewish settlements in the West Bank and the Gaza Strip. Hence, the very clear Arab–Jewish polarization depicted in table 4.4. The sharpest polarization between doves and hawks within the Jewish population concerns the question of settlements. Thus, Netanyahu supporters tended to object to any evacuation of settlements, while Barak supporters tended to accept the idea of evacuation of at least some of the settlements.

The bottom line is that Israelis are very interested in peace. They support the promotion of peace whole-heartedly even when they are "hawks." At the same time Israelis are very anxious about security issues. This is the reason why so many Israelis have deep reservations concerning a full withdrawal from the Golan Heights and the Jordan Valley. These areas are regarded by many as crucial as far as security considerations are concerned. The majority of Israelis believe that the Arab world does stick – at least latently – to its desire to eliminate the State of Israel. This belief characterizes both hawks and doves. The only significant group that deviates from such a tendency consists of Israeli Arabs. As far as specific policies are concerned, there do exist issues – additional to the settlements question – on which one can easily point at evident differences even among Israeli Jews. Nevertheless, as demonstrated above, past surveys prove that dramatic changes in stands on specific policies do occur following dramatic changes in governmental policy.

In a democracy one expects the existence of a strong link between the beliefs held by voters and beliefs held by their leaders. Hereafter the influence of stands on the Arab–Israeli conflict on coalition behavior will be discussed. In addition, it has been proved in a number of surveys that voters attribute priority to issues associated with security and foreign policy in their preference for political parties. Political leaders, who are aware of this fact, respond adequately not only because of their own positions, but also because of this awareness.

In a public opinion poll conducted prior to the 1996 elections 1,064 citizens, who represent the whole population (including non-Jews), were interviewed face-to-face between May 7 and May 17. The respondents were asked the following question: "What, in your opinion, is the main reason why voters prefer a specific political party in general elections?" Table 4.5 compares the answers of Jewish and Arab voters.

Table 4.5   Reasons for support of political parties given by Jewish and Arab voters prior to the 1996 general election (in percentages)

Reason of support	Jewish voters	Arab voters	Total
Security and Foreign policy issues	53	22	48
Party stands on other issues	6	19	8
Belief in party leaders	14	21	15
"The party represents people like me"	18	33	20
Other reasons	9	5	9
N	848	178	1026

The findings of table 4.5, as well as findings of similar investigations conducted in the last two decades, demonstrate the supreme influence of "security and foreign policy issues" on voting behavior. Although the results differed over time, the conflict between Israel and its neighbors, and especially the Israeli–Palestinian conflict, always emerged as the most prominent reason for partisan affiliation. Findings concerning the Arab population are different. It seems that many Arab voters tend to support not only "dovish," but especially "Arab" parties. This is apparently taken for granted by most of them. Hence, the importance of parties that represent "people like me" to Arab respondents. It is also interesting to note that "security and foreign policy issues" tend to be more important for right-wing voters then for left-wingers. In the survey discussed here, 53 percent of Netanyahu supporters mentioned these issues as their main reason for party selection, compared with only 43 percent of Peres supporters.

The Macro-political Level

In order to understand the macro-political level, it seems that one must concentrate on the quite complicated Israeli party system. Figure 4.1 depicts the party system following the 1999 Knesset elections. It should be noted that a number of changes have taken place since the elections. These changes do influence political tactics, but they are not as crucial as far as the general political tendencies are concerned.

The background to the 1999 elections was the negotiations between Netanyahu's government and the Palestinian Authority. The most hawkish elements in Netanyahu's government – especially the NRP – were not satisfied with the way these were proceeding. They suspected that Netanyahu was about to make concessions, which were regarded by them as exaggerated. Once they decided to defect from the coalition, the government lost its majority in the Knesset and early elections seemed inevitable. Netanyahu lost the Prime-Ministirial elections to Barak, but the right-wing parties continued to control half of the Knesset seats, in spite of Likud's losses. The election of the Labor (One Israel) candidate as Prime Minister became possible because of sharp criticism of Netanyahu's personality, and probably also because Barak, a former chief of staff of the Israeli Defense Forces, seemed to be hawkish enough for voters floating between left and right.

Six of the 15 political parties, which won representation in the 1999 elections, should be regarded as "main-stream parties." These political parties may be placed on an uni-dimensional model. They differ from European parties in that in Israel they should be placed according to the position of the parties regarding the Arab–Israeli conflict. The "main-stream" parties are depicted in the centerline of figure 4.1. These parties combined controlled only 68 of the 120 Knesset seats. Other parties are mainly "sectarian" parties. The stands of "sectarian" parties on the Arab–Israeli conflict are not latent, but their main goal is to represent different social groups. Thus, there are "religious" parties, "Arab" parties, and "Russian" immigrants' parties. The "central parties" depicted in figure 4.1 are political parties that would have joined Barak in almost any coalition formed by him following the 1999 elections. Conversely, "third circle" parties are those, the participation of which in any coalition formed by Barak seemed almost impossible. "Second circle" parties are those that would have participated in a Barak coalition under certain circumstances.

Barak formed an "impossible" coalition with a very wide ideological range. The most dovish party in his cabinet was Meretz – a party that also expressed very extreme anti-clerical positions. The most hawkish party in his cabinet was the NRP. In fact, all three religious parties – that had never

Figure 14.1 The party system following the May 17, 199? Knesset Elections

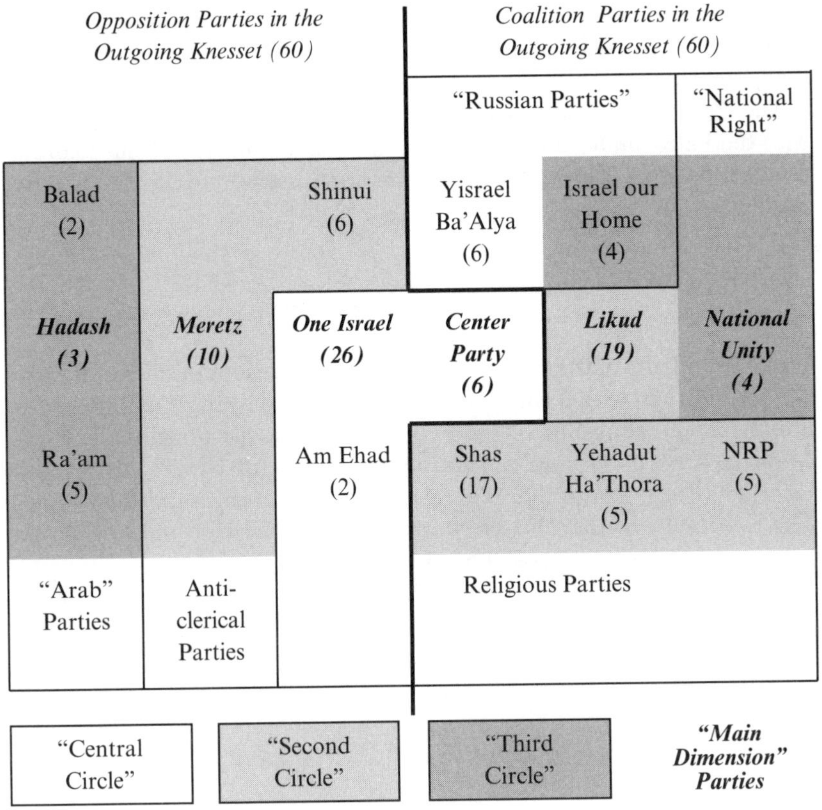

Opposition Parties in the Outgoing Knesset (60)   *Coalition Parties in the Outgoing Knesset (60)*

gained such a wide representation in any previous elections – became members of Barak's coalition. It was clear that once the government made a significant move on any issue, some of its members would find it impossible to remain in the coalition.

Barak seemed anxious to reach a "comprehensive peace." He declared his intention to achieve this goal "within a year." His policies were attacked more than once, even by more dovish members of the Labor party and Meretz (e.g. Shimon Peres and Yossi Sarid). He crossed all the previously known "red lines" in his negotiations with the Syrians and with the Palestinians, but failed. Many criticize Barak for having a "zigzag" policy on many issues. There is more than a grain of truth in such criticism. Nevertheless, the only policy issue on which Barak remained very consistent was the Arab–Israeli conflict. Some criticize Barak for declaring his readiness to make concessions without implementing such inclinations. Given the fact that under Barak Israel withdrew its forces from Lebanon, and given the deep involvement of the American administration and President Clinton himself in the negotiations, there is not much ground to such criticism.

The final blow to Barak's government came with the Camp David talks with the Palestinians (July 2000). All the "right-wingers" of the coalition decided to defect, leaving Barak with a formal support of only 30 Knesset members.

The 2001 Elections

With the collapse of the Israeli–Palestinian negotiations in spite of Barak's concessions, and with the wave of violence initiated by the Palestinians two months later, the results of the February 6, 2001 elections of the Prime Minister seemed inevitable. The lowest turnout in Israel's history was recorded (62%). Out of the valid voters only 38 percent supported Barak. The full results of the 2001 elections are compared with the 1999 Prime Ministerial elections in table 4.6 below.

Table 4.6   The 1999 and the 2001 Prime Ministerial Elections

17 May 1999			*6 February 2001*		
Eligible Voters	4,285,428		Eligible Voters	4,504,769	
Voters	3,372,952	(78.7%)	Voters	2,805,938	(62.3%)
Valid votes	3,193,494	(94.7%)	Valid votes	2,722,021	(97.0%)
Invalid votes	179,458	(5.3%)	Invalid votes	83,917	(3.0%)
Candidate	*Number Votes*	*Percentage*	*Candidate*	*Number Votes*	*Percentage*
Ehud Barak	1,791,020	56.1	Ehud Barak	1,023,944	37.6
Benjamin Netanyahu	1,402,474	43.9	Ariel Sharon	1,698,077	62.4

It seems that the elected Prime Minister did not have many difficulties in forming a new "national unity" government. The Sharon coalition government included seven party lists, with a total of 72 of the 120 parliamentary seats. The three largest parties in the parliament were included – One Israel (23 MPs), Likud (19), and Shas (17) – along with the merged National Unity–Israel Our Home (7), Yisrael Ba'Aliyah (4), and Am Ehad (2). The vote of investiture was supported by these 72 MPs and opposed by 21, with 27 abstaining. Within the first month of the new government, the 5 MPs of the Yehadut Ha'Torah party and a single member of the Centre Party joined the coalition, raising its majority to 78 MPs. The parliamentary opposition is to the left of the government coalition (the Arab parties and Meretz), in the middle (Shinui and the Center), and on the religious right (National Religious).

The new government includes three women (out of a total of 26 ministers), the largest number ever, and one Arab (Druze) for the very first time. This government can survive for no longer than two and a half years. The reason is that the next parliamentary elections are scheduled for November 2003 (notwithstanding Barak's resignation and the election of Sharon).

On the same day that the new government was sworn in, the Israeli parliament passed a bill that abolished the separate election of the Prime Minister and returned the country to a pure parliamentary form of government. This new electoral and political system will go into effect with the next scheduled elections.

The developments narrowed in many ways not only the polarization between the different political camps on both the micro and the macro political levels, but also the difference between Israeli voters and Israel politicians. Everybody, including many of the more extreme members of Sharon's government, willingly accept now the establishment of a Palestinian state. At the same time only a small percentage continue to believe that "real" peace is achievable. The Palestinians have an opportunity to gain not only an independent state, but also most of the territories that would be handed to them by a relatively "hawkish" government.

Abba Eban used to say about the Palestinians that they "never miss an opportunity to miss an opportunity." The question now is whether a retreat from the Palestinian policies of July and September 2000 is possible or whether another missed opportunity should be expected.

A Concluding Personal Note

In 1967 I was even younger than my father in 1929. Ever since the Six Day War I have believed that a Palestinian State should be established. Several months before Prime Minister Eshkol's death, I even had the opportunity to ask him about it in an event that took place at the Hebrew University. "Young man," Prime Minister Eshkol answered in Yiddish, "I wish I could do what you ask me to do."

I strongly believe that the establishment of a Palestinian State – under the most generous conditions possible – serves the interests of Israelis and Palestinians alike. Jews and Arabs are destined to share this tortured ancient piece of land. In principle, I am confident that the better is the situation for one of the communities, the better it is for its twin community.

At the same time, I must admit that, like most Israelis, I do not believe that a real peace is possible in the coming decades. An agreement can be reached and should be desired, but the depth of the hostility toward Israel leaves the goal of a "real" peace – in which one gives up violence as well as the dream to eliminate the other – in the hands of future generations.

The Arab–Israeli conflict in general and the Palestinian–Israeli conflict in particular remind me of a famous biblical story. Two prophets, Hannaniah, the son of Azur, and Jeremiah, the son of Hilkiah, held a public debate. Nebuchadnezzar, the king of Babylon had just exiled the king of Judea. The question about which the prophets argue is when peace will return. Hannaniah claims that peace will come within two years. "Amen, the Lord do so," responds Jeremiah. But he does not believe in an instant peace. "True prophets," says Jeremiah, "are those whose prophecies are about war, evil and pestilence." "Peace will come," he continues, "but it will take seventy years, not two."

References (Data supplied by the secretary of the government of Israel)

Diskin, A. "Israel – Political Data and National Issues 1991–2000," *European Journal of Political Research: Political Data Yearbook*, Dordrecht: Kluwer, 1992–2001.

—— "The New Political System of Israel," *Government and Opposition*, 34 (4) (Autumn 1999): 498–515.

——, *Jerusalem's Last Days: Guidelines for Examining the New Israeli Democracy*, Jerusalem: The Floersheimer Institute for Policy Studies, 2001.

Diskin, A. and Hazan, R. Y., "The 2001 Prime-Ministirial Elections in Israel," *Electoral Studies* (forthcoming).

Divrei Ha'Knesset, Jerusalem: The Knesset, 1999, 2000 (Official Knesset Records in Hebrew).

Ha'aretz (2000–2001, daily newspaper, Hebrew).

Hazan, R. Y. and Diskin, A. 2000. "The 1999 Knesset and prime ministerial elections in Israel," *Electoral Studies* 19 (4): 628–37.

Israel's Government Yearbook 5760 (2000), Jerusalem: The Government of Israel (Hebrew).

Jerusalem Post (2000–2001, daily newspaper).

Jerusalem Report (2000–2001, weekly magazine).

Who's Who in the 15th Knesset, Jerusalem: The Knesset, 1999 (Hebrew).

The following websites have been used to gather information.
www.knesset.gov.il (Knesset); www.pmo.gov.il (Prime Minister's Office)
www.mfa.gov.il (Ministry of Foreign Affairs); www.meretz.org.il (Meretz Party)
www.oneisrael.co.il (One Israel); www.likud.org.il (Likud Party)
www.hadash.org.il (Hadash Party); www.shinui.org.il (Shinui)
www.haichud-haleumi.org.il (National Unity Party);
www.hamercaz.org.il/ (The Centre Party)
www.Palestine-Net.com

5

Foundering Illusions: The Demise of the Oslo Process

Yossi Ben-Aharon

The PLO

To better understand the reasons for the failure of the Oslo process, a look at the background of the Palestinian partner to the Oslo Accord is necessary.

The Palestinian Authority (PA) that came into being through the Oslo Accords, is the governing organ that was created by the PLO. Its chairman is at one and the same time the chairman of the PLO. Most of the members of the executive body of the PA are members of the Executive Committee of the PLO and many, if not most of the members of the PA Legislative Council, are members of the Palestinian National Council (PNC).

The PLO was established in 1964, reorganized in 1968, and was initially dominated by Arab governments, primarily those of Egypt and Syria. Its declared purpose was the "liberation" of Palestine, which meant the elimination of Israel in its pre-June 1967 borders. At the PNC conference in Algiers in 1988, the Council declared the establishment of a Palestinian state, basing its decision on the UN General Assembly Resolution 181 of 1947, which had then been totally rejected by the Palestinians and by all the Arab states. The Algiers resolution was erroneously interpreted as an indirect, de facto recognition of Israel and the acceptance of the partition of Palestine into two states, one Jewish (Israel) and one Arab (Palestine). In fact, although the Algiers meeting based its declaration of an independent Palestinian state on the UN Partition Resolution of 1947, it made no reference, much less extend any recognition, explicit or implicit, of the State of Israel.

The PLO Covenant and the 1974 Resolutions

The basic, guiding platform, or constitution, of the PLO is the Palestinian National Covenant of 1968.[1] Some 25 out of 33 articles of that covenant called for the elimination of Israel by means of an "armed struggle" and supplanting it with an Arab Palestinian state. At the 21st conference of the PNC in Gaza on April 25, 1996, the articles that contradicted the Oslo Accords were supposedly struck from the covenant. However, the process by which those articles were eliminated was not in accordance with the rules set down by the covenant itself and was therefore questionable, if not altogether invalid.

At its 12th meeting, on June 9, 1974, the PNC decided, after a bitter debate that caused a split in the organization, to adopt political, in addition to military means, to achieve its goals. Paragraphs 2 and 8 of that decision stated, inter alia, that the PLO would "establish the independent, combatant national authority . . . over every part of Palestinian territory that is liberated." Once it is established, "the Palestinian national authority will strive to achieve . . . the aim of completing the liberation of all Palestinian territory . . . " This resolution later became known as the "stage by stage" approach toward the "liberation" of Palestine, meaning, in effect, the elimination of Israel.

At the beginning of February 2001, one hundred Palestinian personalities, including members of the Palestinian Authority's Executive Council and members of the PNC, met in Cairo under the chairmanship of the Speaker of the PNC, Saleem Za'nun. The participants decided to establish a National Independence Authority under the PNC. They passed a number of resolutions, one of which maintained that "the Palestinian National Covenant was still in force, because the PNC had not been convened for the purpose of approving changes in the Covenant and, especially, since the legal committee that should prepare the changes had not been set up."[2]

The Oslo Accords

The basic document in the Accords is the Declaration of Principles on Interim Self-Government Arrangements (DoP),[3] which was signed in Washington on September 13, 1993. The DoP set down the arrangements for the establishment of the Palestinian Council, the transfer of powers and responsibilities to it, its jurisdiction, and the transitional period pending the conclusion of permanent status negotiations. Article VIII empowered the Council to "establish a strong police force, while Israel will continue to carry the responsibility for defending against external threats, as well as the responsibility for overall security of Israelis . . . " Article XV stipulated that disputes "shall be resolved by negotiations" and failing that, the sides could have recourse to a mechanism of conciliation or submit the dispute to arbitration.

More pertinent to the subject of this paper is the exchange of letters between Prime Minister Yitzhak Rabin and PLO Chairman Yasser Arafat, which was attached to the DoP and became an integral part thereof.

In a letter to Rabin dated September 9, 1993, Arafat committed the PLO to "a peaceful resolution of the conflict between the two sides" and declared that "all outstanding issues relating to permanent status will be resolved through negotiations." Arafat stated further that the PLO "renounces the use of terrorism and other acts of violence and will assume responsibility over all PLO elements and personnel in order to assure their compliance, prevent violations and discipline violators." In another letter to Rabin of the same date, Arafat undertook to include in his public statements a call upon the Palestinian people in the West Bank and the Gaza Strip "to take part in the steps leading to the normalization of life, rejecting violence and terrorism, (and) contributing to peace and stability . . . "

The Gaza–Jericho Agreement laid down the mode of implementation of the first stage of the Oslo Accords.[4] Under that agreement and its Security Annex, Israel withdrew its forces from the Gaza Strip and Jericho and the PA was to establish a police force comprising 9,000 men. Israel undertook to release some 5,000 Palestinian prisoners.

The provisions of the Gaza–Jericho Agreement included:

- an undertaking by the PA to give Israel the names of the members of the PA and to inform and gain Israel's consent for any change therein (Art. IV);
- a commitment by the PA not to conduct foreign relations, except in economic, scientific, cultural and educational spheres and foreign aid (Art. VI);
- an undertaking to coordinate legislation with Israel (Art. VII);
- a solemn obligation that the Palestinian Police would be the only body permitted to bear arms and no other organization or person will be permitted to acquire, possess or import firearms or explosives (Art. IX).

Annex I to the Agreement limited the number of firearms possessed by the Police to 7,000 light personal weapons and up to 120 low-caliber machine guns (Art. III); Israeli settlements in the areas transferred to the PA will be under Israeli authority (Art. IV). Two important issues were postponed, to be addressed in the permanent status negotiations: Jerusalem and the Palestinian refugees. Contrary to repeated charges by the Palestinians, there was no undertaking by Israel in the Oslo Accords, or subsequently, with regard to the existence, the expansion, or the establishment of settlements.

Barring foreign relations and external defense and security, the Gaza–Jericho Agreement empowered the PA to conduct its affairs, in the territories under its jurisdiction, in total independence. This principle was subsequently applied over all territories that were transferred to the PA.

The First Cracks

The DoP and the signing ceremony on the White House lawn were universally hailed as a turning point in the history of the century-old Arab–Israel conflict. At the ceremony, the Prime Minister of Israel addressed the Palestinians and said that Israelis and Palestinians "are destined to live together on the same soil in the same land . . . we are today giving peace a chance . . . we wish to open a new chapter . . . of mutual recognition, of good neighborliness, of mutual respect, of understanding."

Addressing the people of Israel, PLO chairman Yasser Arafat said that the two sides "will need more courage and determination to continue the course of building coexistence and peace" and added that "the two peoples are awaiting today this historic hope, and they want to give peace a real chance."

In the course of the Knesset debate on the Oslo Accords, Prime Minister Rabin assured the house that the PLO "had undertaken to enforce the cessation of terror and violent activities on its members and to bring violators of its commitment to justice."[5]

Shortly after the implementation of the Gaza–Jericho Agreement, Rabin sounded optimistic, when he said that "in the six weeks following the implementation of the Gaza–Jericho Agreement, the results are altogether positive, even with regard to security."[6] A month later, four Palestinian terrorists were caught attempting to enter the Gaza Strip in Arafat's entourage illegally.[7]

A few weeks later, Rabin's tone began to change. Referring to the killing of three Israeli soldiers by Palestinians since the Gaza-Jericho implementation, the Prime Minister went on to attach grave significance to the killing of an Israeli civilian near Kissufim, adjacent to the Gaza Strip. Rabin criticized the PA and charged that it was not making a serious effort to deal with the terrorist organizations operating from within PA-held territory. "It does not stand to reason that we continue with the (peace) process without a clear indication that the PA is making a serious effort to quell the groups responsible for terror attacks. This would be the test of the process."[8] Rabin then went on to warn the PA that failure to deal with the terrorist threat will force Israel to draw the consequences.[9] Shortly thereafter, Rabin levelled his criticism at Yasser Arafat personally. If Arafat cannot impose his authority on his people, said Rabin, it is doubtful that he can speak for them.[10]

By the end of January 1995, Rabin had reached the conclusion that the Palestinian terror was a strategic threat. In a cabinet meeting, the Prime Minister reportedly said that "the terror has assumed strategic proportions, because it is threatening the peace process."[11] Foreign Minister Shimon Peres, architect of the Oslo Accords, went a step further. He threatened to halt the negotiations with Arafat if the Palestinian leader would fail to extend his control over the PA-held territory. "If (Arafat) is too weak or unwilling, why should we negotiate with him . . . (and) why should we withdraw from the West Bank?" asked Peres.[12]

In another press interview, the Israeli Prime Minister revealed the agonizing dilemma which he was facing in relation to the peace process with the Palestinians. "Logically, Israelis understand that the time has come to put an end to the conflict in all its aspects. Emotionally, they are not convinced that the PA has the ability, the capacity, or the will to cope with the terror."[13]

Palestinan Violations of the Agreements

Throughout the months and years following the signing of the first Oslo Accord, the Israel government, the media and various research institutes issued a multitude of statements and reports on a wide variety of violations by Yasser Arafat, by the PA, and by individual Palestinians.

Probably the most telling and most serious type of violation were the statements by Yasser Arafat, Chairman of the PA and the PLO, the person who signed all the main agreements between Israel and the PLO/PA, on behalf of the Palestinians.

On September 1, 1993, two weeks before the signing ceremony on the White House lawn, Yasser Arafat made the following statement on Radio Monte Carlo: "The agreement [i.e. the agreement with Israel] will be a basis for an independent Palestinian state in accordance with the Palestine National Council resolution issued in 1974 . . . The PNC resolution issued in 1974 (see above, p. 60), calls for the establishment of a national authority on any part of Palestinian soil from which Israel withdraws or which is liberated."[14]

The 1974 resolution to which Arafat referred, also known as the "phase by phase" resolution, laid down the PNC's "political programme." (See above, p. 60.)

Another type of statement by Yasser Arafat was the often repeated reference to Jihad as a way of achieving Palestinian objectives. Thus, in a speech he delivered in a mosque in Johannesburg on May 10, 1994, he said: "The Jihad will continue . . . You have to understand our main battle is Jerusalem . . . You have to come and to fight a Jihad to liberate Jerusalem, your precious shrine . . . No, it is not their capital. It is our capital."[15] In the course of a speech at a large demonstration of support for Arafat that was organized by the Fatah movement in Gaza, Arafat said: "The Palestinian people are maintaining their Jihad, but the process will continue until one of the Fatah youths or a Palestinian boy will raise the flag over the walls of Jerusalem . . . "[16]

A typical statement by Yasser Arafat is the repeated reference to the extremely controversial issue of the "right of return" of Palestinians to the territory of Palestine in its entirety, including pre-June 1967 Israel. Thus, at a reception in his honor in Gaza, Arafat said: "Be blessed, O Gaza, and celebrate, for your sons are returning after a long celebration. O Gaza, your sons are returning. O Jaffa, O Lod, O Haifa, O Jerusalem, you are returning."[17] All the towns Arafat mentioned, except for Gaza, are in Israel proper.

Another example is Arafat's references to the seventeenth-century Khudaybiyya armistice agreement which was concluded between the city of Mecca and Islam's prophet, Muhammad. In an interview with the *al-Quds* Jerusalem daily, Arafat was asked if he felt he may have made a mistake in concluding the Oslo agreement. Arafat replied: "No . . . no. Allah's messenger Muhammad accepted the al-Khudaybiyya peace treaty . . . "[18] Arafat was thus drawing a parallel between the Oslo agreement and Muhammad's ten-year armistice agreement with the Mecca rulers, which he broke after two years. The clear implication was that the agreement with Israel was of a temporary nature and the Palestinian side can abrogate it whenever it ceased to meet its interests.

On December 13, 1994, the IDF Judge Advocate-General's Assistant for International Law issued a report detailing Palestinian violations of undertakings under the agreements with Israel.[19] Each category of violations was measured against the relevant clause in the various agreements concluded between Israel and the PLO/PA.

Among the more serious violations in the sixteen-page report were: refusal to transfer to Israel Palestinians suspected of involvement in terror attacks; refusal to report to Israel on investigations of terror incidents; non-compliance with the commitment to prevent acts of incitement against Israel; refusal to submit names of policemen who were recruited by the PA; illegal arrest of Israeli citizens by Palestinian police; Palestinian policemen driving (Israeli) stolen vehicles; use of weapons belonging to the Palestinian Police in the course of a terrorist attack in Jerusalem on October 9, 1994; recruitment of former prisoners to the Palestinian Intelligence service; non-compliance with the requirment to prevent infiltrations between Gaza and

Egypt; reports of Palestinian civilians openly carrying weapons; abuse and brutalization of persons suspected of collaboration with Israel by the PA authorities; PA activites in Jerusalem, in which the PA has no authority; passage of legislation by the PA without coordination with or approval by Israel; lack of action by the PA to put a stop to the practice of forging documents for the purpose of entering Israel; use of the title "Palestine" in stamps and official documents in contravention of the agreement.

Another serious violation of the Gaza–Jericho Agreement was the constant growth in the size of the Palestinian Police. In February 1995, Terje Larsen, UN Coordinator on PA Affairs, confirmed that the police had reached the size of 15,000, that is 6,000 above the limit set down in the agreement.[20] By the year 2000, it was estimated that the various police, military, and intelligence organs under the PA had reached the size of 40,000. Senior IDF officers characterized the PA armed apparatus as a veritable army, armed and trained for offensive purposes.

Contrary to the expectations of the Israeli architects of the Oslo Accords, attacks on Israelis increased alarmingly following the implementation of the Gaza–Jericho Agreement and the deployment of Palestinian police. In a three-month period, from November 1, 1994 to January 29, 1995, the Israel military authorities recorded 44 incidents of shooting, 12 cases of use of explosive devices, and six confrontations between Palestinian police and IDF soldiers, all in the Gaza Strip area alone. Israeli casualties in those incidents amounted to 4 killed and 8 wounded.[21]

During the five years that preceded the Oslo Accords, 134 Israelis were killed in terror attacks. In the five years following the Accords, 305 Israelis were killed – more than double.

PA Cooperation with Hamas and Islamic Jihad

Not long after the implementation of the Gaza–Jericho Agreement, Yasser Arafat's tactics began to assume a clear pattern. On the one hand, he mobilized international pressure on Israel to speed up negotiations. With this goal in mind, he repeatedly called for an early and full implementation of a final and comprehensive agreement, encompassing total Israel withdrawal from the West Bank and Gaza. At the same time, he kept charging Israel with deliberately slowing the process and using security as a pretext for delaying the withdrawal from territory. On the other hand, Arafat signalled first to the Islamic terrorist groups – Hamas and Islamic Jihad – and later to Fatah and Tanzim, which are under his direct command, to keep up the pressure on Israel.[22]

In the Spring of 1994, before the Palestinian Authority had established itself in Gaza and Jericho, there were reports of coordination between

Fatah, Yasser Arafat's personally led organization inside the PLO, and Hamas, which rejected all agreements with Israel and openly espoused a sustained Jihad toward the elimination of the Jewish state. The reported objective of this coordination was to reach an understanding and prevent competition that might cause friction and clashes between the two movements. Hamas was bent on maintaining attacks on Israel, while Fatah was anxious to prevent incidents that might delay the implementation of the Oslo Accord and the Gaza–Jericho Agreement.

In the event, the two groups signed a "conciliation agreement" which was reportedly intended to enable Hamas to continue its activities, barring attacks that might cause embarassment to Arafat and his group.[23]

Addressing the Knesset, Prime Minister Rabin voiced a warning: " . . . Any . . . understanding between the PLO and the Hamas on the possibility of continued terrorism by the Hamas . . . would preclude an agreement and prevent its implementation."[24]

Rabin's warning went unheeded. In the face of the absence of any concrete reaction from the Israel government beyond words, Fatah later went ahead and signed a formal agreement with Hamas, the full text of which appeared in the Cairo daily "al-Ahram" on September 20, 1995. Under the terms of the agreement, signed "under the sponsorship of Chairman Yasser Arafat and Sheikh Ahmad Yassin [leader of Hamas]," the two movements undertook "to respect the . . . agreements which require the cessation of all military operations in, or lauched from, the areas under the PA . . . " This formulation was designed to sanction attacks by Hamas inside the territory of Israel, which Fatah and the PA could disown.

This double-edged approach by Arafat was entirely consistent with the decisions adopted by the PNC since 1974 – a stage by stage strategy, combining political and military means, toward the total "liberation" of Palestine.

The Arab-Muslim Dimension

Throughout the years of the wider Arab–Israel conflict, Arab leaders and spokesmen declared often that the Palestinian problem was the root cause of Arab hostility to Israel. Once the Palestinians regained their rights, so they said, Arab enmity to the Jewish state would subside.

The White House lawn ceremony featuring the signing of the Oslo Accords by Rabin and Arafat was hailed throughout the world as an historic breakthrough that had put an end to a century-old conflict. A number of Arab states, including Oman, the UAE, Tunisia, Morocco, and Mauritania established some diplomatic representation with Israel. The rest maintained their hostility, while some, like Syria, Iraq, Sudan, Libya, and Iran openly supported the "rejection front" which continued to oppose the very existence of Israel. Syria was especially active in enabling, if not encouraging, the Hizbullah organization to maintain military pressure against Israel in Sourthern Lebanon. At the same time, the Syrian government pressed the other Arab governments to break off relations with Israel, until its own demands of Israel received satisfaction.

With the passage of time and the escalation of violence between Israel and the Palestinians, Arab governments' relations with Israel gradually turned cooler, until some even broke them off. Egypt recalled its ambassador and the media throughout the Arab countries raised the volume and intensity of criticism and castigation of Israel.

The Arab angle in the Arab–Israel equation cannot be separated from the religious Islamic dimension. Until the decade of the 1980s, Arab expressions of hostility to Israel could be defined as secular and nationalistic. Arab ideologues depicted Israel as an outpost of Western Imperialism implanted in a region that was Arab and on territory usurped from the Arabs. The Palestinian National Covenant made no reference to a religious motivation in the Palestinian quest for the removal of Israel and the establishment of an Arab Palestinian entity in Palestine. PLO ideology looked to the eventual creation of an Arab united front, with the PLO as its spearhead, which would join the Arab forces in the final "liberation" of Palestine.

The rise of fundamentalist Islamic movements in the 1980s added a religious, sometimes fanatic, dimension to the Arab antagonism toward Israel. Some of the emphasis in this hostility assumed a religious expression, with movements such as Hamas, Islamic Jihad, and Hizbullah each giving its particular tone to the ideology of rejecting the creation and existence of the Jewish state. The key code word in this ideology was Jihad – a holy war against an infidel entity that had been implanted on land that belonged to the Muslim nation, land defined as an endowment – *Waqf* – that could not be sold, bequeathed or given away. In the eyes of the fundamentalist movements, Israel was a spearhead of a conspiracy of the Judeo-Christian civilization against the Muslim world, a kind of a new Crusader invasion.[25] Historically, the territory of Palestine was never defined by Islam in any way that was different from other lands that were conquered by the Muslim-Arab armies in the seventh and eighth centuries, except for the Hejaz, where the twin cities of Mecca and Medina, holy to Islam, are situated.

Except for Iran, all Arab governments were wary of fundamentalist movements and considered them a destablizing, if not revolutionary, element and a threat to their regime. Domestically, they took stern measures to curtail them. With regard to their activities against Israel, however, Arab governments' attitudes varied from tolerance to outright support.

Soon after he moved to Gaza, Yasser Arafat adopted a careful, two-pronged approach to the fundamentlaist groups. Facing strong pressure from the Rabin government to quell them, he would order PA security organs to take measures. Some were arrested, brought to trial and imprisoned. At the same time, Arafat lauded the suicidal martyrs of the Hamas movement, expressed special praise of Sheikh Ahmad Yasseen, leader of Hamas, and left no doubt in the minds of the Palestinians that he was not opposed to attacks on Israel, providing they did not embarrass him and the PA. Activists from the fundamentalist movements who had been sentenced to prison by the PA courts never spent more than a few months in jail. These included terrorists who were known publicly to have participated in bombing attacks that killed Israelis.

Evolution of the Process

Throughout the years that followed the first agreement with the PLO and under four Israeli governments, negotiations were held and several agreements were signed. In September 1995, Israel withdrew from six main towns in the West Bank, as well as from a major part of Hebron. In January 1997, Israel withdrew from an additional 9.1 percent of the territory of the West Bank. Under the Wye River Memorandum that was signed on October 23, 1998, Israel undertook to transfer additional territory to the PA. Thus, some 40 percent of the area of the West Bank and the Gaza Strip were delivered to the Palestinian Authority and approximately 90 percent of the Palestinian population came under the authority of the PA. Israel retained security control over the remaining territory, which was sparsely populated by Palestinians, and retained full control over Israeli settlements.

The entire process, however, was punctured by attacks on Israelis by various Palestinian organizations. The first spate of attacks was attributed to the two Islamic fundamentalist groups – Hamas and Islamic Jihad. Both groups belonged to the "rejectionist front," which was opposed to any accommodation with Israel. Expectations that the PA would take measures against these groups progressively faded, until it became clear that Yasser Arafat and his apparatus had no intention of inhibiting their activities. Toward the end of the 1990s, Israeli governments, whether Likud or Labor, were openly charging Arafat with encouraging Palestinians to attack Israel. Notwithstanding, the governments in Israel maintained the commitment to the Oslo Accords. Attempts at getting Arafat and the PA to forsake violence and terror as a means of achieving their objectives all failed. Israeli concessions, direct negotiations, diplomatic pressure, intercession of Arab and American mediators – all failed to produce a Palestinian undertaking to concentrate exclusively on negotiations toward the desired objective of a mutually acceptable compromise.

The Breakdown of the Barak Effort

Together with the intensive involvement by US President Bill Clinton, Israel's Labor government under Ehud Barak made a sustained effort, throughout its 18 months in office, to reach an accommodation with Yasser Arafat and the PA. Top-level meetings were held in Camp David, then at Sharm al-Shaykh and finally at Taba, on the Israel–Egypt border. All of them were designed to bring about a final status accord between Israel and the PA. Under the proposed terms, Israel offered to deliver more than 95 percent of the territory of the West Bank and all of the Gaza Strip to the Palestinians, was set to agree to Palestinian control over substantial portions of East Jerusalem, and proposed a solution to the problem of the Palestinian refugees. President Clinton made a last-minute effort at presenting a bridging proposal of his own. They all ended in failure.

The last stage in the efforts at achieving an agreement was accompanied by an outbreak of violence in October 2000, initiated by the Palestinians and openly encouraged by Arafat and his colleagues. The negotiations, which focused initially on the political issues, shifted progressively toward attempts at bringing about an end to Palestinian violence, which was described as the "Temple Mount Intifada" or the "al-Aqsa Intifada." This name was given by the Palestinians when they charged the then leader of the Opposition in Israel's Knesset, Ariel Sharon, of having deliberately triggered the renewed violence when he conducted a highly-publicized visit to the Temple Mount.

Frustrated at the repeated failure of its quest for a meeting of the minds with the Palestinians, the Israel Government finally issued in November 2000 what the media called a White Paper. Officially the document was named "Palestinian Authority and PLO Non-Compliance – A record of bad faith." The opening sentence in that report said:"The present wave of violence – led by the Fatah 'Tanzim' – is essentially *an attempt by Arafat to achieve, **through violence**, his maximal political goals;* and avoid the choices necessary to bring the negotiations to a successful conclusion."

The document went on to catalogue a long list of violations by the PA, including: direct use of violence by the Palestinian Police; ambivalent attitudes toward terrorism, and at times – outright complicity; failure to collect illegal weapons; incitement to hatred; the (inflated) size of the Palestinian Police force; Palestinian security organs operating outside the agreed areas; illegal use of Gaza Airport; ignoring agreements pertaining to economic and infrastructure issues; criminal activities on a large scale under PA auspices; and failure to protect Jewish holy places.

Analysis of the Breakdown

The following analysis of the breakdown of the Oslo Peace Process will address first the Palestinian approach, then the Israel government policy, and finally touch upon a possible alternative, which was begun by the Shamir–Likud government in 1991–2.

The Palestinian–PLO approach

Yasser Arafat and PA leaders have maintained that under the Oslo Accords, which were a five-year interim agreement, Israel should have withdrawn from the entire territory of the West Bank and the Gaza Strip by the end of the five-year interim period. Furthermore, Israel should evacuate the settlements that were established in those territories and agree to carry out the 1949 UN Resolution on the refugee issue.

It goes without saying that the agreements between Israel and the PLO/PA were reciprocal undertakings that obligated both sides. However from the very beginning of the process, the Palestinian side expected Israel to carry out its obligations under the accords, irrespective of the Palestinian conduct. The record has shown, without a shred of doubt, that the PA violated virtually all of the main undertakings under the agreements. This was especially the case with regard to acts of violence and terror, the size and conduct of the Palestinian Police and the consistent preaching, indoctrination and incitement to hatred and violence by the PA leadership, by religious functionaries, by the Palestinian media, and by educators in the Palestinian school system.[26]

The governments of Israel, and especially those that were led by Labor, made serious attempts at meeting Palestinian demands in the negotiations. The Barak government went far beyond the positions that were taken by previous governments in an effort to reach accommodation. President Clinton testified that Prime Minister Barak had gone the extra mile in order to satisfy Palestinian desires. The Barak government lost its majority in the Knesset and was voted out of office primarily because of what the Israeli public considered to be exaggerated and unwarranted concessions to the Palestinians. To the very end of his term in office, Ehud Barak attached maximum priority to bringing about an agreement. The attempt failed because the PLO/PA insisted on demands that were considered by Israel to constitute a danger to the security – and even the existence – of the state.

The breakdown of the process cannot be attributed to misundertandings by Arafat and the PLO or a misreading of Israel's policy by the Palestinians. Actions and statements by the Palestinian leadership have demonstrated, from the beginning of the process, a supercilious attitude toward commitments under the agreements with Israel. The Barak government's characterization of the Palestinian conduct as "a record of bad faith" implied a final judgement that Arafat had deliberately misled his Israeli and American interlocutors all along.

Reading the record of the last eight years against the clauses of the Palestinian National Covenant and the PNC resolutions, particularly that of the 12th congress in 1974, one discerns a pattern of conduct that coincides with the policy of the PLO from its inception. Yasser Arafat said as much in his own words. Furthermore, he made consistent efforts to drive a wedge between the US and Israel and to isolate Israel in the international arena. He appealed to Arab governments, in the name of Arab solidarity and traditional Arab support for the Palestinian cause, to exert pressure on Israel, directly and through international avenues.

Arafat and the PA have also manipulated the media so as to depict Israel as the aggressive Goliath attacking a defenseless David. Toward this objective, Palestinian schoolchildren were directed by the Tanzim to confront Israeli soldiers, hurl rocks and firebombs at them, while the Tanzim and Fatah members positioned themselves behind them with firearms, shooting at the soldiers.

Apologists for the Palestinians will argue that Israel was dragging its feet on the peace process and the Palestinians were only reacting to attacks that were initiated by the IDF. These and similar arguments in the same vein simply fail the test of the facts on the ground and the conduct and statements of the Palestinian leadership.

Finally, one may ask why did Arafat reject all of Israel's compromise proposals, including the far-reaching ones of the Barak government? Why not take what was being offered and wait for the opportunity to resume pressure for more? There is no clear-cut answer to this question. Arafat is the sole, uncontested leader who makes all the decisions. He had always preached for unity in the Palestinian ranks and warned against a split, similar to that which triggered fighting between Palestinian factions during the 1936–9 disturbances. Consequently, he went out of his way to praise attacks on Israel by Hamas and Islamic Jihad. He lauded especially the suicide bombers, calling them "shaheeds" or religious martyrs. He never made a serious effort, contrary to explicit undertakings, to quell the fundamentalist terror groups. Even those who were apprehended and sentenced to jail were soon released and permitted to resume their terror activities. In Arafat's eyes, the need to maintain unity at all costs outweighed an agreement that would expose him to attack by the rejectionist front organizations.

Two main issues turned out to be the deal-breakers in the negotiations. Arafat was probably convinced that he could not accept, or justify, any concession on Jerusalem. The area that had been under Jordanian occupation between 1948 and 1967, especially the Temple Mount (or *al-Haram al-Shareef*), had to be delivered to Palestinian ownership. No government in Israel could agree to such a demand. Second, Arafat had to extract from Israel an undertaking to accept the principle of the "right of return" of the four million or so Palestinian refugees. For Israel, this meant an end to its independent existence as a Jewish state.

Apparently, Arafat and the Palestinian leadership perceived Israel as a weak and spineless giant that could be neutralized and brought to its knees by hitting at its weak points. They took courage from Israel's territorial withdrawals from neighboring Arab countries, especially from Lebanon, and from Israeli leaders' declared readiness to withdraw further. Like the other, equally totalitarian governments in the Middle East, they had difficulty in reading Israel's democracy and decision-making processes, which they interpreted as weakness. They had probably figured that they could afford a confrontation, pay a price, and still come away without sustaining meaningful loss in terms of advancing toward their goals.

The Israel government policy

Approaching the PLO in Tunis and offering to negotiate with its leadership for an agreement with Israel was a revolutionary turn of events. It was a 180-degree departure from a traditional policy, followed by both Labor and Likud governments, of official opposition to any recognition or negotiations with the PLO. Until then, contact with the PLO was forbidden by law and membership in the PLO, or any of its constituent groups, was a punishable violation.

In the Knesset debate following the signature of the Declaration of Principles with the PLO, the late Prime Minister Rabin said that "the risks were taken into account and they do not entail a danger to the security and existence of Israel." He went on to say that Israel was turning toward "days without worry and nights without fear" as there was a chance of seeing "an end to the mourning that visited our homes, an end to wars."[27] Shortly thereafter, Foreign Minister Shimon Peres declared that "we are approaching a stage at which it will transpire that there is no future for terror and it will vanish."[28]

Clearly, the Labor government believed that its unprecedented reaching out to the PLO was a coup that responded to the Israeli people's yearning for an end to terror and violence, toward the advent of peace. It had taken the bull by the horns, so to speak, tamed its most extreme enemy, began to accommodate its demands and could safely believe that it had removed the sting from the almost century-old Arab vendetta against Israel.

Rabin took seriously protestations throughout the Arab world that once the Palestinian problem was addressed by Israel, Arab hostility to the

Jewish state would subside. What in fact took place was reminiscent of the 1948 scenario. Arab governments had then adopted extreme positions that led the Palestinians to believe that the combined Arab power would eliminate the newly-established Jewish state. In the event, however, the invading Arab armies were defeated and the Palestinans, including those who had fled, were left to face the consequences. Now Arab governments and Iran were again supporting the most extreme wings in the Palestinian camp and warning Arafat not to compromise in the negotiations with Israel.

In retrospect, it is evident that the Israeli negotiators with the PLO betrayed lack of experience and a tendency to take irresponsible risks. They did not take into full account Arafat's long career of terror, manipulation, and cunning deceit. They labored under the illusion that once the PLO was established on Palestinian soil and allowed to carry out the normal functions of government, violence and terror would become pointless, and cooperation and mutual confidence would take root. This, in turn, would provide a positive setting for the solution of the more difficult issues, such as Jerusalem, settlements, and refugees. It turned out to be a miscalculation. Arafat and the PA took advantage of their physical emplacement on Palestinian soil to establish an entity that was poised, primed, and indoctrinated against Israel. A plethora of armed groups, posing as police and security organs, were trained and prepared to use their arms, some of which were provided by Israel for police purposes, as soon as the stone-throwing Intifada deteriorated into a shooting battle.

The Rabin–Peres government's tactical approach was flawed in other respects. It placed exaggerated trust in Arafat and attached too little importance to verification. It made gestures and concessions without regard to reciprocity. It agreed to a time-table of Israeli withdrawals from territory, without linking them to parallel Palestinian performance. It did not insist on the inclusion of objective standards of implementation in the agreements. Nor did it insist on concrete and specific steps that would be taken in case of violations. Spokesmen for that government argued that the entire agreement was reversible, and did not attach serious consideration to the price and consequences of taking such a course. They prematurely catapulted Yasser Arafat's standing and image from a leader of an outlawed organization to that of head of a near-sovereign entity and paved his way to the White House as an equal partner to the Israeli Prime Minister. Finally, they agreed to an elaborate White House ceremony and the involvement of the US in the process, thus enabling Arafat to acquire prestige and use it to play off the US against Israel.

Having crossed the Rubicon and established the Palestinian entity right at their doorstep, the Labor and other left-wing politicians could not bring themselves to admit to having committed a monumental blunder. They kept arguing, step after step, that one more concession would change the course of events and turn the clock back to their original scenario. To admit to failure would have spelled total bankruptcy of the Left-wing bloc and removed its chances of leading a government coalition for a long time.

Five Israeli governments have had to contend with the results of the Oslo agreements and their aftermath. There were differences in nuances, different reactions to Palestinian violations, but all of them remained within the parameters of the Accords and tried to make the best of a difficult situation, despite a mounting escalation that was invariably triggered by Palestinian gunmen.

A word on American performance on this issue, under President Clinton, is necessary. The US government was certainly aware of the tremendous risk that Israel had taken in the agreement with the PLO. It was also aware of Arafat's record, including his involvement in acts of terror against Americans and the assassination of American diplomats. Furthermore, it must have been plainly evident to Washington, shortly after the establishment of the PA, that Arafat was not living up to his commitments. Yet instead of taking him to task and supporting Israeli attempts at requiring him to quell the terror and carry out his other obligations, President Clinton chose to treat Israel and the PLO symmetrically. His intimate involvement in the process raised Arafat's stature and encouraged him to maintain his course and multiply his efforts at putting Israel on the defensive. Clinton finally publicly launched a blueprint ("a bridging proposal") which backfired, dealt a heavy blow to the entire process, and helped bring down the Barak government. Finally, the Clinton Administration's intervention in Israeli domestic politics – supporting the Labor government and trying to bring down the Likud – turned out to be a blunder that served neither the peace process nor the US–Israel relationship.

The Shamir government's policy

In 1991, the Bush-Baker Administration made a serious attempt at moving the Arab–Israel process forward. Prime Minister Shamir agreed to negotiate with a Palestinian delegation, providing it was composed of residents of the territories – Judea, Samaria (the West Bank) and the Gaza Strip only. Shamir insisted that the PLO would have no say and no representation, open or symbolic, in the Madrid Conference and in the ensuing negotiations. Secretary of State Jim Baker, as well as the Arab delegations to the talks, accepted these conditions.

Shamir explained that the primary objective of the process, as it pertained to the Palestinians, was to achieve an accommodation with the inhabitants of the territories. There was a solid basis on which agreement could be founded, because the Palestinians in the West Bank and Gaza had a vested interest in maintaining and developing their assets – their personal security, their property, their services and their way of life, free of a military government which they despised. Of course, they had political and national desires, but these could not be met at that stage. The four-year-old Intifada was dwindling and manageable. On its part, Israel did not want to run the lives and affairs of the Palestinians and was willing to work together with them toward removing the Israeli Military Administration of the territories and the establishment of full autonomy.

The Palestinian delegates were known to be beholden to the PLO leadership in Tunis. Nevertheless, faced with the choice between cooperating toward the establishment of autonomy and maintaining the status quo, there was a chance – slim as it may be – that they would opt for the former and convince the PLO leadership to agree and bide their time.

Prime Minister Shamir further argued that there was no practical basis, even the most minimal, for an accommodation with the Tunis PLO. Arafat and his colleagues were all, in a sense, representatives of the refugee constituency, whose inherent uppermost priority was the exercise of the "right of return" for themselves and for the Palestinian diaspora. Furthermore, the PNC had already declared its statehood (in the 1988 congress in Algiers) with Jerusalem as the capital. Shamir suspected, and events later proved him right, that the PLO remained dedicated to the Palestinian Covenant, in spirit and substance, and permitting it to set foot in any part of Mandatory Palestine would, sooner or later, pose an existential danger to Israel.

The Rabin–Peres government thought otherwise. It plunged Israel into the risky road of inviting the PLO to the process. Israel, the Palestinans, and the chances of success in the peace process have since been paying the price.

The Oslo process is a proven, dismal failure. In a deeper sense, it has highlighted the immense gulf between the Arab-Muslim concept of peace with a non-Arab, non-Muslim, Jewish state, and the Western, democratic and Jewish concept of peace with a former enemy. This realization has raised the question whether the "territory for peace" equation, that lay at the foundation of the entire Arab–Israel peace process, was the correct approach in the first place. Delivering territory is an irreversible act, while peace can be overturned overnight and at will. Since the Arab side continued to oppose Israel's right to exist, even after signing agreements with it, a different approach should have been considered. The territorial aspect should have been held in abeyance, perhaps under some outside guarantee, until Israel and the international community were satisfied that the Arab governments in question demonstrated their acceptance of Israel as a legitimate entity and its right to exist in the region, equal to that of the other states. Only after incitement and education to hatred and violence against Jews and against the Jewish state were effectively outlawed and forbidden, a process of true give and take, of direct negotiations toward a peaceful accommodation, could be undertaken.

Notes

1 "The Palestinian National Covenant," English rendition, Leila S. Kadi (ed.), PLO Organization Research Centre, Beirut, December, 1969. Reproduced by the Israel Information Centre, Jerusalem, May 1978.

2 *al-Hayat al-Jadidah*, February 2, 2001. MEMRI – The Middle East Media and Research Institute.

3 "Declaration of Principles on Self-Government Arrangements," Israel Information Center, Ministry of Foreign Affairs, Jerusalem, September, 1993.

4 "Agreement on the Gaza Strip and the Jericho Area" Cairo, May 4, 1994, Israel Information Center.

5 "Divrei haKnesset," Knesset debates, translated from the Hebrew version, September 21, 1993.

6 *Ha'aretz*, July 4, 1994.

7 *Ha'aretz*, July 15, 1994.

8 *Ha'aretz*, August 16, 1994.

9 *Yediot Acharonot*, August 31, 1994.

10 *Ha'aretz*, November 6, 1994.

11 *Ha'aretz*, January 30, 1995.

12 *Ha'aretz*, March 5, 1995.

13 *Ha'aretz*, July 9, 1995.

14 Source – IMRA – Independent Media Review and Analysis.

15 Israel Radio, May 17, 1994; *Jerusalem Post*, May 18, 1994.

16 *Ha'aretz*, November 22, 1994.

17 *Ma'ariv*, September 7, 1995.

18 *al-Quds*, May 10, 1998.

19 "Concatenation of Palestinian Violations," a report by Col. David Yahav, Assistant to the Judge Advocate-General for International Law, December 13, 1994.

20 *Ha'aretz*, February 6, 1995.

21 Extract from a report by Col. David Yahav, Assistant to the Judge Advocate-Genral, published by the Research Dept, Regional Council of Judea, Samaria and the Gaza Strip, February, 1995.

22 Interview with General Moshe Yaalon, Head of Military Intelligence, *Ha'aretz*, May 11, 1997.

23 *Ha'aretz*, April 25, 1994.

24 "Divrei haKnesset," Knesset debates, translated from the Hebrew version, April 18, 1994.

25 For a deeper analysis of the clash between the Islamic and the Western civilizations, see Samuel P. Huntington, *The Clash of Civilzations and the Remaking of World Order* (New York: Simon & Schuster, 1996), chs 9 and 10.

26 (a) See "MEMRI – Middle East Media Research Institute," especially "Inquiry and Analysis" No. 26 and Special Dispatches Nos. 1, 2, 3, 26, 137 and

151; (b) See also "IMRA – Independent Media Review Analysis," A Compendium of Hate: Palestinian Authority Anti-Semitism Since the Hebron Accord, Israel Government Press Office, Jerusalem, 16 December, 1997 (www.imra.org.il).

27   "Divrei haKnesset," Knesset debates, translated from the Hebrew version, September 21, 1993.

28   "Divrei haKnesset," Knesset debates, translated from the Hebrew version, October 21, 1993.

Islamic Perspectives on the Oslo Process

Mustafa Abu Sway

This chapter explains the position of Islamic movements and Muslim scholars regarding the Oslo Process from within the Islamic worldview. It will show that contemporary movements and organizations such as Hamas and the Islamic Jihad, in their opposition to the Oslo Process and their continuation of the struggle against the "Israeli" occupation, conform to the centuries old theological and legal (i.e., Shari'ah) framework. The same worldview shaped the position of their predecessors, including scholars and Islamic organizations, during the twentieth century and beyond.

Historical Palestine

The history of the conflict between Zionists and Arabs is a little more than a century old. It can be dated to the time the Zionist conference took place in Basel, Switzerland, at the end of the nineteenth century. The conference adopted the establishment of a Jewish national home in Palestine. That decision ignored the fact that Palestine was never devoid of a people living there. It also failed to recognize and make use of the history of the relationship of Jews to the whole region, which was shaped by the Islamic presence since the seventh century CE. Such a decision by the Zionist movement meant that a clash with the inhabitants of the land was inevitable. More than a century later, the clash is still going on.

The Jewish presence in Islamic lands predates the beginning of the Zionist movement and indeed the Zionist immigration to Palestine to establish a state of their own. Islamic literature reflects the distinction between Judaism and Zionism. There is no organic relationship between the two; Judaism existed for thousands of years without Zionism as an ideology, with the establishment of a Jewish nation-state forming its backbone. There are ultra-orthodox Jews who do not recognize the Zionist state, Zionists who are atheists, and postmodernist Jewish intellectuals who think of solutions in terms of a post-Zionist paradigm. The latter position recognizes the fact that nation-states are modern political forms that need to be deconstructed. It should be obvious that it is not possible for divine revelation, which took place millenniums ago, to adopt and advocate a modern notion such as the "nation-state,"

The Zionist project aimed at establishing a Jewish polity in Palestine; it did not aim at restoring Jewish presence in a way that would accommodate the Jews without raising any kind of tension. The Islamic Caliphate has had a Jewish presence throughout its entire history, over fourteen centuries, including a Jewish presence in the Holy Land. This coexistence with the People of the Book, including Judaism, is deeply rooted in the Qur'an and the traditions of the Prophet. Muslims in North Africa and the "Middle East" accepted the Jews who fled the Inquisition in Spain, where exemplary relationships had developed between Jews, Christians, and Muslims. Indeed, Muslims could have easily done the same to the Jews fleeing modern European persecution, though one should note that the decision to establish a Jewish state in Palestine took place decades before the rise of Nazi Germany. The Jews, and obviously the gypsies, the Poles and almost everybody else needed to be protected from the Nazis. Yet, the problem was and still is the erection of a sovereign state against the will of the Palestinian people who were displaced by force to accommodate the Zionist entity. It is puzzling how a people who suffered so much at the hands of the Europeans would not break the cycle of violence! The Zionist approach was, and still is, a maximum acquisition of Palestinian land and a minimum Palestinian presence to secure the "Jewish" nature of the state. The exclusive approach of Zionism, Thou or I, was translated into a systematic assault on the sanctity of life and, when spared, its quality.

Until 1948, the Palestinians, both Muslims and Christians, formed 75 percent of the total population of historical Palestine and owned 93 percent of the land. "Israel," or rather the land within the 1948 Green Line, is 78 percent of the total area of historical Palestine and "Israeli" Arabs (i.e., Palestinians) are only 20 percent of the total population of "Israel." The other 22 percent of the land fell under "Israeli" occupation in 1967. Palestinian land in the West Bank, including East Jerusalem, and the Gaza Strip was confiscated by the "Israeli" military. The military then passed it to Jewish settlers who eventually built their settlements surrounding Palestinian towns, cutting off any natural continuum between them, and choking them to prevent natural growth. The location of these settlements made sure that these Palestinian towns were reduced to Bantustans, with no freedom of movement between them.

A solution, in order to be legitimate, should undo the injustice that befell the Palestinian people. If and only if the Palestinian individual is recognized and recategorized as a human being entitled to all the rights that should be enjoyed by humanity, we might see a light at the end of the tunnel. The question is: Does the Oslo process entail that kind of justice? An example of which is the inalienable right of return of all Palestinian refugees to their homes. Why does it make sense for the Jew to "return" after thousands of years, and not the Palestinian who is still alive and literally holds the keys of her home from which she was deported in 1948?

Foundations for Acceptance and Rejection in the Islamic Worldview

What has been mentioned earlier regarding the acceptance of Jews living in Islamic lands is not an extraordinary act where Islamic theology and the Shari'ah are concerned. Islam reflects the stage in which the line of monotheism culminated. The Islamic worldview as manifested in the Qur'an and the Sunnah (i.e., the way of the Prophet as reflected through the traditions) recognizes the previous prophets and messengers, including those sent to the Children of Israel. The books[1] of Revelation that their messengers brought them are also recognized; hence they are "People of the Book." In addition to their freedom to exercise religion and conduct their private life according to the teachings of their respective religions, their status is usually described as *dhimmis* (i.e., People of the Book who have a covenant with the Islamic state defining their rights and obligations). To reflect the extent of the protection they enjoyed, the Prophet said: "He who harms a *dhimmi*, harms me." Thus hurting a Jew or a Christian is tantamount to hurting the Prophet himself. These teachings, in contemporary language, are nothing but theologically motivated affirmative action, which aims at protecting the rights of the "People of the Book." Muslims have such teachings inculcated deep in their consciousness; indeed, believe that such teachings form the cornerstone for a potential solution, one that depends on a different kind of Jewish presence and relationship with the land and the people.

Yet, the above-mentioned status of the *dhimmis* is valid as long as those Jews and Christians are considered part of the society and do not collectively commit acts of aggression against the state, or import ideologies and implement them in a way that endangers the social fabric. The Qur'an says:

> God forbids you not, with regard to those who fight you not for [your] faith *nor drive you out of your homes*, from dealing kindly[2] and justly with them, for God loves those who are just. (60:8)

The same Shari'ah that declares kindness to the People of the Book imperative during peaceful times also makes it obligatory, upon every Muslim, to defend Islamic land if it falls under occupation. Therefore, the religious background of the occupier is accidental. This is also true in the case of Palestine. All Islamic authorities rejected the Zionist project and subsequently its realization as a state at the expense of the Palestinian people. It is for this reason that Al-Azhar in Cairo, one of the most important centers of Islamic learning and a center for scholars, called upon Muslims to save Palestine and declared fighting imperative upon every capable Muslim (1947), and prohibited having a peace treaty with "Israel" (1956). The International Islamic Conference issued a *fatwa* (i.e., a religious ruling) that reiterated the same position similar to that of Al-Azhar (1968). Al-Azhar confirmed its position again in 1977. And in 1990, all major Muslim scholars prohibited giving up any part of Palestine, stressing, at the same time, that no person or institution has the right to legitimize "Israeli" occupation of any part of Palestine. Indeed, it is hard to enumerate all the *fatawa* that were issued in all parts of the Islamic world including remote places as far away as Indonesia.

It is obvious that the general language of the 1990 *fatwa* covers all individuals including Muslim leaders and heads of states, and all institutions including governments. This and many similar *fatwas* prohibit the leaders from recognizing "Israel" regardless of what the latter offers. In simple language, regardless of the size of a "Palestine" as long as it is smaller than historical Palestine. A two-state "solution," therefore, is simply not acceptable. Such a "solution" will not be able to address basic Palestinian rights such as the right of return. "Israel" will reject this right simply because it will want to continue to maintain a "Jewish" character of the state, which means a demographic ratio clearly in favor of the Jews.

The position of specific Islamic organizations or parties simply falls within the parameters of decades' old religious rulings that ultimately attempt to reflect the Islamic worldview. Hamas' position, as an example, reflects a continuum of previous rulings and uses the same language. Article 11 of its charter says: "The Islamic Resistance Movement believes that the land of Palestine is an Islamic land entrusted to the Muslim generations until Judgment Day. No one may [relinquish] all or even part of it . . . " In addition, article 15 states: "When an enemy usurps a Muslim land, then jihad is an individual religious duty [required of] every Muslim . . . "[3] The rejection of "Israeli" occupation, as reflected in these articles, is identical with the position of Muslim scholars and institutions throughout the history of the Palestinian issue.

It is rather obvious that the issue of land in the articles of Hamas's charter is in line with Islamic theology and jurisprudence. Accepting the same terms of reference, which in the Islamic worldview means accepting and following the Qur'an and the Sunnah as the only sources of law governing Islamic life, applies to all Islamic movements in terms of how they relate to political activity. Khaled Hroub noted in *Hamas: Political Thought and Practice* that Hamas' understanding and conduct of the struggle is "equally valid for any other Islamic movement."[4]

Hroub's observation is true regarding "Israel." Yet, while the Islamic movements have a unified position regarding the relationship with the occupation forces, they do not have the same political discourse regarding intra-Palestinian relations. One can detect the influence of modern western political thought on the political discourse of some Islamists regarding the relationship within the state, or the future state as in the case of Palestine. This mode of thinking is always done with respect to the interpretation of the texts of the Qur'an and the Sunnah, never by adding additional sources. Knowing that some readers might raise questions about the other "sources" of Islamic Shari'ah, which include consensus [*ijma'*] and reasoning by analogy [*qiyas*], it is obvious for Islamologists that they do not constitute sources on their own, rather they form tools of understanding.

Subscribing to the same framework is the Islamic Jihad Movement. Its leader, Dr. Ramadan Shallah has said: "Considering the Islamicity of the [Palestinian] issue, the position of the Shari'ah is that the liberation of Palestine is an individual religious duty [required of] the people of Palestine, Syria, Jordan, Lebanon and Egypt . . . until the last one of the Muslims . . . "[5] The words of Shallah reflect a clear reference to the Islamic Shari'ah which is based on the Qur'an and the Sunnah as the sources that form the positions that his movement undertakes.

The rejection of Oslo is also the position of Islamic groups such as Hizb Al-Tahrir Al-Islami [The Islamic Liberation Party], which, despite its name, does not participate in armed struggle against the occupation. It limits its action to political activism that includes direct criticism of the Palestinian Authority. They do not refrain from naming individual leaders and have accused some of them of treason. Similar to what usually happens to the political leaders of Hamas, some of Hizb Al-Tahrir Al-Islamic leaders, including Imams of Mosques in East Jerusalem, were arrested by the Palestinian Authority because of their criticism of all agreements that the Palestinian Authority concluded with "Israel."

One can even detect indirect dissatisfaction with the Oslo Process in the prayers of an apolitical group, such as the Da'wah and Tabligh. These are international Islamic movements that "preach and advocate," hence their name, the ethical part of the message of Islam. They do not interfere in political issues and refrain from taking sides in local politics in countries where they have millions of followers. Yet, a subconscious nurtured by Islamic theology and a sense of Islamic history finds room and expression in the supplication that flows spontaneously, since no Muslim recites a supplication from a text in formal prayers.

In addition, one might add that there are numerous influential individual scholars or preachers, in every country, well known to be independent of any particular Islamic group, yet who are highly critical of the Oslo Process. This is true, for example, of all the five or so preachers who deliver the Friday sermon at Al-Aqsa Mosque in Jerusalem and almost every week express their dissatisfaction with the political and everyday situation of their congregation, which has worsened because of the Oslo process.

The above examples demonstrate that Islamic groups, movements, institutions, and individual scholars share the same theological and legal background. To understand such positions there is a need to understand the central position that the Holy Land occupies in the Islamic worldview. The Qur'an itself mentions the Holy Land in the story of Prophet Moses (Peace be upon him) when he attempted to deliver the Children of Israel from Egypt:

> Remember Moses said to his people: "O my People! Call in remembrance the favor of God unto you, when He produced prophets among you, made you kings, and gave you what He had not given to any other among the peoples.
>
> "O my People! Enter the Holy Land which God has assigned unto you, and turn not back ignominiously, for then will you be overthrown, to your own ruin." Qur'an, 5:20–1

The context is that of Moses (Peace be upon him) inviting the Children of Israel to enter the Holy Land after he delivered them miraculously from Egypt across the sea. The Children of Israel refused to enter the land, because it meant that they had to fight its people, who were known for their exceeding strength. This rejection earned them divine punishment:

> God said: "Therefore will the land be out of their reach for forty years: in distraction will they wander through the land: but sorrow you not over these rebellious people." Qur'an, 5:26

The importance of these verses show that assigning the land to the Children of Israel was as a community of believers and not as cultural Jews. It was submitting to God's will, and not specific genetic codes, that determined the relationship with the land. The Holy land, or any land, is a vehicle where one fulfills the covenant with God. Therefore, Muslims qua submitters, as translates the literal meaning of their name, form a continuum of the followers of Moses, Abraham, or Noah (Peace be upon them all). In my opinion, when a specific community of believers transgresses against God, it is deprived sovereignty in the Holy Land. No specific religious group was ever granted the upper hand or sovereignty in the absolute sense. The history of the Holy Land and Palestinians outdate the history of the Children of Israel, but if we restrict discussion to "monotheistic" sovereignty, it should be recognized that none of the three "monotheistic" religions was capable of maintaining a continuous grip over power.

Yet, the most celebrated verse from the Qur'an regarding the relationship with the Holy Land is the first of the chapter of the Children of Israel, or Al-Isra':

> Glory be to (Allah) Who did take His Servant for a journey by night from the Sacred Mosque [Al-Masjid Al-Haram] to the Farthest Mosque [Al-Masjid Al-Aqsa] whose precincts We did bless, in order that We might show him some of Our Signs: for He is the One who hears and sees [all things]. (Qur'an, 17:1)

There are political implications of the story of the journey by night [al-Isra'] and the ascension from Jerusalem to heavens [al-mi'raj]. This story is taken by all Muslim scholars to establish the Islamicity of the Holy Land, before Muslims arrived historically during the time of the second caliph, 'Umar Ibn Al-Khattab, in 15 AH / 638 CE. There are many traditions related to these miraculous events that are in line with the miracles granted to previous prophets to perform exceptional acts such as Prophet Moses' splitting the sea and Prophet Jesus' resurrecting the dead, all by leave of God, reflecting His Omnipotence. The relevant verses in the Qur'an and the many traditions of Prophet Muhammad (Peace be upon him) that are related to his presence in Jerusalem or define the spiritual significance of Al-Aqsa Mosque are interpreted by Muslim Scholars to indicate that Islam is the trustee of Al-Aqsa Mosque, Jerusalem and the Holy Land.

Legal Status of the Holy Land in the Shari'ah

After 'Umar Ibn Al-Khattab signed an agreement with Bishop Sophronious in Jerusalem, he refused to distribute the land amongst the Muslim soldiers and declared it an Islamic Endowment (waqf) for the benefit of future generations, allowing people to use it without owning it. The waqf category, in Islamic law, is by definition a property that belongs to God until the Day of Judgment. It has its own sanctity and ownership; it cannot be transferred even amongst Muslims. Once a piece of land or property is declared waqf, not even the person who used to own it can change its legal status.

Article 11 of the charter of Hamas states: "The Islamic Resistance Movement believes that the land of Palestine is an Islamic land entrusted (i.e., waqf) to the Muslim generations until Judgment Day . . . "

Islamic literature and rhetoric is filled with references to Palestine as an

Islamic trust or endowment. These references contribute to the Islamist's psyche that rejects the Oslo process, because it means that part of this *waqf* will be passed, or rather was passed already, to non-Muslim hands, thereby changing its status.

Other Legal Notions with Implications for the Peace Process

In Islamic political thought, the prevailing idea is that treaties with the enemy could be concluded if they are temporary. The idea of a temporary truce or cease-fire is acceptable from the Islamic Shari'ah point of view if it generates benefit for the Muslim community. There are detailed legal discussions that are centered on the Prophet's treaties with non-Muslims, especially with the tribe of Qureish, in what became known as *Sulh Al-Hudaybiyah*. From the history of Islam, the treaty considered most relevant to the conflict in the Holy Land is the one Salah-ed-Din Al-Ayyubi concluded in Ramlah, near Lod, with the Crusaders. In both cases, the treaty was temporary.

There has been willingness amongst some Islamists to accept a truce with "Israel" if it withdraws to the 1967 borders, releases Palestinian prisoners, and allows the refugees to return to their homes within the Green Line. Yet, such a deal is always temporary and means that the conflict will ultimately resurface again and again. Hroub noted that the creation of a small Palestinian state in the West bank and Gaza Strip is seen by Hamas as an interim solution as against the total liberation of Palestine, which is called by Hamas "the historic solution."[6]

Hamas has attempted to present its ideas on interim agreements with "Israel." Mahmoud Al-Zahhar, who was considered a Hamas leader, presented in March 1988 a proposal to Shimon Peres, then foreign minister. Zahhar's proposal for a short-term solution asked that "Israel" withdraw to the 1967 borders, with the West Bank including East Jerusalem and the Gaza Strip being placed under UN custody, and the Palestinians naming their representatives for negotiations that would cover all rights.[7] Unfortunately, the "Israeli" authorities did not take this proposal seriously. Reasons for this might be the fact that Hamas was still young and that "Israel" was, and still is, not willing to withdraw to the 1967 borders. Also, traditionally, "Israel" has refused to accept a UN role when it is apparent that this is in favor of the Palestinian People.

Another problem emerges from the necessity of concluding a truce with the leader of the Muslims – the problem of representation. Who should this leader be? Sheikh Ahmad Yassin, the spiritual leader of Hamas, stated when he returned to Gaza upon his release from prison in October 1997 that the Palestinian people has one leadership, one address: the Palestinian Authority and President Yasser Arafat. Nevertheless, Sheikh Yassin did not conform to the Palestinian Authority's position and rejected the Wye River Memorandum Agreement for the implementation of the Oslo II Agreement. He maintained that military resistance against Israelis is legitimate as long as Palestinian land remains occupied. The Palestinian Authority put him under house arrest and prevented journalists from interviewing him.[8]

Notwithstanding the diplomatic statements of Sheikh Yassin, it is the charter of Hamas that defines what a leader can or rather cannot do, in relationship to the peace process. Article 11 states: "no king or president nor all kings or presidents, and no organization nor all organizations, Palestinian or Arab, have the right to dispose of it or relinquish or cede any part of it, because Palestine is Islamic land . . . "[9] Hamas has attempted to foster a positive relationship with the Palestinian Authority without losing sight of its long-term plans regarding the liberation of historical Palestine.

Reflections on the Peace Process

It is clear, then, that a peace process that will result, or rather has already resulted, in recognizing an "Israeli" State over 78 percent of Palestine cannot be accepted from an Islamic point of view. In fact, the very existence of "Israel" is considered illegal. Chairman Arafat's letter to Prime Minister Rabin on September 9, 1993 reflected a direct recognition of "Israel." In exchange, Prime Minister Rabin's letter reflected the decision of the "Israeli" government to engage the PLO in negotiations. It was an exchange of ends for means. The "Israeli" government made good on its promise and one round of negotiations led to another: the Palestinian leadership found itself glued to a perpetual table of negotiations.

Today, there are many voices amongst "Israeli" and Palestinian politicians who were involved directly in the Oslo process and subsequent agreements, and who believe that the Palestinians made a grave mistake in not insisting on a freeze on Jewish settlements to be included in the treaties. Just this aspect above shows that the Declaration of Principles was faulty from the beginning. The unprecedented harsh realities on the ground that emerged as a direct result of the Oslo process, and which led ultimately to the new Intifada, are clear proof of the need for a new, creative solution.

The Islamic movements' position, as well as that of individual scholars, are not, and cannot be, against peace. It is treaties that consecrate injustice that they oppose. Justice remains the prerequisite for peace. The solution has to take into consideration the larger Islamic context where Judaism and the Jews should be reintegrated. If not, the other choice for "Israel" is living in a heavily armed ghetto, that will never gain legitimacy except superficially in the form of treaties that do not have any impact on the collective memory of Muslims save in a negative way. It is a choice between a *de jure* integrated existence and a *de facto* occupier status.

Notes

1   The Islamic worldview recognizes the original books while declaring that the current Old and New Testament have suffered from human editing.

2   The Qur'an uses *tabarruhum*, the root of which is used in the Qur'an to express the excellent relationship that an individual should have with his or her parents.

3   Khaled Hroub, *HAMAS: Political Thought and Practice* (Washington, DC: Institute for Palestine Studies, 2000), pp. 273–6.

4   Ibid., p. 56.

5   Naser-ed-Din Al-Sha'ir, *'Amaliyyat Al-Salam Al-Falastiniyyah Al-Israilyyah: Wijhat Nazar Islamiyyah* [The Palestinian-Israeli Peace Process: An Islamic Perspective] (Nablus: Markaz Al-Buhuth wal-Dirasat Al-Falastiniyyah, 1999), p. 113.

6   Hroub, *HAMAS*, p. 5.

7   Ibid., p. 74.

8   Al-Sha'ir, *'Amaliyyat Al-Salam Al-Falastiniyyah Al-Israilyyah*, p. 27.

9   Hroub, *HAMAS*, p. 273.

From Oslo to Taba: What Went Wrong?

Ron Pundak

Three approaches can be distinguished regarding the question of what went wrong with the peace process which began in Oslo in January 1993. The first approach maintains that peace between Israelis and Palestinians was, and remains, impossible. The second claims that such a peace can be reached but that the two constituencies are as yet unable to acknowledge that it is the only option and are therefore unready to make the necessary and painful concessions. Finally, the third approach counters that the opportunity for peace did in fact exist, but that it was squandered due to the misperception of each of the sides regarding the real interests of the other party, and to the faulty implementation and management of the entire process. This chapter focuses on the third approach.

The uprising, which began the morning after the visit of the then opposition leader and now Prime Minister Ariel Sharon to the Temple Mount/al-Harem al-Sharif, on September 28, 2000, did not begin with the first rock thrown by a Palestinian youth, or shooting by a "Tanzim" activist. The rock and the rifle, and in particular the demonstrations and clashes of Palestinians with IDF forces, are tied to the events of the past seven years since the signing of the Oslo Agreement. Sharon's visit, and the killing of worshippers on the plaza of Jerusalem's mosques on the following day, was the match that ignited the powder keg which had threatened to explode for years.

In particular, from the moment when the five years of the Interim Agreement period of the Oslo Accords expired and a Permanent Status was not even visible on the horizon, the clock began to tick toward the explosion. For Israel, the only way to prevent the detonation was to implement the agreements signed with the Palestinians rapidly and seriously, and to embark promptly on intensive Permanent Status negotiations. Prime Minister Ehud Barak failed to understand this. Indeed, his error was twofold: he decided not to implement the third redeployment, which represented the single most important element in the Interim Agreement; and although he entered into negotiations on Permanent Status earnestly and in goodwill, he did so on faulty basic assumptions which caused their collapse.

The tenure of former Prime Minister Binyamin Netanyahu (1996–9) made it clear to the Palestinians that an elected Israeli Government might actually not be interested in reaching a peace agreement on the basis of the principle of United Nations Security Council Resolution UNSCR 242 (land for peace). This, together with the immense gap between the expectations raised by his successor Ehud Barak's Government and the grim reality (the continuation of settlements, lives in the shadow of checkpoints, an unstable economic situation, and other elements which will be described below) had an unmitigated effect on Palestinian public opinion. The Palestinian public and the "street" leadership – which originally was a supporter of the peace process and of the need to reach reconciliation with Israel – came to the conclusion that Israel did not in fact want to reach a fair agreement to end the occupation and grant the Palestinian people "legitimate rights." It is in this psycho-political-historical context that the conflict found itself in September 2000. The Palestinians had lost hope.

Historical Background

Political leadership is tested when it is confronted with decisions of historic proportions. At the conclusion of British rule in mandatory Palestine, the Zionist leadership was confronted with such substantive questions, specifically in relation to UN resolution 181. The Resolution called for the partition of Palestine between Jews and Palestinians on the basis of the concept of "two states for two peoples." With regard to Jerusalem, the Resolution declared that it should be an international enclave, neither under the sovereignty of, nor the capital of, either state. A majority of the Zionist leadership had for years opposed proposals of partition of Palestine and separation from Jerusalem. Eventually, however, and largely due to the far-reaching vision of David Ben-Gurion, this basic Zionist dispute was finally settled. The proposal for partition was accepted and the establishment of the State of Israel declared on May 14, 1948. Discussions relating to the remaining areas of biblical "Eretz Yisrael" (The Land of Israel) were marginalized, as were the Zionist right-wing's dreams regarding control of the East Bank of the Jordan river. The establishment of Israel opened the gates to Jewish immigration from the Diaspora, consolidating its political, security, economic, social, and cultural foundations.

Ben-Gurion's brave decision was far from being the obvious option it might appear to be today. A great deal lay in the balance. The decision to accept physical separation from parts of Eretz Yisrael, which constituted an important part of Jewish history and tradition, was not an easy task for the Zionist leaders. Ben-Gurion and his supporters among the Labor party (Mapai) leadership, however, chose to focus on the realization of Zionism's basic and vital interest – that of ensuring an independent national home for the Jewish people. Many in the Jewish community in Palestine ("Yishuv"), and in the international community, refused to believe that a Jewish minority, which totaled little more than half a million, could contend with an Arab population double its size, especially in view of the expected attack by the neighboring Arab armies.

Ben-Gurion's resolution in accepting partition was more in the tradition of "realpolitik" and on long-term policies, than based on the clamors of nationalism and messianism. In this sense, there were many similarities between Ben-Gurion and Yitzhak Rabin, who arrived – 45 years later – at a decision of similar caliber, and based on the same conceptual and political thinking. Ben-Gurion clearly understood that the partition plan was a unique opportunity that would ensure international support for the establishment of an independent state. It may be far smaller than the one originally envisaged by the Zionist movement, but it would alter the course of Jewish history.

Concurrently, toward the end of 1947, the Arab leadership, captive of its extremism, announced its refusal to accept the partition of mandatory Palestine, and subsequently led the entire region to war. At the end of the war, the State of Israel had achieved new borders, including Jewish West Jerusalem; the border was wider than the ones designated in UN resolution 181. Israel gained international legitimacy, and its new borders were essentially accepted as the permanent borders of the state. In the Armistice agreements concluded in 1949 with the neighboring Arab countries that had participated in the war, the armistice lines were recognized by all sides. Until the Six Day War, they constituted Israel's internationally recognized de-facto borders. At this point, in 1967, the territorial questions erupted in full force with the occupation of the West Bank and Gaza Strip.

The 1949 war was disastrous for the Palestinians. The Arab state which was to be created next to Israel was not established. The territories originally designated for the Palestinian state and the international area were captured in part by Israel (which increased its size by one-third), in part by Egypt (which placed the Gaza Strip under military rule), and in part by Jordan (which two years later annexed the West Bank and East Jerusalem). The war resulted in the creation of 700,000 Palestinian refugees. They were dispersed in neighboring Arab countries, their lives destined to humiliation, deprivation, and poverty in crowded refugee camps. The Palestinian national leadership was crushed. In the eyes of the Palestinians, this disaster became known as "El-Naqba" ("disaster, holocaust, calamity").

In 1993, the Palestinian leadership faced an historical decision of a magnitude similar to that its predecessors faced in 1947. Decades characterized by ineffective terrorism, violent diplomatic struggle, and an attempt to draw the Arab world into the "liberation of Palestine" eventually led to a watershed event in 1988. A strategic transition by Yasser Arafat and the PLO leadership led to a conclusion that, in December, was translated into an unequivocal political declaration presented in both Stockholm and Geneva.

The PLO recognized the right of the State of Israel to exist, in peace and security, within recognized borders; it denounced terrorism, and announced its desire to establish, by means of political negotiations, on parts of historic Palestine, a state side-by-side with the State of Israel. The "legal" basis for the Palestinian declaration was the Declaration of "Independence" approved in Algeria by the 19 Palestinian National Council, a month earlier, in which Israel was recognized as an independent state in the region.

While 1988 was the ideological turning point, the historic decision to implement this ideology only occurred in 1993, in the course of nine-month negotiations in Oslo. At the end of this process, the Palestinian leadership had surmounted numerous obstacles and difficulties to conclude the Declaration of Principles (DoP), also known as the Oslo Accord. The most notable was that Israel was not prepared to agree that the outcome of the negotiations would be a Palestinian state next to Israel. The Palestinians believed that the agreement should lead to a permanent status agreement on the basis of equality and coexistence, involving a comprehensive peace agreement between Israel and a Palestinian state in the West Bank and Gaza, with East Jerusalem as its capital.

This change, which led the sides to the negotiating table in Madrid in 1991 and Oslo in 1993, was based on a number of processes that matured in parallel: *first*, an understanding by the Palestinian leadership that the conflict with Israel could only be resolved by means of political negotiation, based on the concept of two states for two peoples; *second*, the success of the Palestinian uprising in the occupied territories (the Intifada of the late 1980s) as a popular, national, and authentic struggle; *third*, a shift in mainstream Israeli public and political thinking in relation to occupation and to the national aspirations of the Palestinian people; *fourth*, the rise of Hamas and Islamic fundamentalism in Palestinian society; and *fifth* international geopolitical changes.

The Oslo Accords

As the popular Intifada struggle intensified during the late 1980s, so did the recognition of wide sections of the Jewish population in Israel of the significance of a popular struggle for national liberation. Concurrently, large sections of the Israeli public became gradually detached from the ideology of settling the Greater Eretz Yisrael. The clearest testament to this process is the policy of the Likud governments regarding annexation. They refused to annex the West Bank and Gaza to Israel, not only because they feared international reactions (the Likud government headed by Menachem Begin applied Israeli law to the Golan Heights only in 1981) but also because they understood that such measures would not enjoy the wide backing of the Israeli public. Alongside this process, signs of moderation in Palestinian positions gradually permeated the Israeli discourse. A gradual change in Israel thus began, eventually creating a change of opinion in the mainstream public and in politics leading to questioning the occupation, and to a growing understanding of Palestinian national aspirations.

This change was expressed in the results of the Israeli elections in 1992, bringing to power a new government headed by Yitzhak Rabin and Shimon Peres, and emphasizing the will of the Israeli majority to reach a political settlement with the Palestinians based on an historic separation between the two communities. The preceding Likud government, headed by Yitzhak Shamir, had ostensibly attempted to follow this course in the context of the Madrid Process, but soon hit a dead end. Possibly, the framework set in Madrid, which was based on non-secret discussions conducted in parallel tracks, was itself a barrier to the process. In effect, only after a few months, the Madrid discussions – conducted in Washington – became entangled in a political and legal quagmire. Representatives of the respective sides became entrenched in their known positions, reciting pre-prepared and extreme declarations, basically aimed at their own constituencies and preventing any possible progress. It is important to remember that in the period prior to and during the Oslo process, the Palestinian armed struggle continued and the terrorism of fundamentalist Islamic groups and groups linked to the PLO continued their attacks against Israelis both in the occupied territories and within the Green Line, against civilians and soldiers.

Following the elections in 1992, Yitzhak Rabin established his government with Simon Peres as Foreign Minister and Yossi Beilin as Deputy Minister of Foreign Affairs. It searched for ways of salvaging the Peace Process, attempting to revive the Madrid Process and bilateral negotiations with the Palestinian delegation representing the West Bank and Gaza. Such measures were destined for failure, as they were essentially denying the fact that complete control was in the hands of the PLO/Tunis.

The Israeli law prohibiting meetings with the PLO was revoked (on the night of January 19, 1993). The following day, two delegations arrived in Oslo, Norway – one from PLO/Tunis, the other from Israel – in order to conduct what was to become the first in a series of many meetings. The meeting established the Oslo Channel that culminated with the signing of the historic agreement between Israel and the Palestinians on the White House lawn on September 13, 1993. This agreement opened a new chapter that promised a better future for the entire Middle East.

On January 21, 1993, in a small town two hours from Oslo, under a heavy cover of secrecy, Dr. Yair Hirschfeld and myself met three representatives of PLO/Tunis. From our point of view, the aim of this meeting was to clarify a question that still remains unanswered for many Israelis: can the PLO be a genuine partner in peace? not merely a partner for negotiating an interim agreement or to obtain tactical rewards, but a partner in negotiations that will lead to a comprehensive and sustainable peace agreement between the two peoples.

In his opening statement, Abu Ala, who read a message from Arafat, reiterated what we heard on many occasions in talks with the Palestinian leadership in the West Bank and Gaza: The PLO had made an historic decision, recognizing the need for peaceful coexistence with the State of Israel, to realize the amended strategic aim of the PLO – and negotiate the establishment of an independent Palestinian state in the West Bank and Gaza with East Jerusalem as its capital.

The first meeting was successful. The barrier of mistrust was lifted, as the two sides expressed their commitment to finding pragmatic, creative, and realistic solutions acceptable to both sides. Moreover, a methodology was agreed upon. It was based on a forward-looking approach involving practical discussions, focusing on building a better future for both sides, rather than engaging in debates on correcting the past. The message conveyed by the PLO representatives was quite clear: a wish to end the historic conflict through peaceful measures and to reach a political agreement on the basis of UNSCR 242, the 1967 borders, mutual trust and understanding, taking into account Israeli security interests based on cooperation, openness and coordination, rather than cold peace and hostility. Today, eight years later, I do not doubt that the original timetable could have been met if the process had been implemented based on the principles created during those months of negotiations in Oslo.

At the end of the first meeting, it was agreed to continue with secret, informal, non-committing meetings, under the auspices of the Government of Norway. During the subsequent five months we met – first guided by Deputy Minister Yossi Beilin, and later under the leadership of Minister of

Foreign Affairs Shimon Peres with the knowledge of Prime Minister Yitzhak Rabin – with the Palestinian delegation every few weeks. The second meeting resulted in the creation of a framework within which a draft of a joint Israeli–Palestinian Declaration of Principles was discussed. Our aim was to advance toward a formula that Beilin and Peres would consider politically feasible.

In May 1993, after the first draft was approved within the Oslo group, Rabin and Peres decided to turn the secret and informal track into an official and secret channel of negotiations between the Government of Israel and the PLO, and to adopt the draft that was prepared during the first five months as a basis for these negotiations. Concurrently, Uri Savir (then Director General of the Ministry of Foreign Affairs) and Joel Zinger (future Legal Advisor to the Ministry of Foreign Affairs) joined the negotiating team, with Savir leading the Israeli side.

The negotiations in Oslo carried on for an additional four months, at the end of which the Declaration of Principles between the Government of Israel and the PLO was initialed on August 20, 1993. The surprising announcement leaked through to the public and press a few days later. On September 8 and 9, 1993 Prime Minister Rabin and Chairman Arafat signed letters, according to which the Government of Israel recognized the PLO as the representative of the Palestinian people. Accordingly, the PLO recognized the right of the State of Israel to exist in peace and security. The two parties accepted UNSCRs 242 and 338, and committed themselves to a peaceful resolution of the conflict and all outstanding issues relating to permanent status through negotiations, thus renouncing the use of terrorism and other acts of violence, which endanger peace and stability.

The Declaration of Principles was signed on September 13, 1993, in a ceremony on the White House lawn. In his speech, after his historic handshake with Arafat, Prime Minister Rabin, said the following: "*Let me say to you, the Palestinians, we are destined to live together on the same soil in the same land. We, the soldiers who have returned from battles stained with blood; we who have seen our relatives and friends killed before our eyes; we who have attended their funerals and cannot look into the eyes of their parents; we who have come from a land where parents bury their children, we who have fought against you, the Palestinians, we say to you today in a loud and a clear voice, enough of blood and tears. Enough! We have no desire for revenge. We harbor no hatred toward you. We, like you, are people – people who want to build a home, to plant a tree, to love, live side by side with you in dignity, in affinity, as human beings, as free men. We are today giving peace a chance and saying again to you, 'Enough.' Let us pray that a day will come when we will all say farewell to arms. We wish to open a new chapter in the sad book of our lives together – a chapter of mutual recognition, of good neighborliness, of mutual respect, of understanding. We hope to embark on a new era in the history of the Middle East."* The Prime Minister, who was assassinated just two years later by a Jew from the radical right, concluded his speech with the following quote: *"May He who makes peace on High, make peace for us and all Israel, Amen."* The Israeli–Palestinian peace process had finally taken off.

"The Oslo Spirit" and the Character of the Negotiations

The negotiations with the Palestinians have been significantly different from those conducted with other Arab countries. The hostility and lack of trust existing between the two peoples are sentiments deeply rooted in history, religion, culture and economic interests. Two components of the conflict are particularly salient: the constant friction between the two peoples during 100 years of national struggle over control of Palestine, and the use of terrorism, which sharpened the hostility and increased suspicion between the two sides.

Additional significant elements include: a high level of intolerance toward the other; strong religious sentiments strengthened through a struggle over control of the holy places and in particular those common to Judaism and Islam; the occupation which reinforced Palestinian feelings of dispossession and humiliation and stimulated Israeli arrogance; the obvious gaps in standards of living between the two populations; and finally the economic deterioration in the territories, which deepened the frustration and hatred among the Palestinians.

In contrast to the features above, the talks, already in the first meeting, were characterized by what later was termed the "Oslo Spirit." They were based on the understanding that the negative history between our two peoples, and the existing imbalance of power between the occupier and the occupied, represents an almost insurmountable obstacle for conventional-type negotiations. Our goal was to work toward a conceptual change which would lead to a dialogue based, as much as possible, on fairness, equality, and common objectives. These values were to be reflected both in the character of the negotiations – including the personal relationships between the negotiators – and in the proffered solutions and procedures of implementation. This new type of relationship was supposed to influence the type and character of Palestinian-Israeli talks which would develop between other official and semi-governmental institutions in the future, as well as future dialogue between the two peoples.

For many years, the two peoples had tried to attain achievements at the expense of the other side. Every victory won by one side was considered a defeat for the other, according to the principles of the "zero-sum game" theory. In contrast, "Oslo" was, from the start, guided by efforts to abandon this approach, and to achieve as many win–win situations as possible, notwithstanding that the balance of power was tipped in Israel's favor.

The aim of the "Oslo Spirit" was not only to improve the lives on both sides, but equally to forge ties of trust and to reduce the negative effects of the past. The assumption was, therefore, that it would be easier to search for agreements in areas where the two sides had a clear common interest.

The Process of Implementation and the Netanyahu Government

The relative failure of the Oslo process can be traced back to the beginning of the period of implementation of the DoP Agreement. The "Oslo Spirit" which won over the two leaderships, neither permeated to the level of the Israeli officials who formulated the complicated system of the implementation agreements (the "Gaza and Jericho Agreement" and the Interim Agreement of September 1995), nor to those who were in charge of negotiating with the Palestinians on translating the agreements into concrete actions. Agreements were signed, various responsibilities and spheres of authority were passed on to the Palestinians, but the basic Israeli attitude toward the Palestinians continued unabated, and the patronizing attitude of occupier to occupied remained. It was not replaced by a relationship of equality required of former adversaries headed in a new political and historical direction.

This lack of change in attitudes was reflected in the actions of the military and security apparatuses which maintain high visibility on the ground, and are in tense daily contact with the Palestinian population. The joint patrols of the Israeli Border Police and the Palestinian Police is a typical example. The Israeli side imposed a system of patrols which the Palestinians viewed as problematic from the outset: the joint patrol was conducted only in areas which had been transferred to Palestinian security control (within A areas), and was therefore regarded by the Palestinians as an Israeli means of maintaining its presence, with the "backing" of the Palestinian Police to boot.

Only in hindsight, and after a number of years, did the IDF reach the conclusion that in practice the joint patrol was not needed. The joint patrol, which could have become a spearhead of cooperation, became a source of repeated friction. One reason was the attitude of the Israeli personnel. A substantial part of those who participated in the joint patrols, including some of the officers, were hostile to the Oslo Agreement, to its objectives and to the limited rights it granted the Palestinians. To treat the problem an Israeli army force whose specific responsibility was activities related to the implementation of the Agreement should have been created. This force, perhaps even on a voluntary basis, could have been deployed at checkpoints and passages where it could have significantly reduced the daily humiliations suffered by the Palestinian population – notables and simple citizens alike – in the West Bank and Gaza.

In parallel, the Palestinians tended to underestimate the painful significance for Israel of the murderous terrorist attacks by Hamas and the Islamic Jihad, which only intensified following the signing of the Oslo Agreement, and of the incitement conducted openly by the Palestinian side through its media. Instead of actively pursuing the inciters and demonstrating a 100% commitment to fighting terrorism and its infrastructure, which simultaneously hurt Israel and the Peace Process, the PA attempted a double game: to coordinate counter-terrorist measures with Israel and simultaneously employing a "soft" attitude when dealing with the terrorist leadership, infrastructure and activists.

The three-year tenure of the Netanyahu Government, which according to the timetable should have seen the climax of the implementation of the Interim Agreement and of negotiations on Permanent Status, established new rules of the game that served only to reduce the hope of Israelis and Palestinians alike. From a political point of view this period can be characterized in a single word: failure. Palestinians, the Arab world, and wide circles in the international community asked whether Israel really wanted peace. True to character, Netanyahu sabotaged the peace process relentlessly, and made every effort to delegitimize the Palestinian partner.

Netanyahu's "ultimate weapon" in his campaign against the Palestinians was the mantra that the other side was not fulfilling its part of the agreements and that without mutuality Israel would not implement its part. In practice, during Netanyahu's tenure, both sides committed breaches with regard to the Agreement. The breaches of the Israeli side were both more numerous and more substantive in nature. For its part, the Palestinians did not stop the vitriolic propaganda against Israel by radio, the printed press, television and schoolbooks; did not collect the illegal firearms; did not reach an agreement with Israel on the de facto growth of their Police Force; and did not prove that they were wholeheartedly combating fundamentalist terrorism, including the imprisonment of its activists.

Israel on its part did not implement the three stages of the second redeployment, stipulated in the Interim Agreement; did not withdraw from territories which were supposed to be transferred to the Palestinians; completed only one section out of four with regard to the freeing of Palestinian prisoners; did not undertake the implementation of the safe passage connecting the West Bank and Gaza; repeatedly delayed the permit to build an airport and a maritime port in Gaza; prevented the transfer of monies belonging to the PA for extended periods of time; and continued to establish new settlements, to annex territories for new settlements, and to expand existing ones. At the same time, the political reality forced Netanyahu to continue, albeit reluctantly and in limited fashion, the implementation of the process. The Americans imposed the Wye Agreement on him, which symbolized the implementation of the second redeployment according to the Interim Agreement.

The Palestinians were humiliated. The foot-dragging combined with the arrogance of the Israeli Government, and in particular of its Prime Minister, in their relations with the Palestinian public and its leaders, undermined the latter's belief in the process. The Palestinian message to the Israeli peace camp toward the end of Netanyahu's tenure and the election of Barak was clear: hope and faith was eroding. The Palestinian "street" and its leadership interpreted Israel's policy as seeking to destroy the very core of the Palestinian national dream. Moreover, they warned, if this trend continued Israel would find itself without a partner. The Fatah movement – the cornerstone of the Palestinian support for peace – would be replaced by Hamas as the dominating popular movement.

The Barak Era

The new Government of Barak took office in the spring of 1999. It was met with high expectations. The window of opportunity which had been identified during the Madrid Conference in 1991 and unlocked in Oslo in 1993, was still waiting to be thrown open. In 1999, the political situation in the region was ripe for a breakthrough, but time was scarce. Nevertheless, the Palestinian leadership was still able to contain the violence which could easily have erupted during Netanyahu's tenure. The Palestinian public seethed not merely in response to the delaying of the final dates of the Interim Agreement, but mainly from its growing conviction that the Netanyahu Government – like that of Shamir before him – had no intention of moving toward a permanent status agreement. The average Palestinian in the West Bank and Gaza continued to experience humiliating treatment by the occupation forces, new settlements were established, and land expropriations continued.

Barak should have taken as his guiding principle Ben-Gurion's pragmatic approach, which Rabin employed to such success. This approach is based on the real interests of Israel, rather than on a pressure group or messianic- or security-oriented lobbies: actions were designed to achieve stated goals. Barak quoted Ben-Gurion and wished to emulate him, while in fact he implemented policies which bore the imprint of a Ben-Gurionistic vision but, translated into action, actually more closely resembled those of Prime Minister Golda Meir prior to the October 1973 war.

The version of events which was communicated to the Israeli public during Barak's tenure differed from the reality on the ground. The "Oslo years" under Barak did not change the attitudes which had characterized the occupation under Netanyahu. It did not enable real Palestinian control over the three million citizens of the PA, did not bring an end to building in the settlements or to the expropriation of land, and did not promote economic growth in the territories. In addition, Barak's repeated statements that he was the only Prime Minister who had not transferred land to the Palestinians raised questions about his sincerity. Suspicions increased once it became clear to the Palestinians that Barak would not transfer the three villages on the outskirts of Jerusalem (Abu Dis, Al Eyzaria and Arab Sawahra) to PA control after both the Government and the Knesset had approved the transfer.

The average Palestinian did not enjoy any "fruits of peace" during Barak's administration, and experienced collective punishment such as closures; restrictions on movement which affected almost all Palestinians; a permit-issuing system which mainly hurt innocent people already cleared by Israeli security; mistreatment at IDF and Border Police checkpoints often aimed, on purpose, at PA officials; a dramatic decrease in employment opportunities in Israel, leading to increased unemployment and the creation of new pockets of poverty; water shortages during the summer months as opposed to the abundance of water supply in the Israeli settlements; the destruction of Palestinian homes while new houses were built in the settlements; the non-release of prisoners tried for activities committed before Oslo; Israeli restrictions on building outside Areas A and B; and the establishment of Bantustan-like areas, controlled by Israeli military rule and on occasion dictated by its symbiotic relationship with the settlers' movement. The settlers, for their part, did everything within their power to obstruct the spirit and word of the Oslo Agreement. The result was a relentless struggle over land resources, with the settlers often receiving the tacit backing of the IDF and the Israeli civil administration in the West Bank (a majority of whose staff are themselves settlers).

This difficult situation was magnified by the deep disappointment felt by Palestinians due to the faulty governing style of the PA, the discovery of corruption among politicians, officials, and the security and police apparatus. These institutions treated the Palestinian public in a manner which was far from acceptable democratic norms. The Palestinians came to hate the political elite which was imported from Tunis, as well as the local leadership which rapidly conformed to the corrupt standards of the "Tunisians." Tension between the "street" and the governing elite continued to grow. In this context it proved comfortable for the PA to blame Israel for every problem which arose.

Precisely at this delicate and complex point, the PA should have reassessed its relationship with the Palestinian public, as well as its relations with Israel's population. Without the support of these two constituencies there could be no hope of peace and stability. *Vis-à-vis* the Palestinians, the PA should have implemented radical reforms; "cleaned the stables"; created transparent and trustworthy financial systems; fired corrupt senior officials; reorganized the institutions of the PA; created respect for its elected parliament; and fostered an enthusiastic state-building enterprise which would attract Palestinians from abroad to join the national effort. The PA took none of these measures. Chairman Arafat continued to rule by the obsolete methods he brought with him from Tunis. His attitude permeated the political and public spheres in a destructive fashion, increasing the hatred of the public toward its leadership.

The Palestinian leadership's attitude toward the Israeli public was equally erroneous. Instead of promoting messages which would bring home to Israelis the Palestinian problem and the many difficulties they faced – in humanitarian, national, and political terms – the Israeli public met a barrage of declarations of war (Jihad), terrorist attacks, daily propaganda which could be interpreted as anti-Semitic and the (mistaken) attitude that the Palestinian side did not desire peace. President Sadat captured the hearts of Israelis, and King Hussein brought them to like him as a person. But this approach was completely alien to Arafat. Neither he nor the Palestinian leadership did anything in order to coax and persuade the center-left portion of the Israeli public, a constituency which represented their natural ally.

The situation made it easy for Barak to continue the status quo. Sufficient efforts were not made on the Israeli side – both in the governmental and in the public spheres – to alter the basic assumptions regarding the Palestinians. Official Israeli institutions continued – often without being aware of it – to place more obstacles in the way of implementation of the various agreements, and hinder development in areas and spheres handed over to PA control and responsibility. This trend can for example be illustrated by the various economic restrictions imposed, and by the obstacles put in the way of the development of industrial zones. As a rule, the Israeli side claimed that "security considerations hold priority over all others." This position dictated – in the first period of implementation of the interim agreements – the many closures imposed on the West Bank and Gaza. They prevented the Palestinians from earning, through regular work in Israel, money essential to the Palestinian economy. Imposition of closures became an instinctive reaction, imposed even when not required by security considerations. It has since been proved that the connection between closures and deterrence of terrorism remained minimal. They were instead employed as a psychological device aimed at the Israeli public, proof that "something is being done."

Moreover, the political leadership in Israel was fearful all along – due to mistaken electoral considerations – of revealing to the public what should have been the true message of the period of implementation of the Oslo accords, namely that the entire process was intended to result in a Permanent Status Agreement, its essence being a peace agreement creating a Palestinian state in the occupied territories, with its capital in Arab East Jerusalem, and a respectable solution – practical and symbolic – to the refugee issue.

The Policies and Politics of Ehud Barak

From the outset, Barak caused a feeling of ambiguity in the Palestinian leadership. On the one hand, he appeared serious and determined to reach a permanent status agreement that would include all outstanding issues. On the other hand, he conveyed right-wing messages, particularly with regard to the "price" he was willing to pay in return for an agreement. Former Minister Haim Ramon (in an interview to "Zman Tel Aviv," March 2, 2001) explains that: "When Barak said 'we cannot give assets if there is no permanent status agreement,' he used right-wing terminology. One of the problems was that Barak promised them [the Palestinians] and didn't deliver. Barak refused to implement the agreement on the third redeployment as Israel had promised [in the Interim Agreement of September 1995]. He said, 'if we give, they will receive and will not be satisfied'."

In the article, Ramon refers to Barak's first political maneuver, in which he actually forced the Sharm al-Shaykh Agreement of September 1999 on the Palestinians, according to which the third redeployment would be postponed to a date stipulated in the Agreement. Ultimately, however, and contrary to this agreement, Barak failed to implement the third redeployment. The logic was similar to that which guided him immediately after the Oslo Accords: Israel should not relinquish assets before it was completely certain of the nature of the final agreement. While the basic logic of Barak's approach can be either accepted or challenged, the fact is that this approach was presented to the Palestinians along with public declarations announcing his affinity for the leadership of the pro-settler National Religious Party (NRP). He also made his position clear that the UNSCR 242 did not include the West Bank and Gaza. The Palestinians concluded that Barak – much like Netanyahu – was not willing to reach a fair agreement.

Barak's first strategic mistake, as Prime Minister, was his decision to defer the Palestinian track in favor of an attempt to conclude a peace agreement with Syria. In light of the dismal relations that had developed between the Netanyahu government and the Palestinians, and even though Barak's maneuver might have seemed logical to him and his advisors – but not so to many experts – he should have initiated a special meeting with Arafat, who expected an invitation. At such a meeting the priorities of the Prime Minister could have been explained and possible measures (such as specific redeployment and/or releasing prisoners) discussed, which would serve to alleviate the burden on the Palestinian leadership and public during this uncertain waiting period, thus assuring the Palestinians that one track of negotiation did not exclude the other. This might have dispelled Palestinian fears about Barak's intentions.

Barak did not adopt this approach. He concentrated on the Syrian track, which eventually reached a dead end. Moreover, the Prime Minister rejected Arafat's request to freeze the construction in settlements during negotiations, and did so primarily to maintain his coalition with the NRP, although he did announce that no new settlements would be established. When settlers began constructing dozens of illegal hill-top strongholds, which the Palestinians considered new settlements, Barak missed an opportunity to send a conspicuous message to the Palestinians and the settlers alike by removing the strongholds through legal means or even by force. Instead, he preferred to negotiate and barter with the settlers in order to remove or retain some of the remaining strongholds at other locations. From the Palestinian point of view, Barak's message was clear, although he apparently had not intended to convey it in this way.

Here, too, Barak was captive of misconceptions made by many Israelis, who view political and security developments strictly through a pair of Israeli "glasses." Barak failed to understand that in negotiating with the settlers, he was read differently by the Palestinians than he was by Israelis. He did not understand that in "removing Arafat's mask" in order to "see if Arafat could make tough choices," he actually unveiled the truth under the mask behind which he and a majority of Israelis disguised themselves, consciously or subconsciously. The Israeli public and leadership were not prepared, or had not been prepared, to pay the necessary price for a peace agreement. In the aforementioned article, Ramon describes his answer to the Prime Minister's question whether Arafat was prepared to pay the price for peace. He asked "Are we ready? Did we remove settlements? Have you already divided Jerusalem?" Ramon's conclusion is severe: "Ehud was actually against Oslo, his government abandoned the path for peace. He said 'either there will be peace or we will know who we are talking to'."

Barak was not opposed to a peace agreement with the Palestinians. He was honest, serious, and sincere in his quest to conclude a fair Permanent Status Agreement. Although he was emotionally sympathetic to Gush Emunim, and his mental set-up was formed by 35 years in the military, rationally Barak was "left-wing," positioning himself politically left of many of the leaders of the peace camp in matters relating to permanent status. He understood that the occupation corrupts Israel, and he compre-hended the Palestinian desire for a state. He even admitted on television that if he were Palestinian he would almost certainly have become a freedom fighter in one of the terrorist organizations. However, this ambiva-lence reflecting the contradiction between his emotions and his rationality created a dissonance that further amplified his natural inability to commu-nicate almost any policy, and especially his ideological–rational policy.

One of Barak's problems was that – while negotiating – he rejected the multi-phase strategy developed in Oslo. His "all or nothing" approach brought us to where we are today. The "all or nothing" approach could have succeeded provided that it was accompanied by confidence-building measures toward the Palestinian public and the development of a personal relationship with its leaders. If Barak would have invited them on an "all or nothing" journey, while creating a supportive environment of trust and hope, we would by now have an agreement.

Another of Barak's major faults was his inability to develop personal relations with the Palestinian leadership, and primarily with Chairman Arafat. Rabin and Peres, each in his own way, were able to create intimate working relations with Arafat, the personal nature of which provided a safety net for crisis resolution, overcoming gaps in negotiations. Barak not only disparaged the value of such an approach (during almost two weeks of Talks at Camp David, Barak refused to hold a one-on-one meeting with Arafat). He caused Arafat to distrust him. Arafat was quoted as saying that "Barak is worse than Netanyahu." The alternative to creating "chemistry" with Arafat could have been to create a special relationship with Abu Mazen, his deputy, but here, too, Barak failed. As a result, no relationship was created which could have helped to bridge over the difficulties and distrust which arose during negotiations.

Barak's difficulties in working with the Palestinians were not very different from those he encountered in managing internal Israeli politics. The issues were different, but the approach was essentially the same. It became clear right after the elections when Barak established a non-partisan, non-political team that was designated to negotiate in order to establish a coalition. He essentially excluded the Labor party leadership from the process, thus alienating his partners. In the end, the government was assembled just two days before the 45-day limit expired, leaving everyone except Barak – who remained smiling and haughty – angry, suspi-cious and exhausted. He ruptured his relations with Uzi Baram and Ra'anan Cohen (two pillars of his party); appointed Yossi Beilin and Shlomo Ben Ami to positions (Justice and Internal Security) which did not match their qualifications, and appointed Haim Ramon as a Minister of little importance in the Prime Minister's Office. He also attempted to keep Peres out of the government. After forming the government, however, he was obliged to create a special position for him as Minister for Regional Cooperation. He tried to bypass Avrum Burg by nominating another candidate for the position of Chairman of the Knesset who had little chance of winning, and finally bestowed ministries of high socioeconomic importance upon coalition partners instead of his own party. In response to problems that emerged from coalition negotiations, Barak replied that he could not be pressured or blackmailed. If he blinked now, he added, it would impair his ability to negotiate with the Syrian President Assad.

With the establishment of the government, his course of action did not change. He managed to turn supporters into adversaries. He failed to resolve internal problems, addressing them only when they had reached a point when they could barely be solved. He handled the strike of the physically disabled and the teachers in a similar manner. Toward the Israeli Arabs, of whom 95 percent had voted for him, he was condescending from the onset, establishing no framework for cooperation with the Arab parties or the Arab leadership on the municipal, social, and religious levels. The problem was not one of a lack of will, honesty or vision, but rather the fact that Barak was the poorest of managers.

The Negotiations on the Permanent Status between Israel and the Palestinians

The Oslo Accords basically aimed to set in motion a process which would bring about – through a Permanent Status Agreement (PSA) between Israel and the PLO – peace, coexistence, and reduced probability of confrontation and war. One of the more substantive issues in this context relates to whether a PSA should address and resolve all outstanding issues outlined in the Oslo Accords (Jerusalem, refugees, settlements, security arrangements, borders, relations and cooperation with neighbors, and other issues of common interest titled "generic issues" such as water and economics), or whether the resolutions of complicated issues – Jerusalem, refugees, territorial questions – should be postponed in favor of an agreement which will leave these issues open for later negotiation.

According to the Oslo Accords, all issues, especially those that are particularly sensitive and problematic, will be placed on the negotiating table. Discussions on any of the issues can therefore be postponed only if agreed upon by both sides. From the onset of the negotiating process, it should have been clear to Israel that the Palestinian side was adamantly insistent that nothing was to be postponed and only a comprehensive package addressing all issues of permanent status would be considered. Israeli debate on whether it was correct for Barak to discuss Jerusalem and refugee issues is therefore irrelevant, and demonstrates the dominating feature of

Israeli discourse, which ignored the fact that in order to bring about a real resolution of the Israeli–Palestinian conflict no other choice exists but to resolve all issues on the agenda.

Outstanding issues would leave the agreement hostage to extremists on both sides, who would continue to fight in order to thwart the possibility of concluding these issues in future negotiations, and thereby leave the process of peace and reconciliation at their mercy. A PSA must be clear, while its implementation could be – and perhaps should be – gradual. In any case, and not as was the case in Oslo, the "End State" must be clear to both sides. From an historical–political perspective, being cognizant of possible complexities and complications, all players – Israel, the Palestinians, the Arab World, even the Palestinian rejection front, and the international community – were at this time ripe for an historic step. In this context, Barak's decision to work toward this end was both justified and sound.

Barak was not convinced, upon entering the negotiations, that Israel had a true partner for peace in the present Palestinian leadership headed by Arafat. He still wished to examine whether or not the Palestinian leadership viewed its involvement in the peace process as a strategic decision and whether a critical mass of the Palestinian public supported Arafat and his way. Barak was prepared to go "all the way" in order to reach an agreement, leading Israel toward making the necessary concessions. However, he was not willing to do what was necessary on-the-ground in order to prove his intentions, and he expressed extreme positions in his political statements.

In stark contrast to the hesitations of the Israeli Prime Minister, the Palestinian leadership and a majority of the public were willing to negotiate and to make the necessary concessions, provided that Israel would present clear negotiating positions that would lead to their strategic goal, and that the reality of the occupier vs. the occupied would actually change on the ground.

Barak's negotiating strategy with the Palestinians was mistaken. He should have presented the principles underlying the proposed solutions (mainly regarding the territorial issue) at the early stages of negotiations. This would have provided the Palestinians with an incentive to move forward with the negotiations, and their leadership with an opportunity to convince their long-suffering public that there was light at the end of the tunnel. Instead, in the tradition of "Persian Market" bargaining, Barak engaged in foot-dragging during negotiations. Abu Mazen – the Palestinian architect of the Oslo Accord and a politician with great experience and understanding – who wanted to be the Palestinian figure leading the negotiations, repeatedly recommended that the general principles guiding the Permanent Status agreement be established at the onset of negotiations. An Israeli agreement to this would have turned Abu Mazen into a strategic partner with the political strength to carry the weight of negotiations on his shoulders. Instead Barak rejected this proposal, fearing he would "expose" his positions too early in the game. Barak should have understood that without a presentation of these principles, an agreement could not be reached. Moreover, by introducing these principles he would have strengthened the pragmatic Palestinian camp which claims, even today, that an agreement with Israel is possible. The tragic result was that when Barak "exposed" his positions at the end of the negotiations, it was too late, and done in a manner which was not viewed as trustworthy by the Palestinians. Moreover, by not laying down principles, and leading the negotiations as he did, Barak weakened the Israeli position and had to concede again and again without receiving anything in return.

Barak also relied, mistakenly, on the recommendations of senior Government officials – who in fact were disconnected from the Palestinian reality on the ground and from its policies – who advised him that it would be possible to close a deal on one of two options: either on a Palestinian state in all of Gaza and 80 percent of the West Bank, with an annexation of 20 percent to Israel and without territorial exchanges in return; or on a Palestinian state in all of Gaza and 70 percent of the West Bank, with an annexation of 10 percent without territorial exchange, leaving the rest (20%) for future negotiations. Other experts, and the Intelligence community, in contrast did not believe that the Palestinian leadership had a margin for territorial concessions. They emphasized that Arafat's condition for accepting an agreement was 100 percent of the territories, with certain exchanges of territories in order to accommodate Israel's special needs with regard to the majority of the 200,000 settlers in the West Bank. Barak did not accept this position, and proceded to advance territorial proposals which did not stand a chance.

Barak failed to grasp that from Arafat's and the Palestinian point of view, the Palestinians had already made the most important territorial concession. They had recognized Israel within the pre-June 1967 borders, leaving them with only 22 percent of mandatory Palestine. As a result of misreading the Palestinian perspective, Barak was originally convinced that it would be possible to reach an agreement without territorial exchanges. Later he reached the inaccurate conclusion that an exchange could be based on less than a 1:1 ratio, as Prime Minister Rabin had agreed to in the Peace Agreement with Jordan in 1994.

This highly responsible person – who was able to withstand extremely stressful situations, had amazing powers of concentration and analytical capacity, and who was used to coping with new situations on the battlefield – may have failed precisely because of his qualities. Barak's approach to negotiation was influenced by arrogance, single-mindedness, and the

106

fallacy that "only I have the big picture, and only I know and understand it all." His strategic vision and historical insight collapsed because he failed to understand how to reach his important goal. He attempted to impose his game rules on the negotiations, and forced a Barak-like move on an environment which was unaccustomed to functioning according to his code.

Barak recruited the American administration to this end. In retrospect, it seems that the American administration – in particular the State Department – contributed to the failure of the negotiation process. The traditional approach of the State Department, which prevailed throughout most of Barak's tenure, was to adopt the position of the Israeli Prime Minister. Consequently, the Palestinians suspected the Americans of not being honest brokers. This was demonstrated most radically during the Netanyahu administration, when the American Government seemed sometimes to be working *for* the Israeli Prime Minister, in an effort to convince (and even attempt to force) the Palestinian side to accept Israeli offers. Such a pattern of behavior also was visible during Barak's tenure. The Israeli line was adopted by the Americans without sufficient consideration of the positions and needs of the Palestinian side. With time, President Clinton and the White House staff developed a more profound understanding of the Palestinian position, and a willingness to push the Israelis to alter and roll forward their positions. However, the behavior of the Palestinian side – mainly during the Camp David Talks – psychologically eroded this support, causing the Americans to return instinctively to the traditional pattern of backing Israel's positions.

President Clinton's public statement at the close of the Camp David Talks, to the effect that the Palestinian side was responsible for its failure, was a mistake. The President's position was a reaction to the behavior of the Palestinians during the Talks, and a personal expression of disappointment. He may also have been motivated by a desire to assist a friend – Barak – who was in a difficult political situation at home. The Palestinian Delegation practiced foot-dragging, its representatives on occasion demonstrated an unwillingness to fully engage in the discussions, adopted a passive approach, and contradicted each other. Their behavior left a negative impression on Clinton compared with the frog leaps undertaken by Barak who broke taboos and took great personal and political risks. Nevertheless, Clinton should have been less emotional and more presidential, and should have understood three basic facts: First, the Palestinians could not and from the outset were not prepared to complete the negotiations during a single summit which took place three to five months before the date set for the end of negotiations. Secondly, the proposed Israeli positions, while being far-reaching, remained far from the minimum which would have enticed the Palestinians to sign an agreement. And thirdly, to corner Arafat would always produce the opposite result and push him to commit actions contrary to requirements for a successful conclusion of the negotiations.

It is important to observe that Barak's notion that Camp David was to represent "the" summit to end all summits, an all or nothing approach, was fundamentally wrong. From the beginning, the Palestinians were opposed to the Talks, and were dragged into them by the Secretary of State and the President. The Palestinians believed that the time was not ripe, and that the two sides were as yet not ready for a concluding summit. Arafat was not aware of the intentions of Barak, who produced rabbits and other gifts from his top hat. When these were revealed, the Palestinians were not ready to react with concrete positions. It was therefore impossible to reach an agreement at Camp David. From Arafat's point of view, July was too early a date to reach an agreement. His timeline was September or November, with a preference for the latter. Tactically, his goal was to continue with discreet negotiations (as took place in Stockholm between the Palestinian and Israeli teams in June 2000) until the end of the summer, and then to hold a number of summit meetings which would reach their climax after the American elections, when the President would feel free of the influence of the Jewish vote, and not bound by electoral obligations to his Vice President and the candidacy of his wife in the Senate elections.

When the summit was forced upon him, Arafat requested – but was unable to prevail – that there would be not one but a series of summit meetings which would enable him to build a coalition at home, both within the political elite and with the Palestinian public. His need was not sufficiently apparent to, nor recognized by, the Israelis and the Americans. Toward the end of the negotiations in Oslo in the summer of 1993, Abu Mazen and Abu Ala were also busy building an internal coalition. At the time, this coalition-building enabled Arafat to declare his support for the agreement. The Palestinian leadership was then able to use the combined force of his and the coalition's support in order to market the agreement to the lower echelons of the leadership and to the Palestinian public. Without such an internal coalition composed of elements within Fatah and the PLO, Arafat could not sign an agreement.

In the period leading up to Camp David, the Palestinian leadership was divided over, and engaged in, an internal struggle over who would lead the negotiations, but no less on who would be the heir to Arafat. Israel did not know how to maneuver in this context, and was seen to be involving itself in internal Palestinian politics. One of the Americans' worst mistakes was that they also seemed to be taking a stand on this issue. They appeared to be grooming Mohammed Dahlan, the Head of Preventive Security Forces in Gaza, at the expense of number two in Fatah, Abu Mazen. This struggle adversely affected the functioning of the Palestinian delegation. At certain points – both within the negotiations proper and outside them – various Palestinians presented harsh positions designed to hurt their colleagues by making them appear too lenient.

Insufficient and unprofessional preparation combined with unclear proceedings were not only characteristic of the Palestinian side. The Israeli side, for example, arrived at the summit without being prepared on the complex and sensitive issue of Jerusalem. Barak justified the lack of preparation, stating that he feared "leaks" would result in attacks accusing him of dividing the city. The negotiators were not familiar with the possible models of solutions or with the physical terrain in and around Jerusalem. This mistake was exacerbated when the Prime Minister decided to focus the discussions at the summit to an exaggerated degree on Jerusalem and, specifically, on the most sensitive issue of the Temple Mount/al-Harem al-Sharif. In fact, the logic of the negotiations required the opposite approach. The Palestinians were prepared to reach an agreement on all the other issues, and to leave the two most sensitive issues (the Temple Mount and the Right of Return of the Palestinian refugees) for the end of the negotiations. This set-up would have provided both sides with a clear balance of the gains and losses involved, and would have urged them to reach an agreement. Instead, Barak adopted the opposite approach, adding fuel to the fire in the form of an Israeli demand to change the religious status quo of al- Harem al-Sharif by building a Jewish synagogue within the boundaries of the sacred compound. Such an act had not been contemplated for two thousand years, since the destruction of the Temple in AD 70.

It should be emphasized that the Palestinians made extremely significant mistakes that adversely effected the negotiations, with regard to these issues. These mistakes rendered the Israeli public suspicious of the Palestinians' strategic aims, and advanced a process whereby the average Israeli removed his support from Barak and from permanent status negotiations. On the issue of the Temple Mount, Arafat and the Palestinian negotiating team should not have expressed doubts about the importance and holiness of the Temple Mount for the Jewish people. The legitimate Palestinian claim for sovereignty over the al-Harem al-Sharif was not strengthened by the inconsiderate attempt to ignore the historic Jewish connection to the site.

The second issue proved even worse. Excited Palestinian declarations regarding the Right of Return of every refugee to the State of Israel created a suspicion among the vast majority of the Israeli public, from left to right, that the Palestinian intention remains to eradicate the Jewish state using a Trojan horse in the form of the Right of Return. The extreme Palestinian positions united Israeli–Zionist society. It appeared as an attempt to destroy the foundation on which the Oslo concept was based: the principle of two states for two peoples, the mutual recognition of the right for self-determination of the Palestinian people, and the legitimacy of a national home for the Jewish people. Climbing the high tree of the total Right of Return and the subsequent debate constituted a major blow to the negotiations. The Palestinians touched upon two highly sensitive Israeli nerves: the religious and the national, thus damaging themselves and the possibility of reaching a Permanent Status agreement. It was in total contrast to Palestinian positions in Oslo and in later negotiations.

The Palestinians also failed in the tactical negotiations. In doing so, they did not help those in the Israeli political system who were trying to convince the Prime Minister to go the full distance in order to reach an agreement. The Palestinians changed the head of delegation on several occasions, and presented demands and positions which later turned out only to reflect the interests of the negotiator at the time. Throughout the negotiations, the Palestinian team conveyed a feeling that there was no end to Palestinian demands and that this pressure would continue to increase as the conclusion of an agreement came closer. Those who had negotiated with the Palestinians in the past were familiar with this tactic. Its aim is to exhaust the path of negotiations up to the decision-making point when it is time to sign. The Israeli negotiators, however, felt that the rug had been drawn out from under them, even with regard to proposals that had already been agreed upon.

As negotiations advanced, Prime Minister Barak understood that to reach an agreement he must adopt an approach based on correcting mistakes while in full motion. Such a "correction" was first observed in the nomination of Gilad Sher as Chief Negotiator and that of Minister Shlomo Ben-Ami as the Head of the Israeli Delegation. Further "corrections" occurred immediately following Camp David, when it became clear that the negotiations with the Palestinians could and should be continued, even though the Prime Minister earlier had announced the Israeli Camp David proposals to be null and void. Barak also realized that he should make use of more experienced people, whom he had refused to involve in the past. This resulted in the establishment of the peace cabinet, which included Ministers Shimon Peres and Yossi Beilin – who had gained vast experience since the beginning of the Oslo Process. Beilin's involvement in the last-minute negotiations at Taba – albeit successful – came too late.

The negotiations in Taba, which took place days before Barak's government lost the elections, proved that a permanent status agreement between Israel and the Palestinians was within reach. The distance between the two sides narrowed during the last week of negotiations in Taba, and the climate in which the discussions were conducted was reminiscent of the approach adopted during the Oslo talks. In effect, this led to dramatic progress on all issues on the agenda, including the sensitive issues of the Palestinian refugees and the important territorial issues constituting the basis for any possible agreement. Had the Taba approach been tried from the onset of Barak's tenure, we might today be on the road to peace.

The Intifada

Since September 29, 2000, Israeli–Palestinian relations have entered a new phase of collapse of the peace process paradigm. The second Palestinian Intifada erupted, leaving both publics deeply shaken, and leading to Barak's downfall and the breakdown of permanent status negotiations. This is first and foremost the result of a double misperception. The Palestinian side reached the mistaken conclusion that the Israeli public and Barak were not prepared to pay the price necessary for a genuine agreement and peace. Both the Israeli public and the Prime Minister were in fact willing to cover the necessary distance, on the condition that the Palestinians expressed publicly the conciliatory positions which they had stated privately, and demonstrated non-tolerance and determination in combating terrorism. The Israeli side, for its part, reached the mistaken conclusion that the Palestinians did not want peace, and were bent on destroying the Zionist State both from within and from outside. Israel concluded that there was no partner for peace on the Palestinian side, or at least not one would that had the ability or the will to pursue it. In reality, the Palestinians had not altered their basic position held since 1993, calling for a two-state solution based on a non-militarized state along the 1967 borders with a pragmatic solution to the refugee problem.

The Fatah leadership, which led the uprising and represents the Palestinian "street," was more frustrated than anyone. The Fatah and the Tanzim (the local organizational base of the Fatah) were, and remain, Arafat's main support on the road to peace, which he has followed since September 1993. The Fatah leadership believed in the Oslo Agreement as the stepping stone to a "liberation of the land" through a just peace. They therefore took upon themselves to market the Agreement to the public, and assumed a moral responsibility for its implementation. Consequently, once they reached the conclusion that the process was not leading toward the fulfillment of these goals, they felt that they bore the responsibility for what they viewed as a barren process and even an historical trap. For seven years, they had defended the peace process and fought for it in Palestinian towns, villages and refugee camps, and against opposition from right (Hamas) and left (the rejection front), out of a belief that it would result in a Palestinian state, peace, and economic growth. The explosion was only a matter of time once they concluded that Israel wasn't a partner for peace, that the negotiations were being dragged on, that building in the settlements had accelerated, and that the hope for a state evaporated. The Fatah feared that it would lose its strength opposite Hamas, and preferred in this context, and as a movement for national liberation, to lead the uprising rather than to be dragged into it by Hamas.

It is our duty as Israelis to observe the equation also from the Palestinian perspective. As long as the Palestinian side maintained hope, based on the continuing negotiations, the Palestinian leadership could persuade its public that there is a light at the end of the tunnel, and that its suffering will bear fruit in the end in the form of a fair agreement and a just peace, without settlements or occupation. Once the public realized that this light had been extinguished, frustration and despair led to the eruption of the Intifada.

Conclusion

This chapter presents the problems and obstacles met by the Oslo process since September 1993. It would, however, be inaccurate to conclude from the critical description that the Oslo process and the options it offered for a permanent status agreement were faulty by design. I have argued here that the Oslo approach and its objectives, which were introduced during Yitzhak Rabin's tenure as Prime Minister, were never correctly implemented and should therefore not yet be discounted.

The absence of implementation during Netanyahu's administration, and the problematic management of permanent status negotiations under Barak, are the two main obstacles which prevented the sides from reaching an agreement. Other obstacles included Palestinian insensitivity to the Israeli perception of the daily threat of terrorism to their personal security; Israeli insensitivity to the suffering of an entire people possessed with a collective pride and struggling to gain national liberation from continuing occupation; the destructive effect of anti-Israeli incitement and propaganda; and a fledgling Palestinian political system which acted negligently and employed double talk. These factors were instrumental in causing the deterioration of the situation into violence.

Nevertheless, the possibility of reaching an agreement remains. The Oslo Agreement represents the link between the era of conflict and the era of peace. The Oslo process brought about an historical change in the Israeli-Arab conflict, including the peace agreement with Jordan and a process of recognizing Israel's legitimacy by the Arab world. The process also created an Israeli–Palestinian consensus on a two-state solution based on the 1967 borders and on a reconciliation founded on a fair interim agreement and common interests. The period of the implementation of the agreement and the negotiations on permanent status were supposed to lay the foundation for a comprehensive and lasting peace.

The negotiations were crippled during its initial, promising stages, not from a lack of support of the Israeli and Palestinian publics, but from poor management of the process. If the two sides are able to recognize their mistakes and learn from them, it is this writer's contention that it is possible to renew the negotiations and to reach a permanent status agreement representing the first phase on the long and arduous journey to reconciliation between the two peoples and regional peace.

8

Why Did Oslo Fail? Lessons for the Future

Manuel Hassassian

Peace in the Middle East will be secured only when it takes root in the everyday lives of the people in the region. In addition to securing the appropriate political agreements, securing peace requires establishing a hospitable environment for economic development that will only materialize if peace brings open economic relations and development of the peoples and countries of the region, in the context of a just resolution of the Palestinian question as the core issue of the Arab-Israeli conflict.

Misperception is an important causal factor of conflict. Conflicting parties not only have misrepresentations about each other but also maintain a self-perpetuating and often mistaken conception about the nature of the conflict itself.

Conflict is viewed regularly in terms of right and wrong, in terms of us and them, in terms of win and lose. Such common conceptions, called frames, are unproductive. The prevalence of negative frames about conflict is derived in large measure from past experiences and common assumptions that parties hold about the conflict and each other. Therefore, images, perceptions, cognitions, beliefs, and value systems represent a stereotype conglomerate that impedes the overcoming of psychological barriers. What is required is the establishment in parallel to the ongoing political negotiations of a process of mutual conversion of interests based on the dramatic changes of stereotyped images which have been built up culminatively in this deep historical conflict, and buttressed by ethno-national misperceptions and flagrant distortion. There is a solid conviction prevailing among both Palestinians and Israelis that images dominating their public opinion are prime obstacles to political change and thus dysfunctional to the peace process.

Confidence-building measures through mass communications at the grass-roots level are imperative in setting a frame of reference for a mutual vision of the future, based on equity, parity, and total recognition of rights. Motivated by domestic policy considerations, the Israeli leadership formulated a foreign policy agenda toward the Palestinians and the Arab World on the basis of interdependence and shared benefits. Undoubtedly, the crumbling of the Soviet Union and the diminution of the vitality of territoriality in the Middle East as a function of the Gulf War, and the prevalence of Pax Americana, motivated the Israeli leadership to infuse its national security with economic cooperative considerations and mutual interdependence.

The Palestinians, for their part, convinced that the symbolic achievements desired by the uprising could not fulfill their national aspirations, viewed participating in the negotiations as a pragmatic measure they had to pursue. However, recognition of Palestinian rights by the Israelis was calculated by the Palestinian leadership to be part and parcel of a process in which consequences have to be mutually beneficial.

There were several barriers from the beginning as to the outcome of the implementation of the Declaration of Principles, the first being the economic imbalances between Palestinians and Israelis, and Arabs in general. Israelis have higher living standards and productivity. The second is the structural barriers, with restrictions of Israeli economic policy on the West Bank and Gaza, which puts the Palestinians in isolation economically and in pursuit of economic nationalism. The third is communications and information inequities, where roads and infrastructure in the Occupied Territories are almost non-existent and the information and communications system are inadequate. Fourth is the ideological barrier, with Islam versus modernity/Westernization/Globalization.

Considering this framework as a basis, and comparing it with the reality on the ground, it is inevitable to draw the conclusion that the Oslo process, or the current phase of the peace process as we knew it, has reached a dead end. There is a consensus that the Oslo process failed. It is now defended by people who invested their time and energy into it, as well as their future, while it is not mourned by the people who suffered its consequences, namely the Palestinians – not ignoring the fact that Israelis also suffered during the Oslo process, but to an extent less than that felt by Palestinians. Economic indicators and death tolls prove undoubtedly that Palestinians paid a price resulting from the peace process heavier than that incurred by Israelis.

The Oslo process, which is synonymous with the peace process, failed because it meant different things for the Palestinians and Israelis. Two main issues result: (1) Constructive ambiguity did not work, and (2) the talk of a new Middle East was appealing, but only to those who speak the language of diplomacy.

On the first point, the question for the general public was not a matter of "constructive ambiguity," but rather that the process meant confusion, lack of coherence, and pressure to give up long-held values while not knowing what they will get in return.

On the second point, the Middle East is not a place where the language of diplomacy prevails. In Israel, it is the military language that prevails; on the Palestinian and Arab side, people are still living under traditional political systems that do not necessarily adhere to diplomacy or even to the rule of law.

The Oslo process should not be seen in isolation of the events that led to it, from the moment that Theodor Hertzl thought of the Jewish national homeland in Palestine. Since the very beginning, the conflict was seen as a zero-sum game. At the root of it, Palestinians had to be uprooted so that Herzl's dream could be realized. From the very beginning the ideology of Zionism for Palestinians was a nightmare.

The Zionist movement negated entirely the mere presence of Palestinians, and went so far as to claim that there is not such a thing as Palestine but rather what some called "pre-state Israel." Now let us take a major leap in time from Herzl to the Oslo process. Throughout seven years of peace negotiations, Israeli negotiators toiled with that same old notion and failed to acknowledge that Palestinians have a fundamental right to a free and independent Palestine. In the year 2000, negotiators from both sides were indirectly dealing with the same problem created by Herzl and his followers. Certain steps for accommodation were made by Israel, but only within the context of traditional ideology and not within the context of a new world. For example, Mr. Shimon Peres, as a student of Ben-Gurion, spoke about accommodation and restructuring the region. Delving in historic documents, what Peres was talking about is the same ideology of his mentor Ben-Gurion. So the new Middle East was doomed to failure because its underpinning belonged to a different era altogether. A new Middle East would have materialized if it took into consideration the demise of the former Soviet Union, the Second Persian Gulf War, and the fact that many years have passed since the Holocaust. The new Middle East as marketed by Peres was already out of touch with the contemporary historic context.

As I mentioned before, the Oslo process is not an end in itself but rather a process that should bring peace, justice, and stability. The fact that negotiations went on for such a long time defeated its purpose. Sustaining it became an objective for diplomats while the people on both sides watched, with decreasing patience, the potential loss of their dignity.

Accordingly, it would have been prudent to talk about peace dividends only after peace and justice were achieved. If we jump early on to talking about dividends of peace without addressing the core issues, then the process becomes a sell-out, and the general public will perceive those talks about the dividends of peace as futile. We saw this happening on both sides;

many of those negotiating, or in other words those who speak the language of diplomacy, have been negatively labeled and ill-perceived by their own people. In the Middle East, the language of diplomacy is not supreme. The language of honor, faith, courage, and sacrifice outweigh the western-style art of give and take.

In Israel, where generals swiftly move into the political arena and become Prime Ministers, they must be aware that they do not only move from military fatigue to a suit and a tie; they must make the psychological transition as well. They must show respect for Arabs and Islam, which goes contrary to their long-held values. Whatever constitutes a recipe for success in the army constitutes a recipe for a resounding failure in the office of Prime Minister, and this is the irony of their situation. For generals, it is not the dividends of peace that matter because that is left to the diplomats; they are more concerned about crushing the enemy. A long time ago, Clausewitz said that war is too important to be left to the generals. In our case, it is fair to say that peace is too important to be left to the generals.

In the Middle East, Palestinians and Israelis have to decide whether it is the language of diplomacy and dialogue that will prevail or the language of army generals. Palestinians have not been succesful in adopting either of these two tactics. They went into the negotiations ridden with internal problems. The PLO was a revolutionary organization that adopted guerilla tactics and not institutional and developmental norms and procedures. Moreover, it had to move from one country to another, and that experience weakened its base because there was no institutional or administrative stability. Throughout the years, the best and the brightest within the PLO were lost to assassination or power struggle. Those are the very people that could have led the PLO in running the negotiations and building the National Authority.

Moreover, the PLO had very little experience in dealing with the United States, which turned out to be the only power broker in the peace process. This despite the now commonly known contacts between the PLO and the CIA since the 1970s, and the PLO help in getting US nationals out of Beirut when the civil war broke out, an effort for which it received thanks from then President Jimmy Carter. When the peace negotiations started, the PLO found itself bereft of experience in terms of how to negotiate with the United States, and actually found the arena there occupied by pro-Israel lobbyists. Moreover, European contacts with the PLO, despite having taken place for many years, did not amount in importance to the level of guilt that the Europeans carried towards the Holocaust. The PLO was more familiar with the environment of the Soviet Union, which no longer existed.

In terms of relations with the Arab world, the negotiations could not have started at a worse time for the PLO. Palestinians went to the Madrid

Peace Conference while relations with Saudi Arabia were strained because of the Second Gulf War, as were its relations with Kuwait and all the Gulf Countries. Iraq, as a major Arab force, was out of the equation. Relations with Syria were already strained because of the mistrust between both sides. Egypt already had its peace treaty with Israel. Jordan was focusing on its internal development.

So Palestinians entered into the peace process within an international balance of power not in their favor, a weak and unprofessional administrative system, and the absence of an external power that would support their position. Yet, the Palestinians did not give in on their national platform even under such a dismal situation. Israeli leaders thought mistakenly that they could exploit this environment in order to impose a settlement on the Palestinians. At the same time, the Palestinians thought mistakenly that they could capitalize on their own weakness by proving to the Israelis that they had nothing to be afraid of. Both sides were wrong. Israel could not impose its will on the Palestinians, and the Palestinians failed to win the trust of Israelis.

On the popular level, since the time that the Palestinian Authority was established, two factors generated an angry response among the Palestinian public: corruption and mismanagement within the Palestinian Authority, and Israel's oppressive attitude toward Palestinians.

The Palestinians, despite their efforts to build peace with the Israelis, still witnessed a continued and frenzied construction of settlements in a race against time. This defeated the very essence of the peace process. If there are settlements being built, then it is not Israel's intention to return the land to Palestinians. At the same time, Palestinian negotiators were perceived as unable to do anything through diplomatic means to stop Israel from taking such unilateral steps.

Moreover, the Palestinian public, after the euphoria that accompanied the entry of Palestinian forces, found that the Israeli Army was still in control of every aspect of their daily lives. This came as a surprise and a disappointment to the Palestinian public. The Israeli Army withdrew only from the city centers, not from the cities; they were literally just around the corner. Palestinians still needed permits from the Israelis in order to travel, while Palestinian liaison coordinators served as mere messengers. The Israel Army still sealed off the cities, arrested Palestinians, and wasted no opportunity to remind them that the Occupation is still there. In brief, the political leadership in Israel, and the Israeli Army, did not allow Palestinians to feel proud of their National Authority.

On the Israeli side, what seemed as an insatiable Palestinian appetite for more Israeli concessions surprised the public. Palestinians seemed unappreciative no matter what they were given. But Palestinians felt that they had already made a historic compromise by accepting the State of Israel within the 1948 borders. In retrospect it is obvious that the public on both sides was not ready to accept what the negotiators tried to achieve. Israelis were asked to declare unequivocally that there is no such thing as Greater Israel, and Palestinians were asked to declare unequivocally that there is no such thing as Palestine from the river to the sea. Formally, both sides were bound by agreements, in principle; but implementation mechanisms were too ambiguous and the agreement meant different things to each side.

It was a process that could not bring justice for Palestinians nor security for Israelis. It was a process that capitalized on the imbalance of power. Palestinians were expected to make more concessions because they were the weaker party; if they had been treated on an equal footing, that would have ensured justice and security. In order for any future peace agreement to succeed in the Middle East, security for Israelis and justice for Palestinians must be seen as two faces of the same coin.

Peace has to be sustained after a change in the balance of power that brought it into existence. In other words, people must feel that they have an interest and an investment in peace, and should not feel that they are better off by resorting to violence or unilateral actions. In fact, Palestinians and Israelis saw themselves as *victims* of the peace process. By and large, Israelis felt that despite their generosity, buses were still exploding and shopping centers and café shops were no longer safe. From their point of view, Palestinians were unappreciative of the Israeli generosity. On the other side, Palestinians could not comprehend how the peace process could reach a successful conclusion while settlements were still being built. If there is one single reason that can be pointed to as the main reason why Palestinians lost faith in the Oslo process, it is the fact that despite seven years of negotiations, Israel continued to build more settlements. Palestinians did not perceive any generosity in Israel's actions. While Israelis felt that they were giving too much, Palestinians felt that they were getting too little.

What made the situation more incomprehensible to the public on both sides is that agreements were signed one after the other, yet on the ground things were not improving. Palestinians were worse-off economically, and Israelis were worse off in terms of their domestic security. After agreements were signed, and the handshakes and the hugs, the next day was business as usual in terms of the actual conflict on the ground. An agreement was followed with an implementation protocol, then another protocol for the implementation of the implementation protocol. The process was simply no longer credible, but the people waited patiently and swallowed their pain.

On the Palestinian side, as well as the Israeli side, people felt that they were better off before the peace process.

During the period that preceded the peace process, any Palestinian would have been able to drive his car from his home anywhere in the West Bank to visit relatives and friends in any other town or village, travel to Gaza, and return home in the afternoon. When the Oslo Agreement was implemented, Palestinians were confined to ghettos, their freedom to travel and their economic well-being were diminished. Worst yet, because of the situation created by the peace process, Jerusalem was off-limits to them. They could no longer go to Jerusalem not even when they wanted to pray. And this at a time when Israel, despite the peace process, was bringing immigrants from Russia and Ethiopia, who even before landing at the airport had the right to live in Jerusalem and in settlements in the West Bank, while Palestinians were treated as foreigners.

Instead of building trust, the situation prevailing during the period between 1993 and 2000, when the Oslo process was in implementation, resulted in deeper mistrust and a sense of frustration on both sides.

On the Palestinian side, this frustration reflected itself in attacks against targets inside Israel, with the Palestinian Authority unable to curb the violence. On the Israeli side, frustration reflected itself in the leadership crisis. Since the Madrid Peace Conference, Israel had been under the premiership of Shamir, then Rabin, then Peres, then Netanyahu, then Barak, and now Sharon. Part of the reason for the failure of the Oslo process is the inability of Israel to chart for itself a strategic approach to peace. Negotiating positions were left to the personal whims of the Prime Minister and his uncritical and blind acceptance of Army recommendations, rather than operating instead on clearly planned objectives. And because prime ministers were being changed rapidly and dramatically, the positions Israel carried with it to the negotiations were changing each time with no commitments to previous agreements.

In a book entitled *Is Oslo Alive?* I co-authored an article with Edy Kaufman, entitled "Civil Society and the Peace Process." We spoke about grass-roots perceptions and events taking place that shaped Israeli and Palestinian public opinion regarding the peace process. We focused on the role and function of civil society, and its ability to influence both policy-makers and the general public. Within this context, we tried to analyze and critically evaluate the effect of interaction between Israeli and Palestinian academicians in the peace process.

Furthermore, we asserted that around the time of the October 1991 Madrid Peace Conference, some unofficial initiatives were undertaken to encourage civil society dialogue, this time with a regional Middle East scope. Palestinian–Israeli cooperative efforts, discontinued temporarily through the polarized situation during the Gulf War, were resumed. But overall, their effect was somewhat marginal, aside from assuaging intellectual guilt about "something" being done. Soon, the lack of progress in the Washington, D.C. formal "Track I" negotiations showed that the parties were still stuck in their old attitudes of mutual delegitimization and demonization. Particularly then, "Track II" inter-academic conferencing acted as a legitimating forum where both sides could meet, thereby avoiding officially sanctioned restrictions. The guise of academic conferencing protected the participants, and even drew considerable (albeit silent) official observation by both the PLO and the Israeli governments. Several notable conferences and efforts at academic collaboration deserve recognition here.

For over a decade, Harvard University Professor Herbert Kelman conducted programs in which scholars from both sides of the conflict participated in conflict resolution. Harvard's "third party" status served as a "positive environment where protagonists could exchange views and express their beliefs in an uninhibited manner." At the time, it was difficult to assess the efficacy of the Harvard groups' efforts. Later, however, it would be proved that they did have a personal impact as well as policy relevance, when some of them, such as Sorbonne professor Camille Mansour, or Jerusalem journalist Ziad Abu Zayyad, would later become members of the Palestinian delegation to the Madrid Conference in 1991 and ACRS (Arms Control and Regional Security Talks.)

Another notable example was a dialogue sponsored by the Stanford Center on Conflict and Negotiation in 1990. Together, prominent intellectuals from both sides published a document entitled "Principles and Provisions of a Palestinian-Israeli Agreement," in which the participants endorsed and outlined a two-state solution to be implemented in stages. Prominent Israelis who participated in the conference were the former ranking members of the Israeli military: Moshe Ma'oz, Galit Ghasan-Rokem, Giora Ram Furman, and Oded Megiddo. On the Palestinian side, participants included Mamduh Al-Aker, Rihab Essawi, and Nabil Shaath.

Palestinian–Israeli academic collaboration can take many different forms. Considerable work has also taken place in the spheres of co-publishing and co-teaching. In 1988, two doctoral candidates at the American University in Washington, D.C., Yehuda Lukas and Abdallah M. Battah, published a joint anthology entitled "The Arab–Israeli Conflict: Two Decades of Change." Its introduction cautions that "the conflict has been taking place not only on the battlefield, but also in the halls of academia... This tug of war between scholars has led to a lack of consensus and has manifested itself in contradictory arguments along the same lines which the belligerents themselves use."

Having cited a few examples about academic cooperation between private citizens as part of Track II before the peace process, the next step is to examine efforts exerted during the peace process itself. Reference is made again to the paper I co-authored with Edy Kaufman on "Civil Society and the Peace Process." The peace process refers to the period between

September 1993 (when Israel and the PLO signed the DoP) till the present (May 2001). In some sense this period could initially be considered a denouement of sorts for the academic communities of both sides. The success of Track II negotiations at Oslo meant that academics were now to take more of a back seat position to the "real" policy-makers. Such a second-class status is humorously reflected in the true story of how, after the DoP was concluded in Oslo, Israel's leaders forgot to invite Hirschfeld and Pundak to join them for the trip to the Washington signing ceremonies. This omission was only discovered after Rabin's plane took off. Both academics subsequently traveled to Washington at their own expense on a commercial airliner.

The Role of the Arab Countries

In the absence of an Arab strategy toward the peace process, the underlying philosophy became that "each will remove his own thorns." In fact, the Arabs never had a strategy in facing up to the challenge posed to them by Israel, and the peace process was no different. When the Palestinians signed the Oslo Agreement, Iraq and Libya were under siege, Egypt had long had its peace agreement with Israel, and Syria was advocating a cautious approach and taking reciprocal steps depending on Israel's proving its good intentions. Among the Gulf countries, some were eager to establish ties with Israel while others did not show that eagerness publicly. Jordan and Morocco have had some kind of peace with Israel for many years. To make matters even worse, Iran, as a powerful Islamic power, did not enjoy the trust of any Arab country. In fact, many Arab countries were not even talking to each other. When Palestinians entered the negotiations, their own backyard could not have been more chaotic. Naturally, this weakened the Palestinian negotiating position and resulted in an agreement that is far from satisfying the requirements of a lasting peace with justice.

When Palestinians went to the secret talks in Oslo, the chaos had already been fueled by the structure of the Multilateral Peace Talks. The position of Arab countries ranged between being overly eager to participate, to preferring not to attend at all. The Multilaterals created a serious rift among the larger Arab community.

Palestinians felt that they had to "remove their thorns with their own hands," and thus felt that the only option open to them was to enter into a phased system of solving the conflict, even if that meant making too many compromises for the time being.

The Palestinian approach was poorly accepted by Arab public opinion. Yet Arab governments were satisfied as long as there was a process that constituted a tranquilizer, in the hope that in the future Palestinians and

Israelis might reach an agreement that could be marketed as the long-sought peace.

The problem with the approach of Arab countries is that they were willing to accept what the Palestinians and Israelis accepted. However, this meant that the Palestinians were left alone to deal with the Israelis. Palestinian leadership tried to overcome this weakness by forging close ties with Egypt. In fact, Egypt and the Palestinians enjoy historic and positive ties. Egypt, with the political weight that it carries, would serve as the Palestinian's source of strength. In addition, there was Egypt's close ties with the United States and its peace with Israel. Looking back, the Palestinian leadership made a perfectly wise decision by turning to Egypt for advice and support.

The absence of a unified Arab position contributed to the failure of the Oslo Process. As Palestinians went on the path of incrementalism, they felt increasingly that they had no Arab front behind them, and this led them to try to appease Israel. Israel exploited that situation, first by establishing ties in the Arab countries, second by pressing Palestinians for more and more concessions, third by trying to negate all the terms of reference of the Madrid Peace Conference, and fourth and most importantly, by building more settlements. It is evident that Israel's disregard for the Arab World constituted a major factor that led to the failure of the peace process.

It is noteworthy that the current Intifada has produced reactions in the Arab World through constant supportive popular action along with Islamic solidarity. Although the resolutions of both Arab and Muslim summits provided the minimum support politically and economically to the sustenance of the Intifada, the actual implementation of that support did not meet the expectations of the Palestinians.

The Role of Europe

Europe, with its political and cultural ties with the Middle East, its enormous dependence on Middle East oil, and its geographic proximity to the region, was positioned to play a unique role in the peace process. In addition, the regional geo-political structure was created by the European colonialist powers in the early part of the twentieth century. Moreover, Europe carries a moral obligation toward Palestinians, because it was precisely the European powers that supported the creation of Israel.

The Madrid Peace Conference, the peace conferences held in Geneva, and even the cease-fire agreements negotiated in Rhodes, in 1948, indicate that Europe is capable of playing a crucial role in Middle East peace efforts.

In order to keep the Oslo effort secret, FAFO, a Norwegian research institute headed by Mr. Terjie Larson, then a staff member for the late

Foreign Minister Johan Jorgan Holst, organized the talks. FAFO was simply doing "research" that involved, among others, the Deputy Foreign Minister Mr. Jan Egeland and Mrs. Mariana Heiberg, wife of Mr. Holst. Palestinians working inside the West Bank and Gaza did not know that this was not a research team, but rather a team carrying out a most crucial mission: to prepare the documents needed for infrastructural development and to see on the ground where and how a new reality could emerge. Local Palestinian leaders working with the researchers were never told about the secret talks in Oslo. Secrecy contributed to the success of the talks in Oslo, yet at the same time, secrecy led the negotiators to fall victim to groupthink; a symptom well known in the discipline of conflict resolution.

The tremendous gap between the Palestinians and Israelis necessitated that an incremental approach be adopted, so that eventually the talks could reach a successful conclusion. However, there should have been general agreement from the beginning on the key issues. It is the details that can be worked out step by step, but not the guiding principles. In fact, the problem with the guiding principles adopted in Oslo is that they were too vague.

It is important to note here that Palestinians were encouraged to forge ahead, because of the support they received from the Europeans, and even the friendship and trust that developed between Palestinian and European leaders throughout the years, and in particular during the secret talks in Oslo. Palestinians felt understood, and the Europeans felt appreciated.

When the outcome of the talks became known, there were many visits by European leaders to the region, thus encouraging and supporting the Palestinians even more, at least on the economic level.

The first visit ever by a head of state to the Palestinian Authority was that of President Jacques Chirac. He delivered a speech in front of the Palestinian Legislative Council in Ramallah, and for the first time ever, Palestinians heard a world leader acknowledge their suffering and dispossession. That visit should not be regarded as credit only to Chriac and to France, but also to the credibility of Europe as an honest mediator.

For reasons that are vague, Europe gradually conceded its role to the United States. While the EU continued financing the peace process, its role in the political arena was overshadowed. Some attribute this to the lack of a unified foreign policy and feelings of guilt regarding the persecution of Jews in Europe; which still prevented Europe from exercising a decisive role towards Israel even after all those years.

At the same time, the EU's role has been visible in second track diplomacy, thus bridging gaps in opinions between the Palestinians and Israelis. Yet with all the assistance rendered, the EU fell short in pressing Israel economically on the latter's stand regarding the building of illegal settlements, the confiscation of Palestinian land, and the demolition of homes. And above all, there is no clear-cut pressure put by the EU on Israel to lift the blockade through checkpoints and closures imposed by Israel on the Palestinians.

The Role of the United States

The Oslo process was not an American design. Actually when the scheme was first announced, the United States did not express enthusiasm about it. Yet, stemming from its policy of accepting what the parties accept themselves, the United States went along. With the signing ceremony taking place on the While House lawn on September 13, 1993, the center of political influence shifted from Europe to the United States. Since then, the US has played the contradictory role of arbiter, staunch supporter of Israel, and promoter of peace and regional stability. The three roles were irreconcilable.

Ironically, with the historic handshake of Arafat with Prime Minister Rabin and Foreign Minister Shimon Peres, the region was supposed to embark on a new direction/a new Middle East.

However, the United States, under the Clinton Administration, was unable to free itself from the influence of the pro-Israel lobby. Many of the US negotiators were not merely supportive of Israel, but they were actually active in promoting Israeli interests in the United States. Palestinians felt that they could not trust the US mediators, especially Dennis Ross. President Clinton exerted tremendous effort in trying to reach agreement, but the pro-Israel lobby prevented an equitable agreement. An observer of the situation raised a question as to how Israel would feel if all the US negotiators were Arab Americans? In Congress the situation was even worse, when Netanyahu visited, he received a standing ovation!

Palestinian leader Yasser Arafat was the most frequent international visitor to the White House, compared to all other world leaders. Yet this did not facilitate reaching an agreement, because Palestinians failed to address the US in the manner it understands. Palestinians were newcomers and they did not know their way inside the Washington establishment or in the media.

As talks progressed, the United States seemed to be retreating from all its previous positions. Settlements were no longer illegal, but merely an obstacle to peace. According to Dennis Ross, the West Bank and Gaza were not occupied, but rather disputed territories. It was and still is impossible for Palestinians to accept such a position as the basis for negotiations.

The situation dragged on with no tangible results but with no alternative to the negotiations either, especially under Netanyahu. So the parties went to Wye River and signed yet another agreement. Palestinian leaders viewed security cooperation, with the active participation of the CIA, as a positive step that would bring in a professional element from the United States, and would create a balance with the Administration's biased representatives.

Moreover, in hindsight one can tell that another undeclared intention of the Wye River talks was to lead to the downfall of Netanyahu. When he gave up part of Hebron, he upset his constituency and at the same time there was no way he could receive endorsement from the pro-peace camp. Wye River made Netanyahu look inconsistent, and when he tried to avoid implementing what he himself signed, he looked even worse.

When Barak became Prime Minister, the United States was hopeful. Barak was favored by the United States, and he enjoyed full support of the US mediators in everything he did. Palestinians felt alienated in return.

Actually it was Barak's idea to go to Camp David II, while Arafat felt the initiative came at a time when he was not yet ready. At a meeting with Mrs. Albright in Gaza, Arafat told her that he needed more time. However, Barak convinced Clinton that it was better to bring Arafat to the final status talks when he was not ready, in order to squeeze far-reaching concessions from him. Invitations were issued, so Arafat went to Camp David.

At Camp David the Palestinians felt that the United States was coordinating all its positions with Israel, and then conveying Israeli positions to the Palestinians as if those proposals were American. One Palestinian member of the negotiating team wrote afterwards that before and after every meeting with Arafat, President Clinton met with Barak. In Camp David, Palestinians felt that they were dealing with a joint US–Israeli delegation, with Israel having the upper hand and the final say.

On the issue of Jerusalem in particular, President Arafat was subjected to enormous pressure, but he stood firm. He knew that the proposals made to him were not going to lead to peace.

On the issue of water, there was nothing tangible, which means that water would remain in the hands of Israel. The borders would also remain under Israeli control, and on the question of the refugees, there was no sign of accommodation by Israel. In brief, there were no serious proposals Arafat could market to Palestinians, to Arabs and to Moslems. The fact that Arab leaders refused to pressure Arafat during the Camp David talks is concrete evidence that his position was sound and wise.

That pressure failed, so Palestinians scored a diplomatic victory, contrary to Barak's intention. President Clinton spoke on television praising Barak and indirectly blaming Arafat for the failure of the talks. Clinton stated that Barak made concessions that are far reaching, more than what has been ever offered by an Israeli Prime Minister. He failed to consider that the terms of reference of the peace process were the requirements of international legitimacy, and not the positions adopted by Israeli Prime Ministers. Barak should have been judged by his adherence to UN Resolutions 242 and 338 and the terms of reference of the Madrid peace conference, and not by the positions adopted by his predecessors in the premiership.

The Second Intifada

The diplomatic victory had to be taken away from Arafat and the Palestinians. Ariel Sharon smelled blood. He and Barak colluded together. Sharon would enter Al-Aqsa Mosque, under the military and diplomatic protection of Barak, in order to prove to Arafat, to Palestinians, to Arabs and Moslems, that Israeli had effective control over the sight.

The night before Sharon's infamous visit, Arafat flew at night to Barak's home in Tel Aviv and asked him to prevent the visit. Arafat reportedly said to Barak that by allowing Sharon to go into the Mosque, "we all know how this will begin but we do not know how it will end." Barak did not listen because he thought that this humiliation would create a feeling of defeat among Moslems. Right after the visit on September 28, 2001, the Palestinian leadership bit the bullet, but it was next day that Israeli soldiers entered Al-Aqsa Mosque and started shooting indiscriminately at the worshipers. The Second Intifada had begun.

Sharon's forceful entry into the Mosque put an official end to a process that was stagnating politically, unacceptable to the public, and impossible to implement under the terms of reference on which it was based.

The Intifada did not weaken the Palestinians; instead it put the issues forcefully on top of the international agenda. It was the Israeli Government that was weakened and embarrassed because of blatant human rights violations and the loss of personal security among Israelis. So President Clinton, in desperation, called the parties to Sharm Al-Sheikh. He was trying to accomplish the impossible, namely to have the Palestinians acquiesce to Israeli demands, without any tangible evidence that Barak would adhere to the terms of reference of the peace process. So the talks in Sharm al-Shaykh failed. Any talks will fail as long as the legitimate aspirations of Palestinians are not addressed equitably.

Barak and the Israeli public behind him treated the Palestinians with the utmost brutality. Israelis involved in violence against Palestinians have received lenient sentences, while helicopter gun-ships were used against defenseless Palestinians. Such an approach made Palestinians more determined and less convinced about Israel's sincerity towards peace making. The closures made the Palestinian areas into ghettos or South African apartheid townships. In October/November 2001, the military siege against Palestinians has been intensified and the rhetoric heightened against the Palestinian Authority following the bus attack in Tel Aviv where eight Israeli soldiers and one civilian were killed. However, it was precisely the

Israeli security establishment that gave a permit to that particular Palestinian to drive in Israel. Yet all the blame was thrown on the Palestinian Authority.

Future Prospects

I want to conclude with several recommendations.

(1) The role of intellectuals in processes of change and major political crisis is of great importance. While no one can deny the responsibility of such groups in generating extreme nationalism, chauvinism and xenophobic feelings among the masses, the existence of a vibrant civil society can become a major vehicle for advancing democratic values. A commonality of concerns has induced a significant number on both sides to become part of an embryonic epistemic community which is likely to continue working together for the goal of strengthening both human rights and democracy. Academics in both societies overwhelmingly adhere to these principles as a necessary condition for their societies and their professional freedom.

(2) The need to focus on peace building by civil society as a complement to peace making by the leaders involved in the Arab-Israeli peace process has dramatically become more obvious than ever with the tragic assassination of Prime Minister Rabin by a Jewish extremist and the concurrent threats on the lives of Arab leaders. Leaving aside the isolated expressions of rejoicing by extremist Arab groups, while the leadership of significant Arab regimes took an unusual and most supportive role in the days that followed the assassination, the more general reaction in their countries has been defined as a listening silence. Prior to the assassination there seems to have been collusion between Islamic revivalist groups, universities, and the radical left in the Arab world. In Israel, the opponents of the peace process have been acting together, although clear differences can be drawn between those who express adherence to the principles of democracy and the rule of law, and those who declare their total obedience to the "Rule of God" as the ultimate authority for their political action. Even among these, we find an overwhelming majority that rejects the use of violence. Although those who espouse violence are a minority, their high degree of militancy makes the moderate groups seem reactive rather than active. In the absence of a dominant strategy, the extremist groups – particularly those strongly motivated by divine inspiration – carry the day and set the tone, which becomes a societal impediment to the peace process. In spite of their differences, these groups are often united in the rejection of the peace process and often act politically together.

(3)   In the pursuit of peace, the "establishments" of the countries in the region need to find stronger sources of support that will generate a true majority among the populations. In order to increase the legitimacy of the peace process, it is essential to identify and analyze the true feelings that arouse hostile reactions to the peace process. In a dialogue with antagonistic individuals and groups within the academic communities, this may result in the development of relevant and constructive lines of argument and discourse. A pragmatic understanding of the irreversiblility of the process may lead current opponents to find new ways to come to terms with it as the only feasible option; if not a win–win solution, at least it may be accepted as the lesser evil by a large majority. The role of civil society in promoting intermediate structures with a high degree of legitimacy may be of utmost importance.

(4)   There is no purpose in stressing symmetric trends in the two societies; rather, there is a need to understand both sides. The consolidation of the peace process and the possible repercussions of this dramatic event call for a sustained effort to study, understand, and act in new circumstances in a creative and constructive fashion in the university communities throughout the region. How far the resistance to the process can be diminished by more systematic involvement, working together, separately, or a combination of the two, needs to be further assessed. The need to identify the main political sources of opposition implies not only isolating and controlling the violent religious groups and instigators, but also trying to address the sources of opposition to the peace process among secular intellectuals, many of them in universities in the region (and in the Arab world, in professional associations of lawyers, engineers, or doctors). In spite of the adverse circumstances, small but growing fissures can be detected in their hostile attitude.

(5)   The suggestion to focus on both students and faculty is because they act as feedback to each others' political attitudes. Often an extreme attitude of the students inhibits potential supporters of the peace process on campus by setting the dominant tone. Students are often perceived by the general population as a sincere voice of discontent and therefore listened to. To a certain extent teachers play a role in shaping their students' understanding of core values. Students, and the young in general in the Palestinian society, form a particular sector that in the past has shown a tendency toward polarization, thus acting as a major source of opposition to the peace process. In Israel, the young vote seems to be more extreme than the average, but lately there are signs of internalization of the death of Rabin, along with a call for more active involvement of youth in the peace process. To what extent there is a change, and what facilitates or obstructs change, particularly in the behavior of the other side, needs to be further examined. I believe that for effective networking Palestinian and

Israeli university communities should be encouraged to work together without any restriction, on an equal basis and with respect for the principles of academic freedom.

(6) While the policy-relevant function of the academic world should not be neglected, at times when the peace process becomes paralyzed it is no less important to further proactive research as a way of increasing understanding of the root causes and concrete arguments for antagonism to the peace process as well as stimulating a constructive dialogue with different individuals and groups across the political and religious spectrum. Building bridges across national lines includes matters such as joint study of documents, interviews and surveys, trust building, and conflict resolution workshops; action research and evaluation; long-term applied research and eventual publication of joint articles and books; team teaching, and so on.

(7) In addition to the importance of policy-relevant work and impact at the grass-roots level, peace-oriented activities among the Israeli and Palestinian civil society currently involve only a small fraction of the total potential of such interactions. Borrowing Shimon Peres' term of "privatizing the Peace Process," namely consolidating cooperation without government stimulation or interference, the components of civil society can embark on joint ventures. In a way we can speak about a "sectorial peace," which can be a cumulative process in the search for common ground based on shared values and interests. Efforts such as "People to People" can be multiplied to include professional organizations (psychologists, architects, social workers, lawyers, etc.); handicapped, children, women and other charitable associations; educators, youth leaders, and so forth.

(8) One of the main challenges is to take advantage of the large adherence within both civil societies to the principles of democracy and extend it to the advocacy of peace based on an historic compromise. The level of frustration, primarily on the Palestinian side, has generated an often indiscriminate antagonism toward Israelis as a whole and hence, a reluctance to cooperate. On the Jewish side, the widespread ability to continue with "business as usual" either by denial or just indifference to the suffering of the other side makes it very difficult to reach out to individuals and groups and persuade them to enhance their commitment to peace-oriented action. In both cases, these and other obstacles seem to confine cooperation to a rather limited but nevertheless meaningful effort.

Final Remarks

It is by now self-evident that lasting peace in the Middle East can be attained only with the establishment of an independent Palestinian state with East Jerusalem as its capital. This is the core issue. Issues such as personal security for Israelis, regional cooperation, and the proliferation of weapons of mass destruction are only the symptoms not the cause.

Given the failure of the Oslo process, we must learn the lessons for the inevitable future phase of negotiations. Ultimately, there is no alternative to peace-making between the Arabs and Israelis. Even if a war breaks out in the region, the parties will eventually have to return to negotiation.

In an official memorandum dated January 1, 2001, presented by the Palestinians to President Clinton, Palestinians stated clearly their position and expectations from any future talks, and I quote "We would like, once again, to emphasize that we remain committed to a peaceful resolution of the Palestinian–Israeli conflict in accordance with UN Security Council Resolutions 242 and 338 and International Law. In view of the tremendous human cost caused by each delay in negotiations, we recognize the need to resolve this conflict as soon as possible. We cannot, however, accept a proposal that secures neither the establishment of a viable Palestinian state nor the right of Palestinian refugees to return to their homes."

Accordingly, both sides must learn the lessons from the Oslo period, draw conclusions, and focus the energy of their think-tanks, strategic thinkers, and security establishments toward doing the preparatory work and to wait for the appropriate time when the negotiations will be re-launched.

Both sides need to keep their channels of diplomatic communication open with each other, even if at a bare minimum, so as not to start from zero once again.

I am personally not pessimistic over the long-term prospects of a settlement. Yet I am concerned that nothing is being done to lay the groundwork for the era after Israeli recognition of Palestinian rights and the emergence of a new Palestine.

It is certainly provocative to talk about peace at this time, but more provocative is the deafening silence among the Israeli left and the Palestinian mainstream. As a whole, both sides are no longer talking to each other, and they forget that it is them jointly who will re-launch the peace process in the future, despite the fact that at this time they both feel betrayed by the other side.

I believe that the concept of stagnation is misleading, because eventually events on the ground get out of hand and the situation deteriorates. This is where we are standing right now. In my judgment this current phase could last for approximately three years. If predictions are true that the Sharon Government will last for a year at best, then afterwards there will be negotiations that will last for another one year, so it will be something like three years from now when things will start picking up again. At that stage, we would all have had enough time to grasp all the lessons learned from the Oslo Process and to embark on a new process based on justice, peace, and security for all.

Acknowledgment

The author acknowledges Mr. George Sahhar's input and assistance in preparing this text.

9

The Oslo Peace Process: From Breakthrough to Breakdown

Moshe Ma'oz

Israel's Prime Minister Ehud Barak, in coordination with US President Bill Clinton, initiated in July 2000 a summit meeting at Camp David with PLO leader Yassir Arafat. Their essential aim was to settle the final status of the Oslo peace accords and bring about the end of the Palestinian–Israeli conflict. Alas, Arafat, who reluctantly attended this meeting, rejected the reportedly generous offer by Barak on the plea that it was far from satisfying the Palestinians' expectations. Previously, on the eve of the meeting Arafat asserted that the Camp David II conference had not been sufficiently prepared and discussed,[1] notably concerning the two crucial issues of Jerusalem and the Palestinian refugees. And as a tense stalemate persisted amidst verbal warfare, Likud leader Ariel Sharon staged on September 28 a grand visit to the Temple Mount/*al-Haram al-Sharif*, accompanied by several hundred Israeli policemen. Palestinian Muslims (as well as many other Muslims throughout the world) reacted to what they considered a gross provocation: on the following day, Friday, September 29, after the midday prayer Muslims on *al-Haram* started throwing stones at Israeli policemen and Jewish worshippers in the adjacent western wall. The Israeli police shot and killed seven Palestinians, wounding many others. These grave events provoked or marked the beginning of the al-Aqsa Intifada – this violent Palestinian uprising against Israel, which has claimed during the following seven months some 400 deaths and several thousand wounded among Palestinians, versus less than a hundred deaths and several hundreds wounded among Israelis, including civilians, women and children on both sides.[2]

In practice, thus, the Oslo peace process collapsed alongside a degree of mutual trust and cooperation that had been achieved between the two parties since 1993. Feelings of frustration, despair, and anger spread even among moderate or pragmatic Palestinians and Israelis. The extremists on both sides have stepped up acts of revenge and violence while demonizing each other.

Attempts by Mr. Clinton to offer a bridging formula between the positions of both parties could not stop the violence. Barak conditionally agreed, while Arafat accepted the formula with serious reservations.[3] Consequently, in their last meeting at Taba (Sinai, Egypt) in January 2001, Israeli and Palestinian negotiators failed to reach an agreement. This occurred one day after the end of Clinton's term as US President, and a few weeks before Israel's national elections, wherein Barak was not re-elected as Israel's prime minister.

The collapse of the Oslo process calls for serious investigation and explanations regarding the major query – What went wrong? Was the concept of Oslo essentially faulty, or have both sides, or one of them, contributed to the undermining the Oslo process? Or have both sides been unprepared to deal with the final status issues – notably the status of Jerusalem and the fate of the Palestinian refugees? Are those issues solvable at all? And thus is it possible to ever achieve an Israeli–Palestinian peace and reconciliation? Finally, what were the developments, factors, and circumstances that contributed to derailing and eventually to shattering the Oslo process which had started in a rather promising way.

Promising Start

Indeed, in the Oslo accords both leaders, Prime Minister Yitzhak Rabin and Yassir Arafat (PLO leader), solemnly pronounced "their determination to put an end to decades of confrontation and to live in peaceful coexistence, mutual dignity and security, while recognizing their mutual legitimate and political rights . . . [and] their desire to achieve a just, lasting and comprehensive peace settlement and historic reconciliation through the agreed political process."[4] To be sure, 60–65 percent of the Israelis and Palestinians (in the West Bank and Gaza) supported the Oslo agreements. Even Israeli Likud leader Netanyahu, who had previously rejected the Oslo accords on ideological and strategic grounds, reluctantly acknowledged them on the eve of the May 1996 Israeli elections. And following his ascendancy as prime minister, Netanyahu also signed the Hebron protocol (January 15, 1997), which confirmed the Oslo agreements and provided for the division of this town between Palestinians and Israelis. The Hebron protocol was approved by 75–80 percent of Israelis and Palestinians.[5] Significantly, the Israeli approval and the new Likud government's positions reflected a major change in Likud's right-wing ideology and policy. For the first time in its history it gave up the claim to the entire "Land of Israel" (Greater Israel) and pragmatically acknowledged the principle and practice of sharing this land with the Palestinian National Community, led by the "Palestinian Liberation Organization" (PLO) – the former "terrorist organization." Formally, this move was taken as a reaffirmation of an international treaty (Oslo) signed by the preceding Israeli government. In fact, however, many Likud leaders and members realized by then that Israel could not indefinitely continue to control the West Bank and Gaza, owing to Palestinian resistance and international criticism. Furthermore, a few Likud leaders and many members agreed now to the establishment of a Palestinian "entity," even a "state," in the Gaza Strip and parts of the West Bank. This assumed, however, that Jerusalem remained undivided and under Israeli sovereignty, the Jordan valley was annexed to Israel, and the water resources controlled by Israel.

On the other side of the political spectrum, growing numbers of liberal–leftist Israelis had already advocated since the late 1970s the creation of a Palestinian state on the West Bank and the Gaza Strip. But for many years, there were hardly public discussions regarding the borders of such a state, let alone the status of East (Arab) Jerusalem which had been annexed by Israel following the 1967 war. Nor was there any systematic thinking, even in government agencies, regarding the fate of Palestinian refugees or Jewish settlements. These issues were rather sensitive, almost "taboos" in Israeli public debate, and thus in the Oslo accords they were left to be negotiated at the final stage, "no later than May 21, 1996."[6] It is likely that an Israeli vague commitment regarding the creation of a Palestinian state in the West Bank and Gaza say, within five years, with a certain status in East Jerusalem to be negotiated could have served as a strong incentive for the PLO to fully and credibly implement its commitments to Israel, particularly in the arena of security. In return the PLO could have allayed Israeli concerns had it committed itself at Oslo to implement the Palestinian refugees' "right of return" in the future Palestinian state, not in the state of Israel proper. Whether or not such commitments were discussed at Oslo, they were not included in the agreements, possibly since both Rabin and/or Arafat feared that they would not gain public support for such bold positions; possibly because both or either of them lacked courage and vision as expected from historic leaders.

At any rate, the Oslo accords, largely dictated by Israel, were open-ended, aiming at gradually settling the Israeli–Palestinian conflict: starting with the relatively simple issues and expecting that their satisfactory implementation would create conditions of mutual trust and cooperation, which at the final stage would enable the two sides to jointly settle the most crucial issues of borders, Jerusalem, Jewish settlements, and Palestinian refugees.

Indeed for over two years the provisions of the Oslo Accords were implemented fairly well. Israeli military and civil administrations withdrew from the Gaza Strip and from about 40 percent of the West Bank, including the major towns; and power was transferred to the newly established Palestinian Authority (PA). It quickly created various administrative, economic, security, and political institutions. They included a democratically-elected (on January 20, 1996) legislative council (Parliament) and president (Yassir Arafat). Financial assistance was granted by the international community to develop the Palestinian economic infrastructure, while Palestinians and Israelis developed dialogues of cooperation – including by NGOs – in areas of economics and academia. Both security services worked in coordination against the Hamas. Israel, consequently, improved its regional position and it signed a formal peace treaty with Jordan (October 1994), followed by the establishment of economic and consular relations with Morocco, Tunisia, Qatar, and Oman. Israel also benefited economically and diplomatically from growing international investments and increasing sympathy among the world community, including Muslim countries.[7] No less important: a growing number of Israeli Jews, feeling personally secure, were more inclined to accept a Palestinian state alongside Israel and even grant the Palestinians sovereign rights in parts of East Jerusalem. In addition to the Meretz Party, which had advocated for years the creation of a Palestinian state alongside Israel, the Labor Party for the first time in April 1996 decided to erase from its platform a long-standing objection to the establishment of a Palestinian state.[8] Labor Minister Yossi Beilin went even further by initiating (early in 1994) and agreeing (in November 1995) with Arafat deputy, Abu Mazin (Mahmud Abbas) on a blueprint for the permanent peace settlement i.e., creation of a Palestinian state on the West Bank and Gaza, with certain border alterations (annexing to Israel about 5% of the West Bank) and with the capital of the Palestinian state al-Quds (Jerusalem in Arabic) located in an Arab suburb (village) of Jerusalem – Abu Dis.[9] Significantly, about half of the Israelis supported that formula, more continued subsequently to support the establishment of a Palestinian state (about 55%) or believed that such a state would emerge (75–77%) – this despite the deterioration of the Oslo peace process during Prime Minister Netanyahu's term of office (1996–9).[10] Some Israelis were even ready at that period to accept a Palestinian capital in a Palestinian suburb of Jerusalem (22%), to share sovereignty in East Jerusalem with the Palestinian state (21%), or to allow Palestinian sovereignty in parts of East Jerusalem (30%).[11]

Critical Setbacks

Alas, the unique currents of mutual trust and cooperation between Israelis and Palestinians, alongside the constructive momentum in implementing the Oslo Agreements – possibly toward creating a Palestinian state – did not gain further impetus. Since late 1995 the reconciliation process has suffered a series of crucial setbacks at the hands of anti-Oslo elements, Palestinians and Israelis alike. Vehemently opposing the Oslo process on ideological, religious and/or nationalistic-chauvinistic grounds, these groups became increasingly alarmed by the productive results of that process. Their violent reactions, notably terrorist deeds, as well as omissions and miscalculations by both Israeli and Palestinian leaders, obstructed the Oslo peace process since early 1996.

Among Israel's Jewish population, opposition to the Oslo Accords included the extreme right-wing parties and groups and their followers, Kahane Chai, Kach, Gush Emunim, the Settlers Council, the National religious Party (NRP), the Tzomet and Moledet Parties, and initially also the Likud Party. They strongly rejected the Oslo agreements and a future Palestinian state for the following reasons: ideological convictions regarding Eretz Israel and the unity of Jerusalem under Israeli sovereignty; security concerns regarding Palestinian terrorism as a strategic menace to Israel; and deep apprehension for the fate of the Jewish settlements on the West Bank and the Gaza Strip. Consequently, some of these right-wing groups launched, beginning in late 1993, several attacks against Arabs, initially in reaction to Hamas' attacks; and on Friday, February 25, 1994, Baruch Goldstein, a Jewish settler, massacred 29 Palestinian Muslims at the Tomb of the Patriarchs in Hebron, which includes a mosque. Simultaneously, a concerted campaign against the Labor–Meretz government and its peace policy was initiated by the right-wing groups, while several rabbis issued religious edicts calling on Israeli soldiers to disobey orders to remove Jewish settlements in the territories.[12] In addition, public protests were organized by militant Jews, who heckled and threatened Labor leaders, particularly Prime Minister Rabin. In political rallies he was labeled "traitor" and "murderer" and shown in posters wearing the Nazi SS uniform. This delegitimization may have motivated or encouraged Yigal Amir, a fanatic right-wing Jew, to assassinate Rabin during a peace rally in Tel Aviv on November 4, 1995.

The enormous wave of sympathy for Rabin and support for the peace process in Israel, in Arab countries, and in the international community did not last long. Palestinian enemies of the Oslo process, notably Hamas, continued their efforts to disrupt this process through a series of terrorist actions, which greatly contributed to reversing support of Oslo among Israeli Jews.

Already during 1995, Hamas, triggered by the Hebron massacre, had launched a series of attacks in Israel – in April, July and August – causing many Israeli casualties. The preventive and security measures of the Palestinian Authority (PA) and of Israel could not abort two devastating suicide attacks by Hamas in Jerusalem on February 25 and in Tel Aviv on

March 3, 1996, killing and wounding dozens of Israelis. These attacks were allegedly carried out in revenge for the killing by Israeli agents of Yahya 'Ayyash, the mastermind behind the wave of Hamas suicide bombings against Israel in previous years. But as it happened, these two violent actions had a cumulative effect among the Israeli Jewish public, and influenced the Israeli national election campaign.[13] Many right-wing Israelis accused Arafat of cooperating with Hamas and not fulfilling his commitment to change the notorious Palestinian National Charter.[14]

Binyamin Netanyahu, the Likud leader running against Labor's Pere for prime minister, used these issues in his election campaign and vowed to bring "peace and security" to Israel. Shortly before his election on May 29, 1996. however, Netanyahu did undertake reluctantly to talk to the PLO, and to honor the Oslo Accords, but pledged to implement them in a much slower, "safer" and tougher way than Labor.

Indeed, Netanyahu as prime minister continued the Oslo process at a slow pace, while attempting to drive a tough bargain, particularly regarding the issue of the withdrawal of Israeli troops in Hebron, which was formally settled in January 1997 ("the Hebron protocol").[15] Similarly, he did meet Arafat for the first time only on September 4, 1996, while he made other gestures such as increasing from 25,000 to 35,000 the number of Palestinians allowed to work in Israel (subsequently increased to 100,000), releasing in early 1997 the remaining Palestinian women "terrorists" from Israeli jails, and undertaking to withdraw the army from a further 9 percent of the West Bank (but in fact he did not implement this commitment).

By contrast, however, Netanyahu stated time and again his objection to the establishment of a Palestinian state and to the redivision of Jerusalem, and vowed to continue Jewish settlement activity in Jerusalem, and "Judea and Samaria." Indeed, the new Israeli cabinet lifted the previous administration's ban on new construction of settlements, and adopted measures to limit, if not eliminate, PA activities in East Jerusalem.[16] To demonstrate Israel's determination to maintain control of the eastern part of Jerusalem, in September 1996 Netanyahu ordered the opening of the Hasmonean tunnel near the Temple Mount (*al-Haram al-Sharif*), and in March 1997 started construction of a new Jewish neighborhood on Har Homa (Jabal Abu Ghunaym) on the southeastern outskirts of Jerusalem. These unilateral actions provoked violent reactions and terrorist actions by Palestinians as well as clashes between Palestinian and Israeli troops, causing many deaths on both sides. The Har Homa construction halted the Palestinian-Israeli Oslo process, drew worldwide condemnation of Israel, and considerably worsened Arab–Israeli relations.[17]

Probably in response to American pressure, to Israeli public opinion, and to Egyptian and Jordanian criticism, and possibly realizing Israel's international isolation and diminishing foreign investments, Netanyahu agreed in October 1998 to sign the Wye River Memorandum[18] as a last interim accord before negotiating with the PLO on the Oslo final status issues. But Netanyahu's government implemented only parts of the Wye agreement, under pressure from the ultra-right parties and in anticipation of Israel's national elections on May 17, 1999, alleging the failure of Arafat to fulfill his commitments, and in view of the possible proclamation of a Palestinian state on May 4, 1999 (which in fact was postponed).

Thus, on the one hand, Netanyahu's policy toward the Oslo process revived deep mistrust and anger among many Palestinians. The construction of more settlements, the periodic closures on the West Bank and Gaza, and acts of humiliation, all contributed to decreasing the number of Palestinians supporting the Oslo peace process to less than 60 percent (the highest was 81 percent in June 1996), while greatly increasing the number of those supporting Hamas' violence and terrorism against Israel.[19] On the other hand, however, Netanyahu's "concessions" to Arafat at Wye lost him the support of his right-wing coalition members and led to his defeat in the national elections. On the left side of the political map, many moderate or pragmatic Israelis, Jews and Arabs alike, voted against Netanyahu for the opposite reasons: they have been deeply concerned about the international and regional repercussions of Netanyahu's policies toward the Palestinians. These policies alienated the Clinton administration, the European community, as well as the moderate Arab states, notably Jordan and Egypt, leading to a growing predicament for Israel. Ehud Barak, the new Labor leader, was elected by 56 percent of the voters who expected him *inter alia* to improve relations with the international community and pursue the peace process with Syria and the Palestinians, while withdrawing Israeli troops from South Lebanon.

Barak's and Clinton's Ventures

Similar to Rabin, Barak initially preferred to achieve first an Israeli–Syrian settlement which could be much less complicated and more promising, particularly regarding the solution of the southern Lebanon problem. And similar to the Syrian issue, Barak sought to settle the Palestinian problem in a comprehensive way, not along the Oslo incremental fashion. Yet his first serious discussion with Arafat took place only in September 1999 (in Sharm al-Shaykh) some four months after his election. They agreed on target dates for negotiating the permanent status issues following the full implementation of previous commitments. But similar to the previous agreement, the Sharm al-Shaykh accord was only partly implemented by both sides. Only in July 2000, following the collapse of the Syrian–Israel track, did Barak initiate, with Clinton's encouragement, the Camp David II meeting with Arafat to discuss the final agreement. But Arafat was reluctant to attend the meeting, maintaining that more preparations were needed if a final agreement was to be negotiated.[20] He nevertheless decided to participate in order not to alienate President Clinton, even though he reportedly did not expect to reach a final settlement, particularly on the issues of Jerusalem and the Palestinian refugees.[21] Indeed Camp David II talks failed because of disagreements mainly on these problems, as well as on other issues. Moderating his initial harder positions, Barak agreed to the establishment of a demilitarized Palestinian state on some 90 percent of the West Bank and Gaza, including granting Palestinian sovereignty over the outer Arab suburbs of East Jerusalem. Yet, the inner Arab suburbs, including those in the old walled city, were to be under Palestinian municipal control, but under Israeli sovereignty. Palestinians would enjoy a special status in the Temple Mount/*al-Haram al-Sharif*, such as trusteeship, or even partial or shared sovereignty. Concerning the Palestinian refugee problem, Barak was ready to acknowledge the "right of return" of the refugees to the Palestinian state, and admit tens of thousands refugees in Israel under a family reunification plan and within 5 to 10 years; compensation was to be granted to the Palestinian refugees by international funds.

Contesting Barak's proposals, Arafat and his aides requested that Israel acknowledge the moral and judicial responsibility for creating the Palestinian refugees problem, admit those refugees who would wish to return to their homes inside Israel, as well as pay compensation to all refugees, returnees or non-returnees alike.

On the Jerusalem issue, Arafat demanded Palestinian sovereignty over the entire East Jerusalem, including *al-Haram al-Sharif*, while the Western Wall and the Jewish quarter were to be under Israeli control – but under Palestinian sovereignty. The new Jewish suburbs around Jerusalem built after 1967 could be transferred to Israeli sovereignty in return for other Israeli territories around Jerusalem to be given to the Palestinian state. Other territorial swaps could be made in the West Bank, not exceeding 2 percent beyond the 1967 lines (to include Israeli settlements) in return for the same amount of Israeli land along the Gaza Strip.[22]

Finally, Arafat rejected Barak's request that the framework agreement include a proclamation concerning the end of the Palestinian–Israeli conflict. Yet, despite the failure of the Camp David II Summit[23] and the eruption of the Palestinian Intifada (September 29, 2000), Israeli–Palestinian talks continued, with strong American inducement. A major attempt to bridge the gap took place at the Sharm al-Shaykh Summit between Barak and Arafat on October 16, 2000, but to no avail. Then on December 23, 2000, Clinton met in the White House with Palestinian and Israeli negotiators and put forward his own bridging formula for a final agreement. A Palestinian state was to be created on 94–96 percent of the West Bank and Gaza, with land swaps that would incorporate most Jewish settlers into Israel, while compensating the Palestinians with 1–3 percent of Israeli land. "Jerusalem should be an open and undivided city, with assured freedom of access and worship to all. It should encompass the internationally recognized capitals of two states, Israel and Palestine. What is Arab [in Jerusalem] should be Palestinian. What is Jewish should be Israeli." The Old City would be managed by a special administration. The Muslim and Christian quarters would come under Palestinian sovereignty and the Jewish quarter would be part of Israel. The Armenian quarter would be divided between the two parties in such a way as to allow free passage from the Jaffa Gate to the Western Wall. The Western Wall and the area below the Temple Mount ("the holiest sites of Judaism") would be under Israeli sovereignty, whereas the Palestinians would have sovereignty over the upper levels of the *Haram* which include the two grand mosques: al Aqsa and the Dome of the Rock.

On the problem of Palestinian refugees, Clinton suggested that their right of return should be acknowledged, but implemented in the new Palestinian state including in the lands to be transferred from Israel. While acknowledging the moral and physical suffering of the Palestinians owing to the 1948 war, Israel would admit some of these refugees. The rest would be absorbed in various other countries, while all refugees should receive compensation from the international community. Finally, Clinton pointed out that "any agreement will have to mark the decision to end the conflict, for neither side can afford to make these painful compromises only to be subjected to further demands . . . And the end of the conflict must manifest itself with concrete acts that demonstrate a new attitude and a new approach by Palestinians and Israelis toward each other . . ."[24]

Upon examining Clinton's proposal, it would appear that they tilted toward Barak's positions regarding the issues of Palestinian refugees and Jewish settlement, although not on the status of Jerusalem (to be sure Barak's new position on Jerusalem had been unprecedented in Israeli political history in its boldness and vision, shattering entrenched taboos among Israeli Jews). No wonder then that Barak agreed to Clinton's proposals on the condition that Arafat would accept them, and hoping that a final peace agreement with Arafat would help him to win the forthcoming Israeli elections in February 2001. Arafat, by contrast, was initially critical of Clinton's proposals that "fail to satisfy conditions required for a permanent peace." For example, Clinton's proposal on the Palestinian refugees problem "reflects a wholesale adoption of the Israeli position . . . " and was "problematic" on the *al-Haram al-Sharif*. Consequently, as the Palestinian negotiating team articulated it: "We cannot, however, accept a proposal that secures neither the establishment of a viable

Palestinian state nor the right of Palestinian refugees to return to their homes."[25]

But on January 2, 2001, Arafat met Clinton in the White House and subsequently his spokesman said that the Palestinians "were ready to accept the proposals with conditions, as the basis for further negotiations."[26]

This new Palestinian position apparently facilitated, along with other factors, the last Palestinian-Israeli negotiations before Israel's forthcoming national elections. On January 21, 2001, one day after the departure of President Clinton from the White House, Israeli and Palestinian delegations met at Taba (Sinai, Egypt) under Egyptian auspices. And for six days amidst acts of violence between Palestinians and Israelis in Gaza and West Bank, they conducted "serious and practical talks" mainly on the issues of refugees, security borders and Jerusalem, "taking into account the ideas suggested by President Clinton" and aiming at reaching "a permanent agreement that will bring an end to the conflict between them and provide peace for both people." But "given the circumstances and the time constraints, it proved impossible to reach understandings on all issues despite the substantial progress that was achieved. The sides declare that they have never been closer to reaching an agreement . . . [and] that the remaining gaps could be bridged with the resumption of negotiations following the Israeli elections."[27]

But as we know negotiations have not been resumed following the Israeli elections which, reflecting anti-Palestinian, anti-Oslo and anti-Barak positions, resulted in a major victory for Ariel Sharon, the Likud leader, who has strongly opposed the Labor-led Oslo process. Among the Palestinians too the support of the Oslo process greatly diminished in favor of continued violence against Israeli occupation and Israel itself.[28]

Why Did the Oslo Process Collapse?

The Oslo concept was rather sound under the circumstances of its inception, notably the stalemate in the Madrid negotiations as well as against the background of a century old Arab–Jewish conflict over Palestine/Eretz Israel. And for the initial two years and beyond, it did develop fairly well and scored significant achievements for both sides; preparing the grounds for a final settlement, at least for the eventual creation of a Palestinian state alongside Israel. Alas, since late 1995, following the assassination of Prime Minister Rabin, the Oslo peace process encountered severe obstacles, and finally broke down when the two parties could not agree on the final status issues, particularly on the problems of Jerusalem and the Palestinian refugees.

It may be argued that these two issues cannot be settled in a mutually acceptable way, given the deep-rooted national ethos, historical narrative and political position of Israeli Jews and Palestinian Arabs – which seem to be irreconcilable . If this is the case, peace between the two nations cannot be expected in the foreseeable future, and thus further violence and perhaps war may occur between them. Alternatively a cease-fire may be achieved when both sides are exhausted.

By contrast, it may be also maintained, as concluded by the negotiators in Taba, that "it will be possible to bridge the differences remaining and attain a permanent peace settlement."[29] And that the two sides were unable to reach an agreement, based *inter alia* on Clinton's proposals, owing to time constraints, the departure of Clinton from the White House, the advanced elections in Israel, and, above all, the eruption of the Palestinian Intifada, and the ensuing cycle of violence.

These explanations can be compounded by several more suggestions or evaluations. To begin with, both Palestinians and Israelis have been psychologically unprepared to reach a compromise on these critical issues of refugees and Jerusalem. They have not developed during the Oslo process significant empathy or sensitivity for the concerns, grievances, individual ethos and expectations of each other. Many Palestinians, for example, were not aware of the Israeli–Jewish attachment to the Temple site as a symbol of Jewish theology, history, and nationality. They were not sensitive enough to the Israeli–Jewish fears and frustrations in reaction to Palestinian terrorist actions inside Israel as well as to the continued anti-Israeli indoctrination in Palestinian schools and textbooks.[30] Similarly, many Israeli Jews have not been aware of the Palestinians' deep attachment to East Jerusalem and to *al-Haram al-Sharif*; the fact that most Palestinians were ready to accept a state on merely 23 percent of historic Palestine (the pre-1967 line); of the Palestinians' frustration, bitterness and anger over the building of Jewish settlements on their lands, partly appropriated by Israel, and the personal difficulties of occasional closures, road blocks, collective punishments, economic pressure and personal humiliation by Israeli authorities and soldiers[31] – all of which contributed to the eruption of the Intifada.

Indeed, Israeli and Palestinian leaders did not seriously address the concerns and grievances of each other's people; nor did they, particularly the PA, educate their own public in a positive and constructive way toward peaceful coexistence. They did not do their utmost to systematically prevent, curb, and punish violent actions by extreme elements – Islamic and Jewish alike. Arafat, for example, was for several years rather evasive regarding the abolition of the anti-Israel Palestinian National Charter.[32] Similarly, Arafat was unable or unwilling to prevent the devastating terrorist attacks by the Hamas inside Israel, notably in early 1996.

He would also occasionally release Hamas terrorists from his jails or praise Hamas martyrs.[33]

Israel, on its part, was not always able to stop anti-Arab violence by settlers and occasionally imposed light punishments on settlers who killed Palestinians. For example, following the massacre of 29 Palestinian worshippers in Hebron by a local Jewish settler, Prime Minister Rabin would not use that grave event to remove Hebron's Jewish settlers who had frequently engaged in anti-Arab actions. Furthermore, not only did the Israeli government refrain from removing isolated and provocative Jewish settlements in the West Bank and the Gaza Strip. Since the Oslo agreement of 1993 the number of Jewish settlers' houses and apartments have increased by 52 percent, while the number of settlers rose from 115,000 in 1993 to 200,000 in 2000.[34] Indeed, settlement activities continued also under the premiership of Barak even though he sought to reach a final peace settlement with the Palestinians.

It is true that the Oslo Accords did not provide for the termination of the Israeli settlement activities; but it is equally true that such activities involved appropriating more Palestinian lands while frustrating and angering most Palestinians – Israel's potential peace partners.[35]

In addition, the Israeli government, like the PA, did not fully implement all clauses and commitments of the Oslo Accords. In particular, Israel did not release all Palestinian prisoners and also failed to carry out the agreed military withdrawals from the West Bank, on the plea that the PA had not stood to its commitments regarding arresting Hamas terrorists, disarming this organization and other Islamic groups, and increasing the ranks of its own police (i.e., military) force beyond the agreed numbers.[36]

Indeed, each side sought by and large to maintain its assets or gains as bargaining chips for future negotiations, but with little concern for building confidence and serving a common cause or strategy. Whereas Arafat's strategy was crystal clear – the creation of a Palestinian state along the pre-1967 lines with its capital in East Jerusalem – Israeli leaders did not have a clear or consistent strategy regarding the final settlement. Not only was the Oslo Accord practically imposed by Israel as an open-ended agreement with no commitment for the establishment of a Palestinian state. The four Israeli leaders who served successively as prime ministers from the Oslo breakthrough until its breakdown, articulated different approaches to this issue but were not inclined to create a Palestinian state. All of them preferred to settle first the conflict with Syria. Furthermore, Rabin, Peres, and Netanyahu and initially also Barak vowed to keep Greater Jerusalem – including its Eastern/Arab section – undivided and under Israeli sovereignty "forever." They made this public commitment because it was a central Israeli–Jewish ethos or taboo since 1967. Wishing to be elected or re-elected, these Israeli leaders, particularly the Laborites, possibly lacked the vision or the courage to acknowledge that without the creation of a Palestinian state on roughly the pre-1967 lines with its capital in East Jerusalem, Israel could not bring about an end to its conflict with the Palestinians as well as with other Arab and Muslim nations. Only Ehud Barak, after one year in power and with little public support, dared to break this sacred taboo regarding East Jerusalem as a capital of the future Palestinian state. No doubt this new position reflected leadership, statesmanship, vision and courage; but as a politician, he also realized that only by reaching a final peace settlement with the Palestinians, could he be re-elected as prime minister. By accepting Clinton's far-reaching compromise proposals, Barak possibly aimed also at testing Arafat's real intentions and exposing his strategic positions regarding a final peace with Israel. Alas, as Barak was short of becoming an Israeli De Gaulle, Arafat was certainly not a Palestinian Mandela. He did not rise to this historical occasion to emerge as a great leader and statesman who achieved for his people a sovereign state along roughly the pre-1967 lines with its capital in East Jerusalem, sovereignty in *al-Haram* mosques, and a practical solution for the Palestinian refugees. Arafat possibly missed this historic opportunity, which may not be available again for many years to come. However, it is also possible that Arafat was not yet ready to sign a final settlement with Israel under the given conditions and circumstances. In particular, he was probably unable to agree to Clinton–Barak's "dictation" or proposals regarding the *Haram* and the refugees' "right of return." To be sure, he had not prepared himself and his people, since the inception of the Oslo Accords, to compromise on these core Palestinian narratives. Reportedly, "Arafat himself has challenged core Jewish beliefs, even claiming there never were Jewish Temples on the Temple Mount."[37]

Arafat was apparently unable or unwilling to accept that compromise, especially in the midst of the Intifada which was partly directed against him on account of his corrupt and authoritarian regime and his poor achievements in establishing a sound socioeconomic infrastructure in the PA.[38] Arafat was thus induced to exploit the Intifada, if not to initiate it, in order to repair his somewhat tarnished image as "constructor" for Israel's security in Gaza and the West Bank. He then used the Intifada – which broke out a day after Sharon's provocative visit in the *Haram* – to squeeze more concessions from Israel. He and his aides, impressed by Hizballah's success in driving out the Israeli army from Southern Lebanon, possibly deluded themselves that such a model can be applied also in the West Bank. Or, alternatively, Arafat perhaps calculated that Israel's harsh response to the Intifada would induce the international community to interfere with UN troops and impose a pro-Palestinian settlement.

Conclusion

It is evident, in conclusion, that the violent Intifada, which has claimed many casualties in Israel proper, and Arafat's "negative" reaction to Barak's "concessions," have greatly alienated most Israeli Jews and destroyed their trust in Arafat and in the PA, as well as in the chance to reach peace with the Palestinians. Indeed, like Israel's Chief of Staff, General Mufaz, many Israelis have labeled the PA a "terrorist entity" and believe that the PLO aims again at Israel's destruction.[39]

Similarly, most Palestinian Arabs – their expectations for a sovereign state being shattered – have suffered a great many casualties during the Intifada, as well as economic hardship and restrictions on movement. They also have lost their trust in peace; many have been and are advocating further violence, including suicide bombings in Israel proper.[40] Consequently, not only did the Oslo peace process break down amidst the Intifada, it will certainly take more than a few years to restore trust and revive the peace process between Israelis and Palestinians – either under the title of Oslo, Camp David II, or Taba. For despite their setbacks, the Oslo Accords brought about an historic breakthrough in Israeli–Palestinian relations, namely recognizing one another's political aspirations and agreeing in principle to share the land between the two national communities. Palestinian national institutions were consequently created on parts of Palestine, serving as a nucleus of a future Palestinian state. While fairly good working relations were established between Israelis and Palestinians – in government, economic, and academic circles – the framework for a gradual peace settlement was created but partially applied. And even though the permanent status issues provided by the Oslo Accords were put on the negotiation table fairly late (July 2000), they have become part of the Oslo legacy.

Indeed, Barak, for the first time in Israel's history, broke the "genetic code" of the Arab–Israeli conflict; namely, the sacred taboo on sharing Jerusalem and the Temple Mount with the Palestinians. He also agreed that the Palestinians were entitled to their sovereign state on 95 percent of the West Bank and Gaza. True, most Israeli Jews rejected the Barak–Clinton proposals; while Barak himself – following the failure of the Taba talks – stated that the "ideas examined in Camp David, Washington, and Taba are null and void . . . and . . . do not bind or commit . . . "[41] Nevertheless, these ideas cannot be squashed or ignored by either Israelis or Palestinians, as they have put forward constructive parameters for a genuine and comprehensive peace between the two peoples. However, these ideas and parameters cannot be applied without first producing fundamental changes in the mindsets of both Palestinian Arabs and Israeli Jews. Thus, while drawing lessons from their mistakes and misconceptions during the Oslo process, both sides must educate themselves to understand – even empathize with – the concerns, traumas, fears, historical narratives and national aspirations of one another. Only then can a durable peace and reconciliation be negotiated and achieved[42] between Israelis and Palestinians, Jews and Arabs.

Notes

1 See Mordechai Bar-On, "The Impasse and the Alternative," *Palestine-Israel Journal* VII (324): 19.
2 *The Economist*, April 28, 2001, p. 44. Ze'ev Schiff, *Ha'aretz*, March 28, 2001.
3 See Yossi Beilin, "The Urgency of Constructing Peace," *The New York Times*, April 18, 2001, p. A13. See also below.
4 Text in *Near East Report*, No. 22, October 9, 1995.
5 See Khalil Shikaki, "The Internal Consequenes of Unstable Peace: Psychological and Political Responses of the Palestinians," in *After the Peace: Resistance and Reconciliation*, ed. Robert L. Rothstein (Boulder and London: Lynne Rienner Publications, 1999), p. 34.
6 *Near East Report*, No. 22, October 9, 1995, p. 120.
7 For example, see Sari Nusseibeh, Moshe Ma'oz, and Johannes Gerster, eds., *Is Oslo Alive?* (Jerusalem: The Konrad Adenauer Foundation, 1998).
8 *The Middle East Journal* 50 (4) (Autumn 1996): 583.
9 *Ha'aretz*, February 22, 1996 and March 2, 1996.
10 Asher Arian, *Israeli Public Opinion on National Security 1996* (Tel Aviv: The Jaffee Center, July 1998).
11 *Ma'ariv*, August 1, 1997.
12 Ehud Sprinzak, *The Israeli Right and the Peace Process 1992–1996* (Jerusalem: Davis Occasional Papers, Hebrew University, 1998), p. 11.
13 Don Peretz and Gideon Doron, Israel's 1996 Elections: A Second Political Earthquake?" *The Middle East Journal* 50 (4) (Autumn, 1996): 532ff.
14 *Ason Yadu'a Mirosh: "Heskem Habenayim" ve-sikuneiya shel medina falastinit* (Imminent Disaster: The "Interim Settlement" and the Risks of a Palestinian State) (n.p.: Haforum Habithoni Lehosen Leumi, January 1996).
15 Text in *Journal of Palestine Studies* 26 (3) (Spring 1997): 131–45.
16 "Chronology," *The Middle East Journal* 51 (1) (Winter 1997): 97; *Journal of Palestine Studies* 26 (1) (Autumn 1996): 116–19.
17 "Chronology," *The Middle East Journal* 51 (1) (Summer 1997): 419–22: John Lancaster, "Arab Frustration with Netanyahu's Hard-Line Policies Turn to Anger," *Washington Post*, January 12, 1997.
18 Text, "The Wye River Memorandum" (Jerusalem: Ministry of Foreign Arrairs, October 23, 1998). On the US role see *American Pressure Against the Background of the Peace Process: Reality or Imagination* (Jerusalem: American Jewish Committee, January 22, 1998); The Washington Institute 1998 Soref Symposium, *The Oslo Impasse: Where Do We Go From Here?* (Washington, DC: The Washington Institute for Near East Policy, May 1998).
19 Asher Arian, *Israeli Public Opinion on National Security, 1998* (Tel Aviv: The

Jaffee Center for Strategic Studies, July 1998); *Ha'aretz*, January 4, 1999.

20 See William B. Quandt, *Peace Process* (Washington, DC: The Brookings Institute, 2001), p. 362.

21 '*Adkan Estrategi (Strategic Update,)* 4 (1): 3 (The Jaffee Center, Tel Aviv University, January 2001).

22 *Ibid.*, pp. 4–6; cf. Quandt, *Peace Process*, pp. 363–5.

23 See "Trilateral Statement on the Middle East Peace Summit at Camp David July 25, 2000." *http://www.israel-info.gov.il/mfa/go.asp* MFAHOnn10.

24 Abridged text in *Ha'aretz*, January 8, 2001, based on Reuters. See also Aluf Ben, *Ha'aretz*, December 28, 2000, Quandt, *Peace Process*, pp. 371–2. Full text in http://www2.haaretz.co.il/special/peaceagreement/f/345024.asp.

25 "The Palestinian Position Regarding Clinton's Proposals," *Le Monde Diplomatique*, January 1, 2001.

26 Quandt, *Peace Process*, p. 372.

27 "Taba Talks – Joint Concluding Statement, Saturday, January 27, 2001. *http://www.pna.net/peace/taba_talks.htm.*

28 *Ha'aretz*, November 6, 2000 and February 4, 2001; *Yediot Ahronot*, February 8, 2001; March 30, 2001.

29 See note 27.

30 "Dennis Ross's Exit Interview" by Clyde Haberman, *The New York Times Magazine*, March 25, 2001, p. 39.

31 *Ibid.*; Ze'ev Schiff, *Ha'aretz*, November 24, 2000.

32 Ma'oz, *Middle East Journal*, *op. cit.*, p. 408; cf. Quandt, *Peace Process*, p. 54.

33 See Uzi Benziman, *Ha'aretz*, March 13, 2001; Akiva Eldar, *Ha'aretz*, February 5, 2001.

34 *The Economist*, April 28, 2001, p. 44.

35 See interview with Dr. Saleh Abdul Jawad of Bir Zeit University. *Ha'aretz*, April 3, 2001 and November 14, 2000.

36 *Ha'aretz*, November 24, 2000; Khalil Shikaki in *Palestine–Israel Journal*, *op. cit.*, p. 9. See also the Mitchell Report, *Ha'aretz*, May 6, 2001 and *The New York Times*, May 7, 2001.

37 Dennis Ross, see note 30.

38 Khalil Shikaki, *op. cit.*; see also Interview with Dr. Abdul Jawad, note 34. See also John Kifner, *International Herald Tribune*, November 20, 2000. See also Amira Hass, *Ha'aretz*, February 20, 2001.

39 Meron Benvenisvti, *Ha'aretz*, March 8, 2001; "Peace Index," *Ha'aretz*, January 4, 2001; *Yediot Ahronot*, March 30, 2001; Netanyahu's article in *The New York Times*, February 7, 2001.

40 See "A Palestinian Survey" by Bir zeit University, *Ha'aretz*, February 20, 2001.

41 *Voice of Israel*, March 7, 2001; "Peace Index," *Ha'aretz*, January 4, 2001.

42 For additional analyses and theories regarding conflict and reconciliation see Robert L. Rothstein's contributions in *After the Peace: Resistance and Reconciliation*; Daniel Bar-Tal, "From Intractable Conflict Through Conflict Resolution to Reconciliation: Psychological Analysis," *Political Psychology* 21 (2) (2000): 351–65.

10

The Middle East Peace Process –
Where To?

Ziad Abu Zayyad

First of all I want to make it clear that in this chapter I am speaking in my personal capacity, and not in my official capacity. The issues discussed here do not represent the Palestinian Authority or any official body on the Palestinian side, and thus what I say here are my personal views: they do not commit anybody and they do not represent anybody.

After I had heard my colleagues, I decided to start with a very brief historical background in order to make a few things clear. After the 1948 war, many Palestinians did not accept the results of the war. They refused to accept Israel as a reality. They continued to live with the dream to liberate Palestine and to establish a Palestinian state in all Palestine. They kept that dream, they sought to create a national liberation movement, and they prepared themselves to liberate Palestine. The Fatah was established in 1958 and mobilized the Palestinian masses. Some Arab governments were upset by this development because they thought that the Fatah movement would undermine Arab governments. The late president Jamal Abdul Nasser of Egypt called for an Arab summit and the PLO was established by an Arab league decision in 1964, in order to prevent radical Palestinian groups from gaining more popular influence. Some Arab regimes thought that perhaps the Fatah would be allied with some other political or religious movements and therefore they wanted to limit the influence of that Palestinian movement. However, after the 1967 war, the national movements, including the Fatah, started working from within the PLO, and gradually became it's leadership.

The dream of liberating all Palestine and establishing a Palestinian state in all Palestine did not dominate forever. The Palestinian national movement, mainly after Black September in 1970, realized that the idea of having a state in all Palestine was not accepted either by the Israelis or by the international community. A new gradual pragmatic process began inside the

Palestinian national movement, calling for realism and advocating the two states solution. And that is why, if we look back on the resolutions of the Palestinian National Council, we see that at the very beginning the resolutions speak about the armed struggle as the only way to liberate Palestine. Later, these resolutions spoke about the primacy of the armed struggle but also discussed other means to liberate Palestine. In 1974, after the war between Israel, Syria and Egypt, and influenced by the talk about an international peace conference, the Palestinian National Council (PNC) adopted a resolution stating that the Palestinians would establish a national authority in every part of Palestine which Israel evacuated. In short, Palestinians started to talk about a national authority to be established in territories evacuated by Israel. They wanted to get themselves involved in the political process, which started at that time with the disengagement of forces after the 1973 Yom Kippur war. This pragmatic trend within the Palestinian political thinking continued to evolve throughout the 1970s and 1980s, despite many internal disagreements about strategy and tactics.

The PNC, the Parliament of the PLO, in its session in Algiers in November 1988, publicly accepted the UN's partition Resolution (181) of 1947 and the later resolutions (242 and 338) of 1967 and 1973. This combination between Resolutions 181 and 242 was intended to imply that the Palestinians accepted the principle of partition by dividing Palestine into two states, but we wanted the Israelis to understand that we were committed to Resolution 242, which rejects the acquisition of territory by force. In other words, this acceptance of Resolutions 181, 242, and 338 meant that the Palestinians insisted on a Palestinian state in the West Bank, Gaza and East Jerusalem, territories which were occupied in 1967.

Later, in December 1988, Chairman Arafat held a press conference in Geneva and launched a Palestinian peace initiative based upon the aforementioned resolutions of the PNC. The initiative was described by Shimon Peres at that time as a "cunning maneuver" and that nobody should take Arafat's offer seriously. I believe that this was a missed opportunity because there was a real chance to start talking and working for a peace settlement.

After the Gulf War new factors emerged as main indicators in the determination of Middle East politics. The collapse of the Soviet Union, the divisions and internal conflict in the Arab word, the defeat of Saddam Hussein, and the portrayal of Arafat as an ally of the defeated Saddam were all significant developments. All these factors, as well as others, created a suitable environment to hold an international peace conference.

The Madrid Conference in 1991 was the result of an initiative by US Secretary of State Baker. Immediately after I was released from jail in May 1991 I joined a Palestinian group which was negotiating Palestinian representation with Secretary Baker. We then came to the point when we had to suggest the names of the delegation; we were in direct contact with President Arafat in Tunis about the names. We had a list of 30 people for our delegation to go to Madrid and we consulted Arafat and the leadership on every name. I record that some of the Palestinian members of the delegation were not really negotiators. They were leaders of the Palestinian community who wanted to achieve recognition of their legitimacy with their own constituencies by being named as members of the delegation. We finally reached a consensus on the delegation, which was actually named by and under PLO influence. Everybody knew that the PLO was supervising the negotiating process. The delegation was in constant contact with Mr. Arafat in Tunis and took instructions from him. This fact was known to the Israelis and Americans, but both pretended that it was not so.

Unfortunately, the Madrid process failed. It was obvious from the start that real negotiations could not be conducted in front of TV cameras and microphones. The Likud government planned to drag the negotiations on as long as possible, while continuing its policy of adding more Jewish settlements in the territories and creating facts on the ground to prevent any future withdrawal. It was in these circumstances that the Oslo secret talks were initiated. We had had a problem in the past with the Israeli effort to develop a local leadership in the occupied territories, thus by-passing the PLO, and we in the occupied territories had always insisted that our leadership was the PLO in Tunis with Mr. Arafat as its head. In spite of that, some of our brothers in Tunis were not sure about the loyalty of the Palestinians in the occupied territories and were suspicious of the likelihood of a separate deal with the Israelis – without the PLO. Thus the Tunis leadership wanted to get into the process directly and to guarantee that there would be no chance for anyone from inside the occupied territories to by-pass the PLO and constitute an alternative leadership to the PLO.

I believe that those who did negotiate in Oslo were more flexible in negotiating with the Israeli delegation than any negotiator from inside the occupied territories would have been. I name specifically two issues: the issue of the settlements and the issue of the prisoners.

Why did the Palestinian negotiating team at Oslo not insist on a statement limiting settlement activity? They wanted to be recognized by Israel as the real partner in the peace process, and as such rule out any possibility of an alternative leadership from the occupied territories, such as the delegation which was negotiating in Washington as part of the process established at Madrid. Another issue which the negotiators did not deal with adequately was the prisoners issue, which afterwards caused a lot of criticism inside the Palestinian territories against Oslo. Israel's failure after Oslo to release enough of the political prisoners damaged the Oslo process – it helped to weaken support for it in the Palestinian community. I want to remind you that Menachem Begin, Israeli Prime Minister at the time of Camp David in 1978, accepted a freeze on the building of settlement for six months. In Oslo, the Palestinian negotiators did not achieve anything on this issue and Israel did not agree to make any concessions. The Palestinian negotiators in Oslo also accepted the idea of an interim solution for five years. But they did not think through that the Israeli government and its negotiators might be replaced by another government that would stop the process of the gradual transfer of land, powers, and authority to the Palestinian side.

Furthermore, both sides did not take into account what their domestic opposition would do, whether it was a Palestinian opposition or a Jewish opposition against the Oslo process. Both sides assumed that everything would remain as it was at the time of Oslo, that Rabin would implement the agreement as it was negotiated, the Palestinians would implement the agreement, and in five years there would be a Palestinian state. This assumption proved to be naive and lacked a realistic vision of the future.

Unfortunately, the enemies of Oslo on the Palestinian side implemented a number of suicide attacks against Israeli citizens and these attacks were used by Israelis opposed to the peace process as an excuse to slow down implementation of the terms agreed at Oslo. The public reaction against terrorism made Rabin give up his slogan to fight terror as if there was no peace and implement the peace process as if there was no terror. The Jewish right-wing opposition assassinated Rabin because he was accused of being a traitor who gave the land of Israel to the Palestinians. His assassination brought to power Benjamin Netanyahu who, with right-wing support, put a complete freeze on the peace process.

However, while the Palestinian Authority started a campaign against the Islamic movement, trying to marginalize it or to liquidate it, to prevent any further violence or sabotage of the peace process, Netanyahu's government increased settlement activity, going beyond merely expanding the existing Jewish settlements. The Israelis were intensively and intentionally trying to create as many facts on the ground as possible before peace was imposed on them. It was the mentality of military leaders facing the possibility of the imposition of cease-fire. They behaved as if they were in the last hours of the fight and tried to improve their positions as much as possible to establish a better position before the cease-fire.

The Israeli leaders dealt with the peace process as if they were conducting a war. The Palestinian side witnessed a continued, and intensive campaign of expanding Jewish settlements and constructing bypass roads, a very modern highway network, to link the Jewish settlements to Israel and make them an integral part of Israel. This policy caused an accumulation of frustration, anger, and fear on the Palestinian side. The settlement activity caused severe damage to the peace process and undermined any possibility of its success. The number of settlers in the West bank doubled from 100,000 in 1993 to 200,000 in 2000.

What the Israelis clearly wanted to do was to prevent any possibility of creating a Palestinian state. This was clear from their map of the new settlements as well as from the expansion of the already existing settlements. It was clear that the aim was to prevent or make extremely difficult any future withdrawal, and to rule out any possibility of creating a Palestinian state.

Perhaps they wanted to convince the Palestinians to have a state on paper and not to have it on the ground, to have a state of institutions and symbols but not a reality on the ground. So the Israelis talked about peace, maybe some wanted peace, but at the same time they wanted land and they refused to withdraw from the occupied territories or to annex the occupied territories and give the Palestinian residents equal rights with Israeli citizens. Of course, the Israelis will not accept the principle of annexation because they wanted to take the land but not the population. They want a Jewish state with maximum land but a minimum of Arabs!

And that is why, in 1967, when Israel annexed Jerusalem, they annexed the land and the buildings, but considered the Arab population of the city as a group of Jordanian tourists who entered Israel. They were given a permanent visa that allowed them to reside in Jerusalem, but they were not Israeli citizens. Now, by the same logic, Israel wants to hold onto the West Bank by annexing the territory and taking the land, but they did not want (and still do not want) the population. It has to be asked, Why don't they want the population? Because they want to protect the Jewish majority in Israel and therefore they don't want Arabs. They don't want Arabs to become citizens of Israel.

As a result of this approach the Palestinians gave up their claim for a binational state. They accepted the two states solution, that is, to share Palestine with the Israelis. To divide it between the two peoples. They accepted the 1967 cease-fire lines as borders, giving Israel 78 percent of the total area of pre-1948 Palestine. The Palestinians have demanded in return the right to establish a Palestinian state on the remaining 22 percent – the West Bank, Gaza Strip, and East Jerusalem. But the righ-wing in Israel have resisted this solution and tried to play with figures in a very misleading way. They say, for example, that the Palestinians will have control over 99 percent of their population, but they do not mention that the 99 percent of the population will control less than 40 percent of the land. The core of the conflict between Palestinians and Israelis is the land, not the population.

The same thing happened when we were negotiating recently (the summer of 2000) at Camp David. The Israelis were talking about giving us 95 percent of the land and everybody said, Why do you want more? It is good that they are giving you 95 percent. But people do not realize that it was 95 percent of the 22 percent of pre-1948 Palestine. The Palestinians accept the principle of a two states solution but we want a Palestinian state in all of the West Bank, East Jerusalem and Gaza, which is about 22 percent of the total area of Palestine. The Palestinians were ready to recognize Israel within its borders on the fourth of June 1967, which would have given the Israelis 78 percent of the land. But the Israelis were not satisfied with the 78 percent: they wanted us to forget what happened in 1948 and to act as if the conflict started only in 1967. We were ready to share Palestine with them, but they wanted to share with us the territories occupied in 1967, and not all of Palestine.

Despite all its failures and deficiencies, I still think that Oslo had very substantial positive attributes. One of its achievements was the fact that it brought to a substantial majority of the Israelis and the Palestinians the principle that this conflict would not be solved by war and it was not going to be solved by terrorism and violence. The Palestinians tried for over 30 years all means of armed struggle and sabotage and terror, and it did not change the situation. The Israelis waged wars and used all means of oppression, but finally realized that there is no way that they can make the Palestinians surrender or give up their claim for their homeland.

It is becoming more and more obvious that this is a political conflict that requires a political solution. It is necessary to understand that there is no military solution, something which more and more Israelis, even on the right-wing, have started to realize. The dream of an enlarged land of Israel is not practical anymore. The dream of a Greater Israel ended when Benjamin Netanyahu agreed to implement some articles of the interim agreement, to redeploy troops in the West Bank, and to deliver more territory to the Palestinians.

In spite of this reality, some right-wing Israelis are still trying to settle in the unpopulated areas of the West Bank. They believe that the Palestinians should have control over the Arab-populated areas only. This would not give the Palestinians any reserve lands for natural growth. The rest of the territories should be settled by Jews, according to the right-wing (both secular and religious). They want to offer the Palestinians a kind of self rule for the population, but not the land. The Palestinians insist on the right of self-determination; we want to practice this right in our own sovereign state, and we want to live in that state as neighbors of Israel and in peaceful cooperation with Israel. The outcome of Oslo was supposed to be a state that had built most of its national institutions, yet most of its land is still under occupation.

After Barak was elected as Prime Minister of Israel, I was asked to carry a message from him to President Arafat. The message was short and clear. Barak said that he wanted to assure President Arafat that he was serious and sincere and keen about going ahead with the peace process. All that he wanted was time. He said, don't worry, don't be suspicious, I assure you I will go ahead with the peace process but give me some time to arrange my home base. I carried the message to Arafat, and Arafat recognized that this was a very important message. It took Barak two months to form his government, and then two more months to nominate the head of the Israeli delegation to the peace talks.

He nominated his ambassador in Amman, Jordan, to lead both the interim talks and the final status negotiations. This decision created a negative impression on the Palestinian side. If Barak was really serious and sincere and wanted to go ahead with the process, why was he dealing with it as a part-time job? This was the first negative signal transmitted to us. Later, Barak started talking about combining the third phase of the redeployment agreed to at Oslo with the final settlement negotiations. Barak thus succeeded in undermining the Oslo process because even Netanyahu had implemented (at least partially) some redeployment. The second phase of redeployment wasn't completed by Barak, the third phase wasn't completed by Barak, and he succeeded in diverting attention from the interim arrangements to the final status talks. And when he failed to achieve an agreement on the final status issues, the result was that he was brought down when he lost the elections.

I feel that there is a fundamental difference between the peace concept on the Palestinian side and the Israeli side. Each side understands the process in a different way. For us, we understood that the final aim of the peace process is to put an end to the Israeli occupation, in short that the Israeli army will withdraw from the occupied territories. The framework of the process is UN Resolution 242, which calls for trading land for peace. For the Palestinians, the outcome of the peace process would lead to the establishment of a Palestinian state in the West Bank and Gaza with East Jerusalem as its capital. The Palestinians were ready to establish normal relations with Israel. And to be the bridge that would open the door for Israel to the Arab world.

Normalizing relations between Israel and the Arab world would be the main security guarantee for the existence of Israel. The real answer for Israel's demand for security guarantees is to become an integral part of the Middle East, to be accepted in the Middle East as a natural element in that area. But this cannot be achieved without making a peace agreement with the Palestinians. Israeli withdrawal to the borders of the fourth of June 1967, and the establishment of a Palestinian state, would solve the issue of stability and security in the region.

From the Israeli side, it seems that many of them believe that the peace process is a vehicle for taking more and more land. Their logic was that if we can not achieve the dream of the Greater Land of Israel, let us take as much land as possible, let us diminish the possibility of establishing a viable Palestinian state on our borders, and let us keep the Palestinians under our control. I shall give two examples. In 1947, at the time of the partition resolution, the Palestinians were two-thirds of the population of Palestine and they owned 93 percent of the total area of Palestine. The partition resolution gave them less than 50 percent and at that time they felt that this was unfair, that they should not have to share their country with foreigners coming from Europe. They were not responsible for the crimes of the Nazis and therefore they should not be asked to pay for those crimes. Isn't it unfair that, with two-thirds of the population and most of the land, they are asked to accept less than 50 percent? It is not good to be wise after the event and I myself do not know what I would have decided if I had been living in those circumstances at that time. But I hope you can see Palestinians feel they have been treated unfairly and why it has taken such a long time to accept a settlement that gives us so little.

To return to Camp David, it was true that Barak made a very courageous steps forward by breaking the taboo on Jerusalem. I know that in Israel no one dared to speak about Jerusalem as an issue to be negotiated or as a city to be shared or divided. Barak was courageous for doing that. He brought to the Israeli street the possibility of talking about sharing Jerusalem or withdrawing from parts of Jerusalem and giving the Palestinians, the Arab neighbors in Jerusalem, some share of the whole city of Jerusalem.

Although these were positive steps, at the same time what Barak suggested in Camp David and Taba did not come to the minimum that the Palestinian leadership could accept and sell to its people. From the Palestinian perspective, this is a national struggle and the rights of our people in Palestine belong also to the coming generations; we do not have the right now to accept something that would be rejected by coming generations. The Palestinians seek a settlement that guarantees stability in the region. We do not want to make an agreement that will collapse after five years or ten years. Therefore what Barak offered was not acceptable: his proposals did not present a good basis for any deal. This was especially the case with regard to proposals about sovereignty over the *al-Haram al-Sharif*, where Barak's proposals clearly angered the Palestinian people, not to mention Moslems all over the world.

Again, when Barak spoke of the Jewish settlements it was suggested that the Israelis would give 95 percent of the land and they would evacuate about fifty thousand settlers. But this offer was deceptive because Barak was really only ready to remove some of the small, tiny settlements in the West Bank, and at the same time to double the size of the settlements in the Jerusalem area and in the block of settlements close to the Green Line (the cease-fire line of 1948).

From the Palestinian perspective, what could we as negotiators tell our people when they see the Jewish settlements expanding and growing all the time? What can we tell them if, as a result of the peace agreement, the size of the Jewish settlements will actually grow substantially? They will inevitably ask, Is this the best deal that you can make with the Israelis? We cannot convince Palestinians to accept a deal when they see the negative results on the ground in front of them.

At the same time the Palestinians who raised the issue of the right of return of Palestinian refugees to Israel itself have misrepresented this demand and failed to understand what it would mean for the Israelis. Because if you insist that 3.5 million Palestinians will return to Israel, this would mean that Israel would lose its Jewish majority and not be a Jewish state anymore. The message that the Israelis got from the negotiations over the right of return caused much confusion and fear on the Israeli side. I believe that it is possible to make a deal on the issue, without raising fears on the Israeli side about the real intentions of the Palestinians. I am worried that after the issue was raised in the negotiations, Palestinian people in the territories and the refugee camps began to talk about the right of return, holding marches and taking part in demonstrations over the issue. I wonder if there will be a time in the future, when there will be a chance for a new agreement, when we will be unable to rationalize or justify to our people what sacrifices we have had to make on the right of return issue.

Where shall we go from here? First of all, I think it will be a catastrophe if the Israelis accept the idea of unilateral separation. We hear some Israelis talking about a unilateral separation between Israel and the occupied territories. Unilateral separation, if it were to be decided only by Israel, means that Israel would annex huge areas of the West Bank and would decide unilaterally where they want to keep their army and how they want to deal with the rest of the occupied territories. This would invite a very strong, extreme reaction from the Palestinians. Therefore, I think that the Israelis must think very carefully about the political costs of unilateral separation and its impact on stability and on future negotiations.

The situation on the ground is that during the current Intifada, the influence of the radicals and the Islamic movement on the Palestinian side has increased. Remember that as a result of Oslo the idea grew on both sides that the only way forward was though a political deal. Arafat was leading a productive peace process and the power of the radicals on the Palestinian side was weak. Some of the leaders of the radical groups even sought ways to work within the framework of the peace process. Now, after the failure of the process, there is a growing influence of these radical organizations, mainly in the power of Hamas. If this trend continues, and especially if there is a unilateral separation by Israel and a continued policy of repression and humiliation inside the occupied territories, we shall all face a difficult future. It will be especially difficult to regain the momentum of the early years of Oslo.

Some Palestinians argue that, whatever happens, we have to realize and

157

understand that it is only through negotiations that we can make peace with the Israelis. There is another group that says that this is a historical conflict, a historical struggle, and we should not give up. This perception is that Palestinians should not look on this struggle in terms of the coming months or years. They believe that the main weapon is to try to destroy the internal feeling of security within Israel and through that policy to defeat Israel. If this view becomes dominant, we can expect more and more violence and bloodshed until ultimate victory. But I believe that the vast majority of the Palestinians believe in a political solution. They do not identify themselves with those who think that it is only by causing damage to the internal feeling of security of Israeli society that Palestinians can achieve their goal. I believe that the majority of Palestinians support the idea of negotiating a political compromise, a political settlement with the Israelis. They still believe, in spite of all that has happened, in spite of the current difficult situation, that peace is possible. But those people who still believe in the possibility of peace talks need a partner. Without a partner on the Israeli side, they can do nothing.

The question at the moment is how Mr. Sharon will behave during the coming months – What signals and what messages will he send to the Palestinian side? Another question is how the new administration in the United States will deal with the peace process and the problems in the Middle East. How will they approach it? What position will they take regarding it? To those who said that it is only by direct negotiations between the Israelis and the Palestinians that an agreement can be reached, I must reply that this is not a negotiation between equals. We were not and are not an equal partner to the Israelis, we are the weak side of this equation. If the Palestinians are left alone with the Israelis, we would not make any deal because the Israelis would try to dictate a settlement upon us and the Palestinians will not accept a dictated settlement. Therefore, there would be no chance for any real progress in the negotiations. Thus, I believe that there must be a fairer party, a neutral third party, that can take the initiative and use its influence to convince the two parties to come to an agreement. It seems to many people now that reaching a final agreement will be very difficult, not to say impossible; therefore it is much easier to seek only an interim agreement, leaving the door open for final agreement later. The danger in this approach and any interim agreement is that the facts on the ground change all the time. If we want to guarantee that there will be a real peace process, guarantees have to be in place that the situation will not change on the ground. In other words, Israeli settlement activity is undermining any chance of making peace. Any talk about an interim arrangement must guarantee that the Israelis will totally freeze any activities in expanding Jewish settlements in the Palestinian territories. This then, is the main condition: there should be guarantees from the very beginning about Jewish settlement activity before peace talks can be resumed. All sides must also take measures to calm down the situation and bring back confidence, especially to the Palestinian people that negotiations can be productive and could bring real peace. The principle of freezing settlement activity in the Israeli settlements applies also to Jerusalem. Israel has to stop this process of Judaizing of Jerusalem. Since 1967 the Israelis have been trying to increase the number of Jews in East Jerusalem, to decrease the number of Arabs in East Jerusalem, and to build Jewish neighborhoods around Jerusalem. Without stopping all these settlement activities inside and around Jerusalem there will be no chance for any interim arrangement. The Israelis have to accept the freeze and also to stop the application of the Law of Return, because applying the Law of Return, which means any Jew, anywhere in the world, can become a citizen of Israel, undermines long-term stability. This law creates a major threat for the Palestinians and is a dangerous measure against them. Therefore, within the framework of a peace agreement, the Israelis have to agree to stop settlement activity and freeze the Law of Return. Under the umbrella of this law, Israel brought back about 300,000 Russian Jews – three hundred thousand new immigrants who are now Israelis. If this number was allowed to the Palestinians, I think it could have contributed much to solve the dispute over the Right of Return of the Palestinians.

Palestine is a small country. Israel is a small country. In the end, Palestinians and Israelis have to live together. And the way to live together could go through two tracks: First, either through the establishment of two states until at the end they become a sort of confederation or federation. I do believe that the two states cannot continue to live separately from each other. Second, the other way to integrate the Palestinians and the Israelis could be through violence because, with the Israelis insisting on having Jewish settlements in the Palestinian occupied territories, there will be a time in the future that there will be no area within which to establish a Palestinian state and, at the end, the conflict would become a violent communal conflict between Arabs and Jews. Altogether the number of Arabs in the West Bank, Gaza, and Israel itself is over four million. The number of Jews is between 4.5 and 5 million. In 10, 15 or 20 years, the number of Arabs will be more than the number of the Jews.

Perhaps we need a Palestinian Mandela to lead the Palestinian Arab majority in the geographical area of Palestine into a bi-national state. If the Israelis insist on keeping the Jewish settlements in the occupied territories, they will contribute to putting an end to the Zionist movement and contribute to the establishment of a bi-national state in Palestine. So, at the end, I think that the Israelis and Palestinians have to live together either in two states developing special relations between themselves or in one state created as a result of the continued policy of occupation and settlements.

If both sides embark on the process of trying to make peace, and if some interim agreements about freezing settlements and population changes in Jerusalem are worked out, and if measures are taken to calm the situation, peace still remains possible. The Palestinians have to start giving clear signals to the Israelis about their intentions, about their desire to build democratic institutions and civil society. The Israelis in turn need to come to understand that they have a responsible and reliable partner for peace.

11

A Fragile Peace: Are There Only Lessons of Failure?

Robert L. Rothstein

The Oslo Accords were controversial from the start. The Israeli right rejected Oslo because they felt too much had been given away (or at least put on the table) and the Palestinian left and the Islamic fundamentalists rejected it because not enough had been gained and/or the ancient goal of destroying Israel could not be surrendered. The controversy deepened as the process of implementation faltered and then dissipated under a hail of charges and recriminations: of mutual bad faith, of insincerity and duplicity, of turning the peace into a new means of carrying on the war – the list, unfortunately, could go on. Indeed, by the time that the al-Aqsa Intifada broke out in the autumn of 2000 "true believers" in the Oslo process were few and far between on both sides and the numbers who were willing to call Oslo a "monumental blunder" (Yossi Ben-Aharon) were on the rise.

This seems to imply that Oslo was a "bad" peace agreement, a peace that increased the probability of a return to violence and made it even more likely that the next attempt to jump start a peace process would be endangered. But, as I have already noted (pp. 1–3), while the peace agreements that begin the process of ending a protracted conflict are bound to be flawed, incomplete and fragile, the descent into renewed and even more bitter conflict is not inevitable or foreordained. Oslo has turned out to be a bad peace but it need not have descended as far as or as rapidly as it has. There is no doubt that the form that the Accords took created problems in the post-Oslo years (a point to which I shall return), but Oslo was a product of its times: distrust and suspicion were rife, both leaders were constrained by domestic weaknesses, and neither was willing (or perhaps able) to attempt a high risk/high gain strategy (like Camp David I) – a "big bang" negotiation to resolve all the central issues at once. Nevertheless, while the implementation process was bound to be fraught, leaders on both sides failed miserably in the task of transforming an exploratory truce into a genuine peace process.

Still, while it is easy to bemoan the absence of strong leadership (Arafat and Netanyahu are not Mandela and de Klerk) – it may be more important to ask whether leaders in such conflicts are only rarely strong because they have been weakened by their inability to win the war or negotiate a bearable compromise. One question leads to another: not whether leaders have failed in implementation but why they have done so. (For an attempt to answer this question, see pp. 10–12.)

Criticisms of one or another aspect of the Oslo peace process have been rampant. This is hardly surprising but what is surprising is another judgment that is widely – but not unanimously – shared: the results of Oslo have been profoundly disappointing to both sides but, despite this, Oslo has had a serious and lasting effect on the conflict between Israelis and Palestinians. Ma'oz perhaps expresses this most vividly when he declares that Oslo broke the "genetic code" of the conflict in that it now became possible and necessary to discuss – face to face – the central issues: land, borders, settlements, the right of return, the Temple Mount/*al-Haram al-Sharif*. It even became possible and necessary to think about the unthinkable, about what one could or could not compromise and what price one was willing to pay for peace. None of this, of course, means that agreement on the issues will be achieved but it does mean that new questions are being asked, old beliefs are being (at least tentatively) reassessed, and the inevitable resumption of negotiations will be heavily affected by what was discussed and provisionally agreed to in the earlier rounds of negotiation after September 13, 1993. Oslo has not brought peace but it has altered the cognitive landscape in potentially important ways.

Oslo and Its Critics

Why were the opportunities, as limited and uncertain as they may have seemed, not grasped? There is no single or simple answer to this question and the answer (or answers) are likely to be as complex as the evolving situation on the ground. All of the explanations proffered seem to have part of the truth, but none suffices by itself, and we should not assume – although some clearly do – that one side or the other is relatively more responsible for the downward slide. There is guilt aplenty for both sides: it could be fairly argued that neither made a genuine commitment to the peace process and neither understood (or even seemed to care about) what needed to be done to strengthen an inherently fragile peace process.

The Nature of the Oslo Accords

Oslo was not a victor's peace but it was also not an equal peace. Israel was clearly the stronger party not only in terms of military, economic and political power, but also because Arafat had been badly weakened by his support for Saddam Hussein's brutal invasion of Kuwait and the resulting loss of financial support from the Gulf states. He had also achieved none of the PLO's goals and was facing increasing disaffection within the Palestinian community, especially the "inside" in Gaza and the West Bank. In this context, while the Oslo Accords guaranteed nothing about whether or how the central substantive and symbolic issues would be resolved in the future, they did provide Arafat and the PLO with crucial gains: recognition as legitimate and official representatives of the Palestinian people, promises of substantial amounts of foreign aid, and – perhaps above all – regular access to the White House.[1]

Perhaps this kind of agreement was the most that was possible at the time. But an agreement that delayed discussion of crucial issues until the future contained the seeds of its own failure (see chapter 10 by Ziad Abu Zayyad). It is hard to build a constituency for peace when the shape of the peace remains unclear and unsettled. This put a tremendous burden on the early years of the peace process: Palestinian support, which was initially fairly high, could be sustained only if the peace brought tangible and significant gains quickly; Israeli support, which was also initially favorable (hopeful, if skeptical), could be sustained only if the security situation seemed to improve and if Arafat seemed willing to comply with the terms. In the event, both communities were disappointed: standards of living deteriorated as foreign aid was dissipated on salaries for the security forces and bureaucracy that Arafat created or wasted through corruption or misused for secret spending on arms imports; and the Israelis were outraged by brutal terrorist attacks during the Peres–Netanyahu campaign and by increasing doubts about Arafat's sincerity.[2] Whatever cognitive legitimacy the peace process might have had was thus rapidly dissipated and any peace process without increasing cognitive legitimacy among the public at large is bound to remain a thin and top-down process.

There is a paradox here worth considering. It seems quite likely that there would have been more Palestinian support for Oslo if the initial agreement contained some outline of the contours of a settlement of at least some of the central issues. For example, there might have been an agreement on the creation of a Palestinian state with defined borders and a capital in East Jerusalem, but to be approached gradually and after Palestinian compliance with obligations to control violence and terrorism – an instance of what I have called "incrementalism plus." The paradox is that this kind of

163

strong commitment was impossible because of the distrust, ambivalent promises, and domestic weaknesses that prevailed during and after the initial negotiations. What needed to be done could not be done and the issues left for later continued to recede into the distance as the peace process deteriorated. This seems to imply that, while Oslo was a deeply flawed agreement, it was the only game in town and it did generate some opportunities that were there to grasp or to provide building blocks for later peace efforts. We shall discuss momentarily why they were not grasped – indeed were thrown away because the risks of peace seemed greater than the risks of renewed conflict.

A slightly different argument about the Accords and their virtual collapse might also be made. From this perspective, the incomplete nature of the original agreement and the subsequent clashes (especially at Camp David II) over key issues merely revealed an underlying conflict of interests that was clearly revealed by, not resolved by, the negotiating process (see chapter 3 by Khalil Shikaki). As bargaining theorists would say, there was no "contract zone" in the negotiations and thus Camp David II and the later talks failed because they were too ambitious. In effect, only temporary truces are possible because there is no agreement on mutually bearable compromises; the conflict must go on until a clear winner emerges; and Oslo itself was thus driven not by a common vision of peaceful coexistence but by a desire for a peace process – which could bring real gains – but not a compromise peace.

This view has gained more and more converts in the past nine or ten months. Arafat's decision to use violence and terrorism to pursue goals that he could not get at the negotiating table destroyed his credibility with the Israelis and generated increasing domestic pressure for severe retaliation; conversely, the Israeli tactics against the violence generated more hatred and bitterness among the Palestinian people, thus fueling more and more extreme demands to compensate for the losses endured. Palestinian demands have gone up as Israeli willingness to make concessions has gone down and (November 2001) it is no longer clear that Arafat can stop the violence if he in fact wants to stop what is clearly a popular response to Israeli control. Still, while this view may have gained popularity recently, it is far less convincing as an explanation of earlier events. In fact, both participants in and close observers of the Camp David negotiations with President Clinton and the last gasp negotiations at Taba believe that they were tantalizingly close to real agreement on all of the final status issues and that there had been real movement by both sides. If so, an extraordinary opportunity may have been wasted and it may be some years before a similar opportunity again arises. In any case, in response to the argument that no contract zone ever existed, we can at least say that there is some reliable testimony that a contract was much closer than the naysayers can believe.

Failures of Implementation

Extremists on both sides believe that victory is the only acceptable option. The other side must either be destroyed or forced to live as dependent vassals of the winner (see chapter 6 by Mustafa Abu Sway). Everyone else, for the most part, believes that failures in implementation bear a major part of the responsibility for Oslo's decline. The Palestinians are united in their belief that the Israelis were the major culprit (failing to meet deadlines, failing to release prisoners, failing to turn over revenues to the Palestinian Authority, etc.). The Israelis are more divided with the peace wing (Ron Pundak, Moshe Ma'oz) willing to criticize Israel's implementation policies but more judicious in spreading the blame around, and the rejectionists (Yossi Ben-Aharon) largely blaming Arafat and doubting his sincerity about peace.

The exchange of charge and countercharge is not very useful or illuminating. To this observer, it seems as if neither side made a strong commitment to the peace process and each used the other's transgressions as a justification for its own: the result obviously was a race to the bottom that does not seem to have ended (as of November 2001). The more important question is why this happened. Even objective analysts (who the postmodernists tell us do not really exist) can disagree about the answer to this question. It seems to me at least arguable, however, that the interaction of a number of key factors was primarily responsible for turning Oslo into an empty shell.

One factor we have already noted. The Accords provided no guarantees about the future and in an environment still dominated by pervasive distrust and festering grievances, it would have been very risky – a leap of faith – for weak leaders to implement commitments, especially when there was so much doubt that the other would or could reciprocate. In effect, cheating was rational. Weak leadership was another factor: for different reasons, leaders on both sides lacked a strong mandate to make the kind of painful sacrifices that a stable peace would require. Whether matters would have been different if Rabin had survived or Peres had been re-elected in 1996 with strong support for peace is an unanswerable question. A third factor was the unfortunate deterioration in standards of living among the Palestinians in the West Bank and Gaza, a compound result of disastrous policies by Arafat's new regime (incompetence, corruption, and foreign aid wasted on salaries or illegal arms purchases, etc.), Israeli border closures after every terrorist incident, and heavy-handed policies by Israeli forces at various border crossings. For the Palestinian people the peace dividend was non-existent and the petty humiliations of Israeli rule continued. Finally, failure bred failure: terrorist incidents leading to retaliation leading to terrorist incidents, etc. Support for peace, which was always thin and volatile, rapidly eroded and a syndrome of linked failures led to an even more bitter return to conflict. A weak and fragile peace was turned into a bad peace.

Domestic Politics

Domestic politics always plays a role in peace settlements, if in large part because the original top-down agreement needs collective legitimization by the public at large. Without the support of public opinion the leader who has risked signing an agreement will usually face challenges from dissident leaders – thus forcing ever more extreme options and hard-line bargaining strategies – or even the outright loss of the leadership (see chapter 4 by Avraham Diskin and chapter 7 by Ron Pundak). Public opinion is only one of many ways, of course, in which domestic politics intrudes on the peace process but it deserves special emphasis in the present context.[3]

Since neither leader had a strong coalition for peace and since the support that did exist was tinged with strong degrees of skepticism, the leaders became equally ambivalent and the peace process never became deeply rooted. In these circumstances, if something had to be sacrificed it would be the integrity of the peace process. Each side was more focused on the domestic audience (the audience that kept one in power) or the external audience (that provided aid and status) than the party across the bargaining table. Since the domestic audience has been further radicalized by the renewed cycle of violence and retaliation, the near-term prognosis for the peace process is grim. In addition, since neither leadership made the slightest effort to educate their followers about the need for peace, the benefits it might bring, and the new attitudes that it required, attitudes and beliefs remained firmly fixed on an ethos of conflict.

In such circumstances the call for new and better leadership has been heard regularly in the media. However, it does not figure greatly amongst those closely involved, perhaps because there is no obvious or superior alternative to Chairman Arafat and because the likely alternative to Mr. Sharon may be Mr. Netanyahu. Thus there is a tacit sense that speculations about new leaders may only distract from the matter at hand: restarting a peace process with the leaders we have, not the ones we would like to have. Still, personal variables have been so consequential in the peace process that it might be interesting to at least speculate about the qualities that are important in effective leadership. We might speculate here that effectiveness is a function of opportunity, power, motivation and skill, with power being defined here as control over a sufficiently broad and deep domestic constituency and sufficiently strong influence over crucial external patrons.

(Perhaps one ought to add credibility as another important variable but, since it does not change outcomes here, I will leave it aside.) We could then rank order these variables in terms of high, mixed and low, producing the following matrix:

	Opportunity	Power	Motivation	Skill
High	O, CD		O	
Mixed		CD	CD	O
Low	P	O, P	P	CD, P

If we try to illustrate the implications of this for Chairman Arafat, we could assess his score at Oslo (O), at Camp David with President Clinton (CD), and at the present time (P). If we score 1 for a high ranking, 2 for a mixed, and 3 for a low, Arafat scores a 7 at Oslo, an 8 at Camp David, and a 12 in the current situation. To illustrate, opportunity and motivation were high for Arafat at Oslo, skill was mixed, and power was low; conversely, all four variables are low at present. In short, in terms of effectiveness in influencing the other side and achieving goals, Arafat's score has gotten progressively worse.[4] Turning this around will require either new or better leadership, a very rapid learning process for an old leader with experiences, beliefs, and attitudes that might be more appropriate for carrying the conflict on, or very strong pressures from important external sources of support.

Third Party Intervention

There has been a prevalent assumption that a relatively unbiased third party may be indispensable in brokering any agreement between profoundly distrustful enemies. This was clearly not true for the original Oslo agreement but it has been true in most other cases. The third party can obviously bring some crucial assets to the bargaining game, including financial resources, the ability to offer guarantees or peace-keeping forces, and some political cover for leaders facing the need to justify painful sacrifices.

Perhaps one reason there was not more focus on this issue was the fact that President Clinton's last direct intervention at Camp David was not only unsuccessful but also left both sides unhappy: the Palestinians because Clinton clearly (and publicly) blamed Arafat for the failure and the Israelis because some of the provisions of his last plan (especially on Jerusalem) were considered unworkable. This episode illustrated one of the potentially negative aspects of third party intervention: the third party may have its own agenda, its own timetable, and its own problems.[5] In any case, while the US will be and is indispensable in any negotiating process in the Middle East, the widespread perception of a negative impact at Camp David –

which is certainly at least partially unfair – has at least had the beneficial impact of making one point clear to both Israelis and Palestinians. This is that they themselves will have to make the peace and sustain the peace, with the help of, but not dictation from, the US and other external supporters. Still, there is general agreement that Oslo did not fail because of any sins of omission or commission by the US.

The Nature of Protracted Conflict

I argued earlier that there was a deeper level of explanation for the failure of the Oslo process. I do not want to repeat or summarize those arguments here, but a brief comment may be useful. To end conflicts in which distrust, if not hatred, has been and continues to be pervasive and where there is no way to guarantee that the other is either able or willing to implement commitments and where the risks of peace seem greater than the risks of a familiar and (usually) bearable return to the patterns of the past guarantees a fraught and fragile peace process. In these circumstances, the fears, the ambivalent behavior, the frequent charges and countercharges of duplicity and failure to comply with terms are not and should not be considered as surprising or aberrant. They are, in short, "what comes naturally" and if one or both sides fail to understand this, or have inflated expectations about the other's behavior or, above all, do not try to build into the peace process mechanisms to try to deal with or ameliorate the inevitable "shocks," the peace will deteriorate rapidly – as Oslo attests. One hopes, of course, that with substantial support from abroad, the growth of awareness about the benefits of peace, a benign learning process among both leaders and the public, and a little luck, the shocks will gradually dissipate. Note that none of these things happened during the Oslo process.

This is not the forum to suggest how some new mechanisms might be developed, but it is clear that the process of implementation could be usefully strengthened if mechanisms were institutionalized that required cooperation to produce joint benefits. Many useful steps are familiar from the literature on conflict resolution (see chapter 8 by Manuel Hassassian) but others may require some innovation and cross-fertilization. Thus interesting things might be learned about how to deal with apparently indivisible issues (say, the Temple Mount/al-Haram al-Sharif dispute) by looking at some of the new literature on equity bargaining.[6] And one might look more closely at the literature on the utility of second-track negotiations or even "pre-negotiations." One might also look at other peace processes (Northern Ireland, South Africa, Dayton, for example) to get some hints about how to build effective joint institutions. Finally, one might investigate the possibility of devising new approaches to bargaining in which working out rules of coexistence are more important than winning a greater share of the pie – or even merely increasing the size of the pie, as beneficial as that might be. Obviously, none of these approaches guarantees peace but breaking through to stable peace after a long and bitter conflict is bound to be a multidimensional project that will require multiple and persistent efforts in a variety of areas.

Notes

1   There are some observers who argue that Oslo actually saved Arafat, a decision (presumably) made knowingly by the Israeli government because it wanted a strong leader to stop terrorism and the use of violence. Moreover, both then and now there was no apparent alternative to Arafat – a factor he has used to his political advantage. Still, since the Palestinian people did not benefit from the Oslo process, it can safely be said that Arafat and his supporters in Tunis were the biggest winners from Oslo.

2   Another factor that angered the Palestinian people was the continued presence of Israeli troops and the heavy-handed and petty harassments inflicted by these troops at border crossings. Frequent border closures were also a major aggravation, although since these occurred after terrorist incidents it is difficult see what the alternative could be.

3   Another key factor was that leaders on both sides had to play coalition tactics and were always under threat of key defections. This not only slowed the negotiating process, but also forced leaders toward more hardline policies then they might have preferred.

4   I have done this only illustratively here and it should be noted that some Israeli leaders might have similar scores – or worse.

5   It is clear that President Clinton and then Prime Minister Barak pushed Arafat too hard too soon – as Arafat himself had warned them. Whether giving Arafat more time would have changed matters greatly is unclear, especially given the fact that both Clinton and Barak had so little time in office left.

6   For example, see H. Peyton Young, *Equity – In Theory and Practice* (Princeton: Princeton University Press, 1994).

Contributors

Mustafa Abu Sway, Professor and Director of the Islamic Research Center, Al Quds University, is an eminent authority on the Islamic position on the Arab–Israeli conflict.

Yossi Ben-Aharon, as Israeli ambassador and former Deputy Director General of the Foreign Ministry, has been involved in the key Arab–Israeli negotiations of the 1980s/1990s.

Abraham Diskin, formerly Chairman of the Political Science Department at the Hebrew University of Jerusalem, was advisor to several Israeli prime ministers, the Ministry of Foreign Affairs, and the Knesset.

Manuel Hassassian is Professor of International Relation and Executive Vice-President of Bethlehem University. He has been extensively involved in the peace process (now as Head of the Jerusalem Task Force).

Aaron D. Miller was Deputy Special Middle East Coordinator for Arab-Israeli Negotiations at the State Department; he has served as an advisor to four Secretaries of State, and has helped formulate US policy on the Middle East.

Ron Pundak played a decisive role in the secret track of unofficial negotiations that culminated in the Oslo Accords, and advised on the blueprint for Final Status Negotiations.

Robert L. Rothstein is Harvey Picker Professor of International Relations at Colgate University. He recently edited *After the Peace: Resistance and Reconciliation,* the product of an earlier Colgate conference on peace processes in several major conflicts.

Moshe Ma'oz is Professor Middle Eastern Studies and Senior Research Associate of the Truman Institute, The Hebrew University of Jerusalem.

Contributors

Ziad Abu Zayyad is Minister of Jerusalem Affairs of the Palestinian National Authority. He is co-editor and founder of the *Palestine–Israeli Journal of Politics, Economics and Culture*, and has been involved in almost all of the Palestinian–Israeli negotiations in the last decade.

Khalil Shikaki is Associate Professor of Political Science and Director of the Palestine Center for Policy and Survey Research in Ramallah. He is widely quoted on public opinion, Palestinian Authority governance, and Israeli–Palestinian second-track negotiations.

Index

Abu Ala (Ahmad Qurie), 41, 93, 108
Abu Mazen (Mahmud Abbas), 41, 105–6,
 108, 136
Academic cooperation, 121–2, 128–9, 130–1
Al-Aqsa Intifada, 38, 44, 88, 111, 127
Al-Husseini, Haj Amin, 47
Al-Qaeda, x–xiv
Arab countries and the peace process, 66,
 117–18, 122–3
Arafat, Yasser, vii–ix, xi–xv, 9, 11–12,
 26 *n*25, 27 *n*31, 27 *n*37, 61, 63, 70–1, 86,
 100, 108, 126, 127, 133, 134, 141–2, 145,
 155–6, 164
Asymmetry of power, 32–3, 95, 115, 119,
 158

"Bad Peace," 1–3, 161–2
Barak, Ehud, 12, 14, 41, 50, 54, 55, 56, 69,
 70, 88–9, 98–110, 126, 127, 139–42, 145,
 154–5
Begin, Menachem, 92, 152
Beilin, Yossi, 92, 93, 103, 110, 136
Ben-Gurion, David, 89–90, 98, 116
Benefits of Oslo to Arafat, 18
Benefits of peace *see* Oslo Accords
Bin Laden, Osama, x–xv
"Big Bang" versus incremental negotiating
 strategies, 15–16, 23–4
 See also Protracted Conflict

Camp David I (1978), 15, 35, 51, 152
Camp David II (2000), 12, 14, 15, 37, 38,
 39, 42, 107–8, 133, 140, 153–4, 156
Civil society and peace-building, 120–2,
 128, 130
Clinton, Bill, 12, 23, 69, 70, 74, 107, 126,
 133, 134, 139–42, 167
Confidence-building measures, 103
Conflict between democracy and Judaism,
 48
Conflict resolution *see* Protracted conflict
Conflictive ethos, 4, 23

Dayton Agreement, 19–20
Declaration of Principles *see* Oslo Accords
Demilitarization of Palestinian state, 40, 43
Domestic politics of peacebuilding, 8–12,
 41–2, 103–4, 166–7
 See also Oslo Accords; Protracted
 conflict

Educational process, 10, 36, 143–4
 See also Protracted conflict
"El Naqba" (The Disaster), 91
Empathy, absence of, 4, 14, 21
Enemy image, 50
Europe and the peace process, 123–4
Existential conflict *see* Protracted conflict
Existential security threat to Israel, 24, 48

Failures in implementation *see* Oslo
 Accords
Fatah, 44, 66, 111, 149
Future of Oslo peace process *see* Oslo
 Accords
Gaza–Jericho Agreement, 61–2, 65, 96
"Gresham's Law" of conflict, 5
 See also Protracted Conflict

Hamas, 44, 65, 67, 84, 85, 86, 112, 137–8,
 157
Haram al-Sharif (Temple Mount), 16, 43,
 44, 72, 109, 133, 140
"Hawks and Doves," 50, 51

Incremental strategies, 15
"Incrementalism plus," 15, 163
International monitors of agreements, 46
Islamic fundamentalism, 67, 82, 157
Islamic Jihad Movement, 65, 67, 82
Islamic perspectives on Oslo, 78–87
Israeli Arabs, 49, 50, 52
Israeli attitudes toward Palestinians, 96–7,
 102, 117, 136, 146
Israeli domestic politics, 54–7, 103–4, 120
Israeli negotiating tactics, 72–3

Index

Israeli policy after September 11, xiii–xiv
Israeli political parties, 54–7
Israeli–Palestinian attitudes toward each
    other, 38, 45, 95
Israeli support for Oslo Accords, 12, 51,
    163, 166
Israeli–Syrian peace process, 34, 35, 36,
    101–2, 139–40

Jerusalem issue, 35, 42, 43, 71–2, 109, 140,
    141, 142

Labor Party, 54–5, 70, 103, 136
Leaders, role of in peace process, 10–12, 18,
    21, 165–7
Learning process in negotiations, 14, 19, 20,
    25 n17, 28 n43
Legacy/Lessons of Oslo Accords see Oslo
    Accords
Likud Party, 56, 92, 134, 137, 151

Madrid Conference, 32, 35, 74, 92, 150–1
Management of expectations, 8
Meretz Party, 54–5, 136
Misperception, role of see Protracted
    conflict
Morley, Ian, 17, 29 n50
Muslims and Jews in the Middle East,
    79–81

National Religious Party, 54–5, 101
Negotiating process in protracted conflict
    see Protracted conflict
Netanyahu, Benjamin, 8, 27 n31, 50, 54, 89,
    96–7, 138
New approach to negotiations, 16–18

Oslo Accords, passim; benefits to Arafat
    and PLO, 18, 163; benefits to Israelis, 38;
    benefits to Palestinians, 38, 99, 154;
    Declaration of Principles, 37, 60–1, 62,
    86, 94, 96, 115; decline and race to the
    bottom, 3, 18, 88; different points of
    departure, 32, 34; and domestic politics,
    41–2, 166–7; failures in implementation,
    63–5, 68–9, 70–1, 75–6, 93, 96–8, 98–113,
    115, 119–20, 135–9, 142–5, 165–6; legacy
    of, 19–20, 31, 112, 147, 162; lessons of,
    20–2; origins of, 91–6, 134, 151; open-
    ended nature of, 34, 40–1, 135, 163–4;
    and permanent status talks, 31–2, 88,
    104–5
"Oslo spirit," 95–6

Palestine Liberation Organization (PLO),
    31, 40, 42, 59, 67, 91, 93, 117, 135, 149,
    151

Palestine National Council (PNC) , 59, 150
Palestinian Authority, 11–12, 41–4, 45, 59,
    73, 99–100, 118, 145
Palestinian internal politics, 108–10, 152
Palestinian National Covenant, 45, 60
Palestinian national movement, 31, 135, 150
Palestinian negotiating tactics, 100, 110
Palestinian policy after September 11,
    xii–xiii
Palestinian refugees, 35, 42, 90
Palestinian support for Oslo Accords, 12,
    146, 163, 166
Palestinian terrorism and violence, 33,
    62–3, 69, 97, 120, 143, 152, 164
Partition Resolution (1948), 89
Peres, Shimon, 72, 73, 85, 92, 94, 103, 116
Protracted conflict, 3–6, 168–9; conflict
    resolution, 120–32, 168–9; conflictive
    ethos, 4; domestic politics of, 8–12; exis-
    tential phase, 4–5; "Gresham's Law" of,
    5; incremental strategies, 15; "incremen-
    talism plus," 15; management of
    expectations, 8, 13; misperception in,
    114; need for new approach to negotia-
    tions, 16–18; negotiating process in, 15;
    "sufficient consensus" in, 11; top/down
    negotiating process, 10, 18, 163;
    "window of opportunity" for negotia-
    tions, 5–6
Public opinion, 41–2, 45, 48–57, 120, 166–7

Rabin, Yitzhak, 21, 61, 62, 66, 72, 73, 86,
    92, 94, 137, 152
Ramon, Haim, 101, 102, 103
Right of return, 37, 39, 43, 45–6, 64, 75,
    109–10, 140, 143, 157
Ross, Dennis, 12, 23, 125

Savir, Uri, 94
Second-track diplomacy, viii–x
Security concerns of Israel, 24, 43, 48, 52,
    155
Settlement activity by Israel, 33, 42, 52, 79,
    102, 119, 138, 152–3, 156–9
Shamir, Yitzhak, 74–5
Sharon, Ariel, 14, 56, 88, 127, 158
Shas Political Party, 41, 56
Six Day War, 90
State Department (US), 107
"Sufficient consensus" domestically, 11

Taba negotiations, 45, 110–11, 134
Taliban, ix–xv
Temple Mount see Haram al-Sharif
    (Temple Mount)
Terrorism, ix–xv
Third-Party intervention, 21, 158, 167–8

Index

Top/Down peace process *see* Protracted
   conflict
Transformational bargaining, 16–18
Two-State solution, 39, 81, 112, 153

United Nations Resolutions, 59, 89, 101,
   127, 131, 150
United States, role of, xi–xii, 74, 107, 117,
   125, 158, 167–8

Water Rights issue, 99, 126
Window of opportunity for negotiations,
   xvi, xvii, 5, 24 *n*12
Wye River negotiations, 86, 125–6, 139

Yassin, Sheikh Ahmad, 68, 85–6

Zartman, I. William, 24 *n*12
Zionism, 78, 79, 89, 116